# REDISCOVERY AND REVIVAL IN ISLAMIC ENVIRONMENTAL LAW

The common ground between religions could be fruitfully promoted in order to call for an effective protection of the climate system. Positioned at a junction of different worlds, this book is a multidisciplinary work on Islamic law, common law and environmental law. Looking at the past, present and future, the author suggests a paradigm shift starting from the common ground in order to propose a better future for environmental law in Muslim countries. As the first book to compare *Sharia'* and common law in field of environmental protection, it suggests a new path in comparative environmental law by recognizing the contributions of both history and spirituality.

SAMIRA IDLLALÈNE is Professor of Law at Cadi-Ayyad University, Safi, Morocco. She was a Fulbright scholar in 2016 as a Courtesy Associate Professor at the University of Oregon, School of Law. She is a partner of Environmental Law Alliance Worldwide and pro bono legal consultant for Moroccan environmental NGOs.

# ASCL STUDIES IN COMPARATIVE LAW

ASCL Studies in Comparative Law is designed to broaden theoretical and practical knowledge of the world's many legal systems. With more than sixty years' experience, the American Society of Comparative Law has been a leader in the study and analysis of comparative law. By promoting the investigation of legal problems in a comparative light, whether theoretical or empirical, as essential to the advancement of legal science, it provides an essential service to legal practitioners and those seeking reform of the law. This book series will extend these aims to the publication of monographs and comparative studies of specific legal problems.

The series has two series editors. David Gerber is Distinguished Professor of Law and Co-Director of the Program in International and Comparative Law at Chicago-Kent College of Law, Illinois Institute of Technology. He is currently President of the American Society of Comparative Law. Mortimer Sellers is Regents Professor of the University System of Maryland and Director of the Baltimore Center for International and Comparative Law. He is an Associate Member of the International Academy of Comparative Law.

## Series Editors

David Gerber *Chicago-Kent College of Law*
Mortimer Sellers *University of Baltimore*

## Editorial Board

Richard Albert *University of Texas*
David Clark *Willamette University*
Helge Dedek *McGill University*
James Feinerman *Georgetown University*
Richard Kay *University of Connecticut*
Maximo Langer *University of California Los Angeles*
Ralf Michaels *Duke University*
Fernanda Nicola *American University*
Jacqueline Ross *University of Illinois*
Kim Lane Scheppele *Princeton University*
Franz Werro *Georgetown University*

## External Advisory Board

Josef Drexl *University of Munich*
Diego Fernandez Arroyo *Institut d'etudes politiques de Paris*
Hongjun Gao *Tsinghua University*
Michele Grazidei *University of Turin*
Ko Hasegawa *University of Hokkaido*
Hisashi Harata *University of Tokyo*
Andreas Heinemann *University of Zurich*
Christophe Jamin *Institut d'etudes politiques de Paris*
Yong-Sun Kang *Yonsei University*
Claudia Lima Marques *Federal University of Rio Grande do Sul*
Bertil Emrah Oder *Koc University*
Amr Shalakany *American University of Cairo*

# Rediscovery and Revival in Islamic Environmental Law

## BACK TO THE FUTURE OF NATURE'S TRUST

**SAMIRA IDLLALÈNE**

Cadi Ayyad University

## CAMBRIDGE
### UNIVERSITY PRESS

University Printing House, Cambridge CB2 8BS, United Kingdom

One Liberty Plaza, 20th Floor, New York, NY 10006, USA

477 Williamstown Road, Port Melbourne, VIC 3207, Australia

314-321, 3rd Floor, Plot 3, Splendor Forum, Jasola District Centre, New Delhi - 110025, India

103 Penang Road, #05-06/07, Visioncrest Commercial, Singapore 238467

Cambridge University Press is part of the University of Cambridge.

It furthers the University's mission by disseminating knowledge in the pursuit of education, learning and research at the highest international levels of excellence.

www.cambridge.org
Information on this title: www.cambridge.org/9781108738842
DOI: 10.1017/9781108772082

© Samira Idllalène 2021

This publication is in copyright. Subject to statutory exception and to the provisions of relevant collective licensing agreements, no reproduction of any part may take place without the written permission of Cambridge University Press.

First published 2021
First paperback edition 2022

A catalogue record for this publication is available from the British Library

ISBN 978-1-108-48878-5 Hardback
ISBN 978-1-108-73884-2 Paperback

*To my nieces and nephews: Salma, Emyliah, Issam, Youssra, and Noah, the New Seeds and the Common Grounds, with love.*

*To my professors: Mohamed-Ali Mekouar and Veronique Labrot.*

*To my students.*

# Contents

| | | |
|---|---|---|
| *List of Figures* | *page* xi |
| *List of Tables* | xiii |
| *Preface* | xv |
| *Acknowledgments* | xix |
| *Glossary* | xxi |
| *List of Acronyms* | xxiii |

**1   Introductory Context and Issues** | 1

1.1  Background: The Ecological Spirituality Movement | 1
1.2  The Particularity of Islamic Law and the Research Gap | 8
1.3  Why Islamic Environmental Law Matters | 12
1.4  Reinvigorating Islamic Environmental Law and Building the Atmospheric *Waqf* Paradigm: Lessons from Comparative Law | 28

**2   What Is "Islamic Environmental Law"?** | 31

2.1  The Sources of Islamic Environmental Law | 33
  2.1.1  The Qur'an: The Principal Source of Islamic Environmental Law | 34
  2.1.2  The Sunnah or Hadith: The Interpreting Rules of Islamic Environmental Law | 38
  2.1.3  *Ijma'*: The Necessary Consensus of *Ulamas* | 39
  2.1.4  *Ijtihad*: The Evolutionary Principle for Islamic Environmental Law | 40
  2.1.5  *Qiyas* (Analogy): A Tool for Comparison | 41
  2.1.6  The Juristic Preference: *Istihsan*, a Tool for Seeking a Better Environment | 42
  2.1.7  *Al Maslaha* (Public Benefit): The Vehicle of the Atmospheric *Waqf* Paradigm | 43

2.1.8 *Al Urf* (Customary Law): Back to the Waqf Roots          44
2.2 Islamic Environmental Law Instruments: The Ingredients of the
Atmospheric *Waqf* Doctrine/Paradigm                         46
2.2.1 *Waqf* as a Landmark General Tool for Environmental
Protection in Islamic Law                               47
2.2.2 Protected Areas: A Specific Tool for the Protection of Natural
Resources under Islamic Law                             50

3    **The Dormancy of Islamic Environmental Law**                   54

3.1 Historical and Political Factors                             55
3.2 Socioeconomic Factors                                   59

4    **A Fruitful Comparison with the Common Law**                   63

4.1 Exploiting the Numerous Similarities between the Trust
and the *Waqf*                                         64
4.1.1 The Religious Foundations                            65
4.1.2 Similar Functioning Modes                           72
4.1.3 The Inalienability of the Assets                        73
4.1.4 Similar Purposes                                   74
4.2 The Fabulous Destiny of Environmental Trusts (from the Trust
to the Public Trust Doctrine)                              75
4.2.1 From the Classical Trust to the Public Trust Doctrine     76
4.2.2 Atmospheric Trust Litigation: The Claim for a Trust for
Future Generations                                  81
4.2.3 An Overarching Principle: The "Trust in the Higher Sense"   83

5    **Potential for Growth of Islamic Environmental Law**            86

5.1 Islamic Environmental Law Principles: The Core of the
Atmospheric *Waqf* Paradigm                            86
5.1.1 Sustainability                                     87
5.1.2 Green *Khilafa* or Stewardship                       90
5.1.3 Adaptive Management                               96
5.1.4 An Early Answer to the Tragedy of the Commons          99
5.1.5 Cutting-Edge Rules: The Recognition of Animal Rights     101
5.2 Current and Potential Applications of Islamic Environmental Law   110
5.2.1 The Evolution of Eco-Islam: From Theory to Practice      111
5.2.2 Environmental Waqf Initiatives and Islamic Green Finance   129

Conclusion                                            141

*Select Bibliography*                                     147
*Index*                                               159

# Figures

1.1 Evolution of the Ecological Spirituality movement and Islamic countries 7
1.2 Map of the Islamic world 10
1.3 Map of legal systems in the world 13
2.1 The sources of Islamic environmental law 34
2.2 Functioning modes of *Waqf* and Trust 49
5.1 The multiple uses of the *Waqf* 97
5.2 Map of the most developed Islamic finance markets around the world 99
5.3 The potential of Islamic finance to foster environmental *Waqf* 132

# Tables

1.1 *Waqf* and the environment in Islamic countries' constitutions
according to their legal systems                                    21
2.1 Environmental *Fatwas* in the world                             37
4.1 *Waqf* laws and their potential application to the protection of
the environment                                                     66
4.2 Comparison between the *Waqf* and the Trust                     70

# Preface

The story of this book started more than ten years ago in France, when I was a PhD student at the University of Western Brittany.

My PhD thesis focused on legal aspects of coastal management in Morocco. This led me to study comparative law on this issue and to learn about the concept of the "Trust" in English law.

My focus on the Trust came from my interest in the Conservatoire du littoral[1] as a tool to protect and conserve the coastal zones in France. I discovered then that the Conservatoire du littoral was inspired by the English Trusts, especially by the National Trust.

Many years later, I started teaching comparative law at the University of Cadi Ayyad in Morocco; I taught then the origins of the Trust concept and how this institution works.

I discovered that there are various similarities between the Trust and the Waqf, an Islamic law institution, which is, like several Trusts, a charitable endowment. I started to collect more information on both the Trust and the Waqf. I was fascinated by the possibility to use the Waqf in the same way the Trust has been used in England for nature conservation.

I found in historical books a wealth of information on how Waqf was also used for the protection of natural resources few centuries ago. More than that, the Waqf was a revolutionary legal concept because it holds animals, not just humans, as beneficiaries.

The combination of both comparative law and environmental law sheds more light on other institutions such as *Agdal* or *Hima*, protected areas under customary

---

[1]  The Conservatoire du littoral is a French institution in charge of coastal protection. Its main work is to purchase coastal lands and keep them for natural conservation purposes. The Conservatoire du littoral was inspired by the national trusts or public trusts in England. www .conservatoire-du-littoral.fr

law that also have a spiritual component. Moreover, these protected areas can be created through the *Waqf*.

More frequently analyzed in scholarship on anthropology and ecology, these protected areas are not sufficiently studied in legal scholarship. Yet it is curious that these institutions can be found in all Muslim countries. In addition, their social and ecological potential still exists in many countries despite their decline. So why are these protected areas never studied or taught in law schools in Muslim countries?

During my hikes in the Atlas Mountains, I could see how the *Agdals* (protected areas) work in real life for the efficient distribution of water between the inhabitants of a village, to ensure good pasture for cattle. It is amazing how well the law is respected when it is governed by customary rules. It's not comparable with what happens in town. In Safi, the city where I work, factories discharge tons of sulfuric acid into the sea, day and night. In Agadir, my hometown, the former Tagazout campsite, where all the inhabitants have at least one memory of a holiday, has been transformed into a beach resort, large areas of the coast have been concreted over and disfigured, and the endemic trees of Argan have been destroyed. How did we move from such awareness of nature to this situation of contempt for it?

It's very difficult to find information on the environmental *Waqf*. I only found scraps collected here and there. But that was enough to learn that this *Waqf* is possible. Why isn't this kind of *Waqf* taught in our law schools in environmental law curricula? We study *Waqf* in law curricula but the connection between this institution and the protection of the environment is not taught anywhere. Sometimes here and there we find a few paragraphs given to the Islamic aspect of environmental law. As for "customary law", it generally has no place in law schools (at least not in Morocco).

Why don't Muslim countries exploit this rich heritage?

In the Atlas Mountains, national parks have been created since the end of the nineteenth century. To better protect these parks, the administration put barbed wire all around. But in some places the barbed wire has been torn away. When I asked a resident of a hilltop village in the Atlas (which is only accessible on foot because there is no paved road), he replied, "I do not recognize this policy. The government is too far from here!" Statutory law was superimposed onto customary law and this most often led to a difficult cohabitation.

In my research on the Trust, I was led to study what is known as the Public Trust Doctrine – a doctrine that has evolved over more than a century in the United States. I considered first that this doctrine was similar to the English Trust. I was wrong.

During my fellowship at the University of Oregon School of Law, in the United States in the fall of 2016, I started to understand that actually the Public Trust Doctrine is a mixture between the English Trust and the *domaine public* in the civil law system of continental Europe.

# Glossary

| | |
|---|---|
| **Agdal**: | Protected area. The equivalent of Hima in North Africa |
| *Aya*: | *Qur'an*'s verse |
| *Fiqh*: | Islamic science |
| *Fuqahas* (**or** *Ulamas*): | Plural of Faqih, person who is specialized in Fiqh |
| **Hadith**: | sayings of the Prophet Muhammad considered as the second source of *Sharia'* |
| *Haram*: | what is forbidden by *Sharia'*; it also has the meaning of sanctuary |
| *Harim*: | areas around bodies of water, or any other places, dedicated to protecting them (sanctuaries) |
| *Hima* (**or** *Hema*): | protected area under Islamic law or customary law |
| *Ijma'*: | consensus of *Fuqahas* (or *Ulamas*) which can be considered as a source of Islamic law |
| *Ijtihad*: | the effort of interpreting Islamic science and sources of *Sharia'* |
| *Istihsan*: | a source of *Sharia'*, literally means "seeking of good", the equivalent of Equity |
| *Khilafa*: | viceregency, trusteeship; it also has the meaning of political authority |
| *Maqasid*: | higher purposes of the *Sharia'* |
| *Maslaha*: | public interest or benefit (is also part of *Maqasid*) |
| *Qiyas*: | a source of *Sharia'* that applies analogy |
| Qur'an: | Muslim holy book and the first source of *Sharia'* |
| **Sharia'** (**or** **Sharī'ah**): | Islamic law |
| **Sunnah**: | acts of the prophet Muhammad considered as the second source of *Sharia'* |

| | |
|---|---|
| **Surah (or Sura)**: | a verse from the Qur'an |
| **Ulama (or Ulema)**: | *Sharia'* and/or *Fiqh* scholars |
| **Urf**: | customary law |
| **Waqf or Habous**: | charitable endowment |
| **Zakat**: | tax alms |

# Acronyms

ARC:        Alliance for Religions and Conservation
IDB:        Islamic Development Bank
IEP:        Islamic Ecological Paradigm
IFEES:      Islamic Foundation for Ecology and Environmental Sciences
IPCC:       Intergovernmental Panel on Climate Change
ISESCO:     Islamic Scientific, Educational and Cultural Organization
IUCN:       International Union for Conservation of Nature
MENA:       Middle East and North Africa region
OIC:        Organization of Islamic Cooperation
PTD:        Public Trust Doctrine
SDGs:       Sustainable Development Goals
UNDP:       United Nations Development Programme
UNEP:       United Nations Environmental Programme
UNFCCC:     United Nations Framework Convention on Climate Change
WANA:       West Asia–North Africa Institute (WANA)

# 1

# Introductory Context and Issues

We often say that Islam is a complete way of life, by which it is meant that our ethical system provides the bearing for all our actions. Yet our actions often undermine the very values we cherish. Often while working as scientists or technologists, economists or politicians, we act contrary to the environmental dictates of Islam.

Islamic Declaration on Nature, 1986

## 1.1 BACKGROUND: THE ECOLOGICAL SPIRITUALITY MOVEMENT

During the last half of the twentieth century, fundamental environmental changes affected the world, brought on by human impacts on natural ecosystems.[1] The holding of the 21st Conference of the Parties under the United Nations Framework Convention on Climate Change (UNFCCC) (COP 21)[2] in a Muslim country, Morocco, served to highlight the link between religion and the protection of the environment, and in particular the contribution that Islamic law (*Sharia'*) could make to protecting the environment.

Indeed, faced with the non-enforcement of "modern" environmental law,[3] some voices in the Muslim world and elsewhere are calling for the revival of ecological spirituality and the ancestral traditions that have always viewed humans as *part of* nature.

[1]   Available at: www.millenniumassessment.org/
[2]   Available at: https://unfccc.int/process-and-meetings/conferences/past-conferences/marrakech-climate-change-conference-november-2016/marrakech-climate-change-conference-november-2016
[3]   On this issue, see the latest UNEP report on environmental rule of law: UNEP, 'Environmental Rule of Law: First Global Report'. United Nations Environment Programme, Nairobi, 2019. Available at: www.unenvironment.org/resources/assessment/environmental-rule-law-first-global-report

As Professors Mary Evelyn Tucker and John Grimm state,

> For many people an environmental crisis of this complexity and scope is not only the result of certain economic, political, and social factors. It is also a moral and spiritual crisis which, in order to be addressed, will require broader philosophical and religious understandings of ourselves as creatures of nature, embedded in life cycles and dependent on ecosystems. Religions, thus, need to be reexamined in light of the current environmental crisis. This is because religions help to shape our attitudes towards nature in both conscious and unconscious ways.[4]

As a matter of fact, politicians and environmentalists are increasingly aware that climate change issues cannot be dealt with away from cultural and religious roots. Climate politics are, indeed, "intricately intertwined with deep-seated lifestyle choices and cultural patterns and practices, which in turn influence attitudes toward the environment and toward governmental involvement in environmental regulation".[5]

The link between religion and the environment is not new. It is part of a wider movement called "Ecological Spirituality", "Religion and Ecology", "Nature and Religion" or "Environmental Ethics". This movement stems from scientific research, philosophy and theology since the sixteenth century.[6] It calls for the integration of values embedded in religion, such as "a sense of the sacred, the intrinsic value of place, the spiritual dimension of the human, moral concern for nature, and care for future generations", which are "often ignored as externalities, or overridden by more pragmatic profit-driven considerations".[7] It is based on the idea that "acknowledging the sacredness of the natural world provides a powerful reason to inspire the masses to protect it".[8]

These ideas based on environmental spirituality resonate with international initiatives such as the Earth Charter and the UN Earth Summit.[9] In fact, the Earth Charter is defined as "an ethical framework for building a just, sustainable,

---

[4] Mary Evelyne Tucker and John Grim, 'Series Foreword', in Richard C. Foltz, Frederick Denny and Azizan Baharuddin (eds.), *Islam and Ecology: A Bestowed Trust* (Cambridge, MA: Harvard University Press, 2003), xvi.

[5] Cinnamon P. Carlarne, 'Reassessing the Role of Religion in Western Climate Change Decision-Making', in Waleed El-Ansary and David K. Linnan (eds.), *Muslim and Christian Understanding: Theory and Application of 'A Common Word'* (New York: Palgrave Macmillan, 2010), 169.

[6] For more details, see for example Roger S. Gottlieb (ed.), *Oxford Handbook on Religion and Ecology* (Oxford: Blackwell, 2006). See also Mary Evelyn Tucker and John Grimm, 'The Movement of Religion and Ecology: Emerging Field and Dynamic Force', in Willis Jenkins (ed.), *Routledge Handbook of Religion and Ecology* (New York: Routledge, 2017), 3–12.

[7] Tucker and Grimm, 'The Movement of Religion and Ecology', 5.

[8] Roger S. Gottlieb, 'Introduction: Religion and Ecology – What Is the Connection and Why Does It Matter?', in Roger S. Gottlieb (ed.), *Oxford Handbook on Religion and Ecology* (Oxford: Blackwell, 2006), 1–21.

[9] Bron R. Taylor and Jeffrey Kaplan (eds.), *The Encyclopedia of Religion and Nature* (London: Thoemmes Continuum, 2008), xviii.

and peaceful global society in the 21st century. It seeks to inspire in all people a new sense of global interdependence and shared responsibility for the well-being of the planet and future generations".[10]

The Earth Charter is basically a United Nations initiative that has been carried forward and completed by civil society. It was launched on June 29, 2000 as a people's charter by the Earth Charter Commission (an independent internal organism) at the Peace Palace in The Hague.

It is based on four main ideas or principles:

- Respect and care for the community of life.
- Ecological integrity.
- Social and economic justice.
- Democracy, non-violence and peace.

In the Islamic world, Muslim philosophers have been addressing the subject of ecological spirituality since the Middle Ages,[11] but the new philosophers seem to be more interested in finding practical applications for ecological spirituality in modern society.[12] One of the pioneers of this "movement" is Professor Seyyed Hossein Nasr, who shared his thoughts in his 1967 lecture at the University of Chicago: "Man and Nature: The Spiritual Crisis of Modern Man".[13] This paper was "path breaking for the entire field of religion and ecology" in the Islamic world and beyond.[14] Professor Nasr calls for a rediscovery of Islamic environmental ethics by using the scriptural basis from the Qur'an and Sunnah[15] but also from the Sufi sources in both poetry and prose (such as works of Ibn Arabi, Jalal al Din Rumi and Mahmud Shabistari).[16]

Since the 1960s, other philosophers and thinkers, including Syed Iqtidar Zaidi, Fazlun Khalid, Odeh Rashed Al-Jayyousi, Ahmed Raissouni (or Raysuni), Ibrahim

---

[10] For more details, see https://earthcharter.org/discover/the-earth-charter/

[11] Ibn Tufail's book on the history of Hay Ibn Yakzan is centered on ecological principles. It is a fable about a child who is raised by a doe on an island and who grows up to discover the world and nature. See, for example, Muhammad Ibn Abd Al-Malik Ibn Tufayl, translated by Lenn Evan Goodman (ed.), *Ibn Tufayl's Hayy Ibn Yaqzan: A Philosophical Tale* (Chicago, IL: University of Chicago Press, 2003).

[12] Richard C. Foltz, 'Islamic Environmentalism: A Matter of Interpretation', in Richard C. Foltz, Frederick Denny and Azizan Baharuddin (eds.), *Islam and Ecology: A Bestowed Trust* (Cambridge, MA: Harvard University Press, 2003), 249–79, at 251. See also on the grassroots movement and the idea of Islamic Ecological Paradigm (IEP), Md Saidul Islam, 'Old Philosophy, New Movement: The Rise of the Islamic Ecological Paradigm in the Discourse of Environmentalism' (2012) 7, 1, *Nature and Culture*, 72–94.

[13] Seyyed Hossein Nasr, *Man and Nature: The Spiritual Crisis of Modern Man* (London: George Allen & Unwin, 1968).

[14] Willis Jenkins and Christopher Key Chapple, 'Annual Review, Religion and Environment' (2011) 36, *Annual Review of Environment and Resources*, 441–63.

[15] Acts and sayings of the prophet Muhammad.

[16] Seyyed Hossein Nasr, 'God Is Absolute Reality and All Creation His Tajalli', in John Hart (ed.), *The Wiley Blackwell Companion to Religion and Ecology* (Hoboken, NJ: John Wiley & Sons, 2017), 11.

Özdemir and many others,[17] continue to praise the merits of the revival of Muslim ethics for environmental protection.[18]

Some philosophers and thinkers act through international organizations such as the International Union for Conservation of Nature (IUCN)[19] or the Islamic Scientific, Educational and Cultural Organization (ISESCO).[20] Others founded dedicated organizations[21] such as the Islamic Foundation for Ecology and Environmental Sciences (IFEES)[22] or Islamic Relief Worldwide.[23] This movement brought about the Islamic Declaration on Nature (September 29, 1986),[24] the Islamic Declaration on Sustainable Development adopted by ISESCO in 2002[25] and in 2012 (adopted at the Fifth Islamic Conference of Environment Ministers held in Astana, Kazakhstan in June 2012)[26], and the Islamic Declaration on Global

[17] See Arthur Saniotis, 'Muslims and Ecology: Fostering Islamic Environmental Ethics' (2012) 6, 2, *Contemporary Islam*, 155–71, at 158.

[18] For a complete bibliography, see for example A. M. Schwencke, *'Globalized Eco-Isam: A Survey of Global Islamic Environmentalism'* (Report, Leiden Institute for Religious Studies (LIRS), Leiden University, 2012). See also Donatella Vincenti, '"Green" Islam and Social Movements for Sustainability' (PhD thesis, Liberta University Internationale Degli Studi Sociali, Luiss Guido Carli, Rome, 2017), 111–39. See also Saidul Islam, 'Old Philosophy, New Movement'; and Saniotis, 'Muslims and Ecology'.

[19] In 1983, the Saudi Arabia government had asked a group of lawyers and thinkers to write a paper on the issue of Islam and the protection of the environment (Abou Bakr Ahmed Bakader, Abdul Latif Tawfik El Shirazy Al Sabagh, Mohamed Al Sayyed Al Glenid and Mawil Y. Izzi Deen, *Islamic Principles for the Conservation of the Natural Environment* (Gland, Switzerland: International Union for Conservation of Nature and Natural Resources, 1983). Available at: www.iucn.org/content/basic-paper-islamic-principles-conservation-natural-environment. This paper was edited by the IUCN for a second time in 1994. Available at: www.iucn.org/con tent/iucn-calls-reviving-waqf-environment-initiative. It explains how the principles of law and ethics in Islam can serve the protection of the environment. *Waqf* and *Hima* are among the suggested tools. See also: www.iucn.org/content/iucn-calls-reviving-Waqf-en

[20] Ahmed Raissouni, *Islamic Waqf Endowment: Scope and Implication* (Rabat: ISESCO, 2001).

[21] For an exhaustive list of these organizations, see Dina M. Abdelzaher and Amir Abdelzaher, 'Beyond Environmental Regulations: Exploring the Potential of "Eco-Islam" in Boosting Environmental Ethics within SMEs in Arab Markets' (2015) 145, 2, *Journal of Business Ethics*, 357–71, at 365.

[22] IFEES is a voluntary nonprofit organization that was established in the United Kingdom in 1994 in order to integrate Muslims with the scientific movement and to explain and clarify the Islamic point of view toward science and the environment. See the website at: www.ifees.org .uk/

[23] Islamic Relief Worldwide is an independent humanitarian organization created in 1984 whose mission is guided by Islamic values in order to mobilize resources, build partnership and develop local capacity. See their website at: www.islamic-relief.org/

[24] In 1986, the World Wildlife Fund (WWF), at its 25th anniversary in Italy, adopted the Assisi Declarations, 'Messages on Humanity and Nature from Buddhism, Christianity, Hinduism, Islam and Judaism', which included insights into the principles governing the environmental ethics and ethos from five mainstream faiths. It included the Muslim Declaration on Nature. Available at: www.arcworld.org/

[25] Available at: www.isesco.org.ma/fr/wp-content/uploads/sites/2/2015/05/Developmt-durable1.pdf

[26] Ibid.

Climate Change (adopted on August 18, 2015 at the Islamic Climate Change Symposium held in Istanbul).[27]

Islamic environmental declarations not only represent ecological statements but also encourage interfaith environmental coalition. This interfaith movement was initiated by academia through famous initiatives such as the Alliance of Religions and Conservations (ARC), Yale's Forum on Religion and Ecology and many other research and grassroots initiatives.[28]

The second encyclical of Pope Francis, *"Laudato Si"* ['Praised Be You']: *On Care of Our Common Home*, is one of the main expressions and impetuses of this growing interest.[29] Its impact goes beyond the sphere of the Christian world. It has been a resounding success for other religious groups but also in the spheres of politics and academia.[30] *Laudato Si* invites us to take a new spiritual approach to the world anchored in environmental conscience that could lead to a profound lifestyle change. According to Pope Francis, the environmental crisis must be dealt with using a holistic approach, both socially and environmentally.

Based on the "integral ecology" paradigm, *Laudato Si* makes a link between development and environment and considers that environmental justice is the key element of this paradigm. In fact, Pope Francis draws an analogy between poverty and the environment, both considered by him as vulnerable and neglected in contemporary paradigm dominance.[31] Therefore, Pope Francis claims a right for the environment based on two grounds: (1) humans depend on the environment in

---

[27] Available at: www.arrcc.org.au/islamic_declaration. See also, for an overview of the global framework of this Declaration: Rosemary Hancock, 'Faith and Creation: Possibilities of an 'Islamic' Environmental Ethic', *ABC Religion & Ethics*, September 11, 2018. Available at: www .abc.net.au/religion/islamic-environmental-ethic/10233070; and Howard S. J. Damian, 'An Islamic Declaration on Climate Change', *Thinking Faith*, October 29, 2015. Available at: www.thinkingfaith.org/articles/islamic-declaration-climate-change#_edn15.

[28] Elizabeth McLeod and Martin Palmer, 'Why Conservation Needs Religion' (2015) 43, 3, *Coastal Management*, 238–52 at 241; Leslie E. Sponsel, 'Spiritual Ecology as an International Environmental Movement' (2014) 15, *Advances in Sustainability and Environmental Justice*, 275–93. See also Jonathan Chaplin, 'The Global Greening of Religion' (2016) 2, *Palgrave Communications* [online], 16–47. Available at: www.nature.com/articles/palcomms201647. Examples of outcomes of this movement are the program of Earth Stewardship Initiative by the Ecological Society of America: www.earthstewardshipinitiative.com/ and the Millennium Alliance for Humanity and Biosphere: https://mahb.stanford.edu/

[29] Available at: w2.vatican.va/content/francesco/en/encyclicals/documents/papa-francesco_20150524_enciclica-laudato-si.html. On the many similarities that exist between the Encyclical and Islamic environmental principles, see, for example, Damian, 'An Islamic Declaration on Climate Change'.

[30] Wolfgang Sachs, 'The Sustainable Development Goals and Laudato Si': Varieties of Post-Development?' (2017) 38, 12, *Third World Quarterly*, 2573–87.

[31] An analogy is drawn between the environment itself and the poor (LS: 170, 190) as both remain vulnerable and neglected in contemporary paradigms of dominance (LS: 2, 48). Jessica Ludescher Imanaka, Greg Prussia and Samantha Alexis, *'Laudato Si'* and Integral Ecology' (2017) 5, 1, *Journal of Management for Global Sustainability*, 39–61 at 52.

that it has instrumental value for all people; and (2) creatures have intrinsic value, both in themselves and in their interconnection with the world.[32]

*Laudato Si'* parallels the Islamic Declaration on Global Climate Change. The same ideas can be found in both texts, and were addressed to the international community and especially the Paris Climate Summit leaders.

In this regard, some authors consider that if the Islamic Declaration on Global Climate Change "appeared to be riding the wave of religious attention to environmental crises", in reality it "reflected decades of work by Muslim scholars and activists eager to find an Islamic response to environmental crises".[33]

In fact, Islamic philosophy encouraging the protection of the environment has also given rise to a growing grassroots movement led by faith-based groups or even by secular groups using Islamic principles. This movement is also called "Eco-Islam" or "Islamic Ecological Paradigm" (IEP).[34] It seems to have been initiated and further developed in the Islamic countries of South East Asia, notably in Indonesia and Malaysia, but also in Iran, Pakistan and Egypt. It is however spreading at a slow pace to the Middle East and North Africa (MENA) region.[35] Eco-Islam predated the Islamic Declaration on Global Climate Change but this declaration was a strong catalyst for the movement.[36]

More recently, while this book was in preparation, the United Nations Environmental Programme (UNEP) adopted a new strategy called "Faith for Earth Initiative", which encourages an interfaith coalition on spirituality and the environment. In March 2019, at the fourth UN Assembly for the Environment in Kenya, the "Faith for Earth Initiative" organized a panel gathering faith leaders and scholars around the theme of cultural and religious impacts: "Innovative Solutions for Environmental Challenges and Sustainable Consumption and Production". In May the same year, the first report was published.[37]

The "Faith for Earth Initiative is based on the idea that the religious community has a vital role to play in the protection of the environment. This initiative echoes the arguments of the Ecological Spirituality movement and complements what has already been done within the framework of the United Nations[38] and other

---

[32] Ibid.

[33] Damian, 'An Islamic Declaration on Climate Change'.

[34] Fachruddin Majeri Mangunjaya, Imran S. L. Tobing, Andang Binawan, Evangeline Pua and Made Nurbawa, 'Faiths from the Archipelago: Action on the Environment and Climate Change' (2015) 19, 2,*Woldviews: Global Religions, Culture, and Ecology*, 103–22. See also Saidul Islam, 'Old Philosophy, New Movement'.

[35] For more details, see Chapter 5.

[36] On the evolution of Eco-Islam, see Section 5.2.1.

[37] UNEP, UNEA, 4, Faith for Earth Dialogue, Synthesis Paper, 2019. Available at: www .unenvironment.org/resources/synthesis-reports/faith-earth-dialogue-synthesis-report

[38] For example, the UNDP's work on how to engage with faith-based NGOs for social and economic development.
   See their guidelines at: www.undp.org/content/dam/undp/documents/partners/2014_ UNDP_Guidelines-on-Engaging-with-FBOs-and-Religious-Leaders_EN.pdf

FIGURE 1.1 Evolution of the Ecological Spirituality movement and Islamic countries

initiatives of private organizations or international NGOs (Figure 1.1).[39] The main objective of this initiative is to mobilize faith leaders and the faith community to achieve the Sustainable Development Goals (SDGs). In fact, engaging with faith-based groups in order to protect the environment is paramount according to the UNEP "Faith for Earth Initiative" for these main reasons:[40]

- History has shown how faith-based groups have participated in providing socioeconomic services to communities.
- Spiritual values have importance for the majority of the world's population.
- Faith-based groups have potential for inspiring changes.
- Religions acknowledge the sacredness of nature and are able to transmit this idea and to inspire the masses.
- Faith-based groups have great funding potential.[41]
- Faith-based groups are often considered by the population as more credible than governments.

In fact, according to the "Faith for Earth Initiative", in many countries "spiritual beliefs and religious practices are interwoven with cultural values, social principles, political engagement, and economic prosperity".[42]

---

[39] Among those initiatives we can cite academia but also NGOs and private organisms. See note 8 above.

[40] UNEP, 'Engaging with Faith Based Organizations' (2018), 4–5. Available at: www.unenvironment.org/about-un-environment/faith-earth-initiative. Those arguments can also be found in more detail in the literature related to Spiritual Ecology. See for example Sponsel, 'Spiritual Ecology as an International Environmental Movement'.

[41] In fact, faith-based organizations are not only spiritually prepared for ecological principles which are ethical principles – they believe in the sacredness of the earth and are good candidates for spreading the ecological faith – but they are also financially strong and can influence the protection of the environment both ideologically and financially. See Mcleod and Palmer, 'Why Conservation Needs Religion'. See also, for an insight on the evolution of this movement and its main arguments, Taylor and Kaplan, *The Encyclopedia of Religion and Nature*.

[42] UNEP, 'Engaging with Faith Based Organizations', 5.

At the fourth UN Assembly for Environment in Kenya, 135 faith leaders attended the Faith for Earth Dialogue.[43] Many Islamic NGOs, officials and scholars participated in this UN panel. Among the officials, ISESCO held a panel entitled "From Theory to Practice: The Islamic Perspective of Environmental Protection and Promoting Interfaith Actions".[44] This experience was shared through the Conference of Ministries of Environment in Islamic Countries held in Rabat two months later.[45]

Ecological Spirituality or environmental ethics is gaining momentum not only at grassroots level, but also at governmental level. In the Islamic world it has, however, a specific connotation. In fact, in the framework of Islam, law is intertwined with spirituality and ethics. Therefore, tapping into the "Ecological Spirituality" movement in order to boost environmental law in Muslim countries is both critical and complex.

## 1.2 THE PARTICULARITY OF ISLAMIC LAW AND THE RESEARCH GAP

Beyond the ecological spirituality reflected by the "Eco-Islam" movement, it is important to emphasize that the particularity of Islamic religion is that it encompasses both spirituality and Islamic law. *Sharia'* is a polysemic word that means at the same time: the way, the source of water and the law. Islam includes both "religion and society". Its "spiritual and temporal dimensions are so closely intertwined that any fragmentation may seem contrary to its vocation".[46]

Therefore, in the Islamic world, the link between religion and the environment is extendable to the sphere of the law. In other words, the Ecological Spirituality movement cannot be understood and analyzed outside of the legal component when it comes to Islam. In fact, "[I]slamic environmental ethic is based on clearcut legal foundations which Muslims hold to be formulated by God".[47]

In spite of this reality, it seems that Islamic law has been approached almost accidentally, and from an ethical angle, while addressing environmental issues, by

---

[43] See the UNEP, UNEA, 4, Faith for Earth Dialogue.

[44] UNEP, UNEA, 4, Faith for Earth Dialogue.

[45] ISESCO was represented by M. Abdelmajid Tribak, who is in charge of the Education for the Environment program in this organization. ISESCO then hosted the fifth meeting of the Islamic Executive Bureau for the Environment. Available at: www.icesco.org/

[46] Omar Azziman, 'La tradition juridique islamique dans l'évolution du droit privé marocain', in Jean Claude Santussi (ed.), *Le Maroc actuel, une modernisation au miroire de la tradition* (Aix-en-Provence: Institut de recherches et d'études sur les mondes arabes et musulmans, Éditions du CNRS, 2013), 251–72. (Translation by the author.)

[47] Izz-Deen Mawil, 'Islamic Environmental Ethics, Law and Society', in Ronald J. Engel and Joan Gibb Engel (eds.), *Ethics of Environment and Development* (New York: University of Arizona Press, 1991), 164.

philosophers not by jurists.[48] Yet, the analysis of Islamic environmental law offers many opportunities to move from a descriptive phase of "why" (why is it important to protect the environment by using the scriptural sources of Islam?), to a more effective phase focusing on "what" (what could this protection be?) and "how" (how can these sources serve the environmental rule of law today?). As Professor Abdelzaher and colleagues put it:

> While prior research has examined the relationship between Islam ... and environmental responsibility, the majority seek to only depict foundational principles (why) of this "theological" relationship through narrative research, citing evidence from authentic Islamic teachings, rather than empirical investigation informed by an analysis of primary sources of the Islamic religion (i.e. the sayings of God and/or the sayings/teachings of the Prophet Mohammed). This religious environmental movement has recently reached a new level by addressing questions of what (what is the environment, its regard, and the role of humans toward it?), informed by empirical research.[49]

Other more detailed studies therefore merit special attention in the field of Islamic Environmental Law as a separate branch of both environmental law and Islamic law. This new branch would require scholars from both sides (Islamic Studies and Environmental Law) to communicate and work together. Not to mention that such a branch will also suppose that scholars from both sides must have a basic knowledge in the field of ecology.

A total of 1.8 billion people in the world are Muslim, representing 23 percent of the world's population in 2015 (Figure 1.2).[50] Tapping into the ecological potential of Islamic religion and law is essential to enforce environmental law and protect the planet's resources. To do so, we can rely on the ethical arguments of the "Eco-Islam" movement but also on purely legal arguments. In fact, as mentioned, if the use of religion to preserve the environment can be valuable, in Muslim countries it is reinforced by the legal rule (as *Sharia'* encompasses both).[51] In fact, if those who argue that religion can shape environmental behavior and be decisive in protection of Earth's living system might "simply [be] exaggerating the importance of religious ideas when it comes to their influence on environment-related behavior",[52] the situation is completely different concerning Islamic religion. In fact, this religion is

---

[48] See for example Ibrahim Özdemir, *The Ethical Dimension of Human Attitude towards Nature: A Muslim Perspective* (Merter/Istanbul: Insan Publications, 2d ed., 2008). See also Fazlun Khalid, 'Islam and the Environment – Ethics and Practice: An Assessment' (2010) 4, 11, *Religion Compass*, 707–16.

[49] Dina M. Abdelzaher, Amr Kotb and Akrum Nasr Helfaya, 'Eco-Islam: Beyond the Principles of Why and What, and Into the Principles of How' (in press) *Journal of Business Ethics*, 1–21, 10.1007/s10551-017-3518-2.

[50] Muslim Population by Country. Available from: worldpopulationreview.com/countries/muslim-population-by-country/

[51] See Chapter 2.

[52] Taylor and Kaplan, *The Encyclopedia of Religion and Nature*.

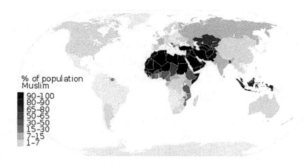

% of population
Muslim
90–100
80–90
65–80
50–65
30–50
15–30
7–15
1–7

FIGURE 1.2 Map of the Islamic world

also intertwined with the legal system. Therefore, there are more opportunities to make a shift to a more effective environmental paradigm.[53] In fact, as mentioned earlier, in Islam, law, morality, politics and religion are interconnected. Thus, before digging deeper into Islamic environmental law, it is important to recall that "Islamic law is the epitome of Islamic thought, the most typical manifestation of the Islamic way of life, the core and kernel of Islam itself".[54] Accordingly,

> The source of laws for water use and animal welfare are the same as for other aspects of human understanding and conduct. Thus, the literature on "Islam and ecology", "Islam and human rights", and "Islam and animals" follows a general pattern ... In Islam this unified approach to thought and conduct is known as *Sharia'* or "the way".[55]

Consequently, it is difficult to separate legal aspects from ethical aspects, especially while making an analysis of environmental law in the framework of Islamic law. Yet, according to Professor Willis Jenkins, "a practical Islamic environmental ethics ... may not first require a theology of nature, but an environmental jurisprudence".[56] This is exactly what the first Islamic scholars did.[57] Indeed, although Islamic law is a "sacred" law, it is by no means inherently irrational. It was established "by a rational and methodical interpretation, and the religious norms or moral rules that were introduced into the legal content provided the framework for its internal cohesion".[58] Therefore, it is essential to promote the significant opportunities inherent

---

[53] But it depends on how this legal rule is enforced. It is not always the case. On this issue, see Chapter 4.

[54] Joseph Schacht, *An Introduction to Islamic Law* (Oxford: Clarendon Press, 1964).

[55] Khalid, 'Islam and the Environment'.

[56] Willis Jenkins, 'Islamic Law and Environmental Ethics: How Jurisprudence (Usul Al *Fiqh*) Mobilizes Practical Reform' (2005) 9, 3, *Worldviews*, 341.

[57] See, for example, Ahmad Raysuni on Imam Shatibi's book on Maqasid *Sharia'* (higher *Sharia'* objectives). Ahmad Raysuni, 'Theory of the Higher Objectives and Intends of Islamic Law' (trans. Nancy Roberts), International Institute of Islamic Thought, 2005.

[58] Joseph Schacht, *Introduction au droit musulman* (Paris: Maisonneuve & Larose, 1983), 13. See Chapter 2 on the sources of Islamic environmental law.

within the Islamic perspective on environmental resource governance including Islamic law.[59]

Examples of using religion to promote ecological behavior are numerous.[60] But law is used less frequently. On the contrary, Spiritual Ecology appears as a critic of environmental law. The particularity of Eco-Islam is that it is at the same time an answer to the lack of enforcement of statutory environmental law and a means of using the law (*Sharia'*) as a solution to environmental law failure. One of the first and most powerful examples that has been promoted so far, in the framework of the Eco-Islam movement, is the environmental *Fatwas*. Fatwas are part of the *Sharia'*. They are religious decrees or opinions given by a religious authority (a *mufti*).[61] Majliss Ulama Indonesia (a commission of Muslim *Fuqaha* or *Ulamas*) is one of the pioneer Muslim institutions in releasing environmental *Fatwas*. This Majliss has also influenced other similar initiatives, mainly in Malaysia.[62] For example, in 2014 a *Fatwa* declared that the trade of wild animals is forbidden under Islamic law.[63]

However, those examples are quite rare. While there are more and more measures being taken to apply religion and Islamic law teachings to the protection of the environment, these measures are not systematic. In fact, the movement of Eco-Islam is still in its infancy.[64] In addition, the legal component of Islamic environmentalism is not sufficiently emphasized by this movement. In fact, although the faith-based ecological movements often call for the implementation of *Sharia'* rules and principles in the environmental sphere, further studies in this area are needed. Only few legal scholars have specifically analyzed the environmental Islamic

---

[59] West Asia–North Africa Institute (WANA), 'Religious Leaders Promoting Environmental Good Governance', December 2016, Amman, Jordan, 22 pp.

[60] See for example the "Green Belt Movement", the "Green Piligrimage Initiative" and the "Alliance of Religions and Conservation (ARC)". For more examples, see Sponsel, 'Spiritual Ecology as an International Environmental Movement'. See also McLeod and Palmer, 'Why Conservation Needs Religion'. For a more detailed overview, see Vincenti, '"Green" Islam and Social Movements for Sustainability'; and Schwencke, 'Globalized Eco-Islam'. See also Abdelzaher et al., 'Eco-Islam'.

[61] Typically, the issued *Fatwa* states the 'issues of the case', and then the position of the law on it. MUI's guide for issuing fatwas states: "It has become clear that to leave questions unanswered, and thus to allow the Muslim community to remain in a state of confusion cannot be validated, whether with respect to *i'tiqadi* (Muslim religious teaching) or [Sharia'] (Islamic law). For this reason, the scholars need to provide a direct answer without delay, and strive to wipe away questions of the community about the certainty of Islamic thought and teachings with respect to the questions that they encounter. In addition, every condition that can obstruct the process of issuing the answer (*fatwa*) must be overcome right away". Cited by Mangunjaya et al., 'Faiths from the Archipelago', 110.

[62] Anna M. Gade, 'Islamic Law and the Environment in Indonesia: Fatwa and Da'wa' (2015) 19, *Worldviews*, 161–83; Mangunjaya et al., 'Faiths from the Archipelago'. See also Shazny Ramlan, 'Religious Law for the Environment: Comparative Islamic Environmental Law in Singapore, Malaysia, and Indonesia', NUS Centre for Asian Legal Studies Working Paper 19/03, Centre for Asian Legal Studies, Faculty of Law, National University.

[63] Gade, 'Islamic Law and the Environment in Indonesia'. For more details, see Chapter 5.

[64] See Chapter 5.

legal rule.[65] Moreover, up to now there has been no work done in the English language on comparative law between major legal systems and Islamic environmental law.

This lack of analysis is probably due to the fact that studying the *Sharia'* from an ecological point of view is a complex endeavor. It needs not only to undertake a legal analysis (on both environmental law and Islamic law), but also requires a historical approach. In fact, most of the ecological aspects of Islamic law have fallen into disuse.[66] Therefore, it is paramount to learn how former ecological legal tools have worked in the development of the *Sharia'* and why they fell into disuse. This look at the past is timely and necessary in order to respond to the global ecological crisis.

This book proposes a research agenda in order to enforce environmental law in Muslim countries through the application of environmental rules embedded within the *Sharia'*, taking into account the essential contribution of comparative law. Islamic environmental law could in fact reveal unsuspected potential for evolution from the standpoint of comparative law, as will be discussed later.

Although it is difficult to separate the legal aspects from the ethical aspects in the fields of Islamic law and environmental law, this book will focus as much as possible on the legal analysis of the law (Islamic law, environmental law and comparative law). For the philosophical aspects, the reader will be able to refer to the numerous and rich references cited in this book.[67]

Before going further, it is important to make some basic observations about the topic addressed in this book. For example, why it is important to study Islamic law from the ecological standpoint?

### 1.3 WHY ISLAMIC ENVIRONMENTAL LAW MATTERS

First of all, it is important to note that the Islamic countries to which this study is referring are countries with a majority of Muslims and/or countries that adopt Islam in their constitutions and law. Islamic countries are located in South Asia and South

---

[65] As far as I know, the only substantive work in this direction is Professor Abd-Ar-Rahman Othman Llewellyn's chapter, 'The Basis for a Discipline of Islamic Environmental Law', in Richard Foltz, Frederick Mathewson Denny and Azizan Haji Baharuddin (eds.), *Islam and Ecology: A Bestowed Trust* (Cambridge, MA: Harvard University Press, 2003), 185–247. More recently, a legal analysis has been conducted by Shazny Ramlan on *Fatwas* (legal Islamic ruling or opinions) and *Khutbahs* (religious sermons), as legal instruments of Islamic environmental law used in three countries (Singapore, Malaysia and Indonesia) (Ramlan, 'Religious Law for the Environment'. In 2012 I also started analysis of Islamic environmental law, especially the institution of *Waqf* (also called *Habous* in Morocco) in a comparative law perspective. Samira Idllalène, 'Le *habous*, instrument de protection de la biodiversité? Le cas du Maroc dans une approche de droit comparé' (2013) 4, 1, *Développement durable et territoires* [online]. Available at: https://journals.openedition.org/developpementdurable/9732

[66] See Chapter 4.

[67] See for example Nasr, 'Man and Nature'; Khalid, 'Islam and the Environment'; Ibrahim Özdemir, 'Toward an Understanding of Environmental Ethics from a *Qur'anic* Perspective', in Foltz, Denny and Baharuddin, *Islam and Ecology: A Bestowed Trust*, 3–37; Gottlieb, *Oxford Handbook on Religion and Ecology*; Tucker and Grimm, 'The Movement of Religion and Ecology'.

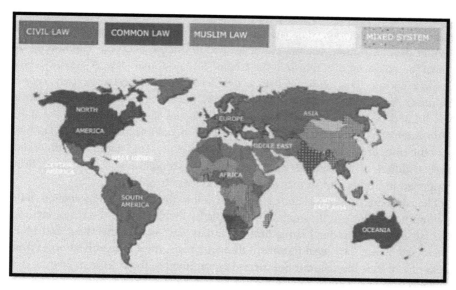

FIGURE 1.3: Map of legal systems in the world

East Asia, in the Middle East and in North Africa (Figure 1.2). However, this book also concerns itself with countries with a minority of Muslims. In fact, the application of Islamic environmental law should not be limited to Islamic countries. A parallel with Islamic finance is relevant here as countries all over the world embrace it in their banking systems ("*Sharia'* compliant funds", for instance).[68] Following this example, Islamic environmental law could also be applied in non-Islamic countries.

Second, although Islamic countries apply Islamic law in many aspects of social life, in general they no longer apply it to the protection of the environment. In fact, several Muslim countries adopt mixed legal systems (Figure 1.3). A large majority of Muslim countries have a mixed legal system including Islamic and Romano-Germanic law (also called civil law system),[69] while a minority combine Islamic and common law

---

[68] See Section 5.2.

[69] See for example Mortimer Sellers, 'An Introduction to the Rule of Law in Comparative Perspective', in M. Sellers and T. Tomaszewski (eds.), *The Rule of Law in Comparative Perspective. Ius Gentium: Comparative Perspectives on Law and Justice*, vol. 3 (Dordrecht: Springer, 2010); and Pierre Legrand, *Le droit comparé* (Paris: Presse Universitaire de France, 3d ed., 2011). See also Vernon Valentine Palmer, 'Mixed Legal Systems', in Maurro Bussani and Ugo Mattei (eds.), *The Cambridge Companion to Comparative Law* (Cambridge: Cambridge University Press, 2012), 368–83.

The Romano-Germanic legal system, also called the civil law system derived mainly from Roman law and especially from the *Corpus Iuris Civilis* of Justinian. It constitutes the predominant legal system in the world. Its main characteristics are that it is based on statutory law as the main source of law. In contrast to the common law system, the Romano-Germanic

legal systems. For historical and political reasons,[70] Islamic law in those countries is generally limited to a few areas such as family law or land tenure law.[71]

After decolonization, Islamic countries had to choose between maintaining the law of the colonizer or a return to the Islamic and customary law. A majority chose the first option. This choice led to a decline in *Sharia'* and customary law. In Morocco, for example, during colonization the field of enforcement of the *Sharia'* was limited to family law, successions, unregistered lands and *Waqf* (charitable endowments).[72] This remained the same after decolonization. Better yet, from 1957 the rules of Islamic law applicable in matters of personal status and inheritance were codified in an official legal code called Moudawana.[73] The same thing happened in Sudan and in many other Islamic countries.[74]

The consequences of this choice were also felt in the field of the protection of the environment. This was illustrated for example by the decline of the major environmental legal tools under Islamic and customary law such as the *Waqf* and *Hima* (protected areas). The legal transplant that took place through codification of these areas of law after the colonization period contributed to their decline.[75]

Third, the environmental situation in all Islamic countries is not the same. On the one hand, Muslims live in the regions most affected by climate change, water scarcity, droughts and pollution. But on the other hand, "many Muslim-majority countries continue to contribute to climate change by burning fossil fuels such as coal, gas and oil in copious amounts".[76] In fact, seven of the top fifteen oil-producing states in the world are Muslim countries, members to the Organization of Islamic Cooperation (OIC): Saudi Arabia, Iraq, the United Arab Emirates, Iran, Kuwait, Nigeria and Qatar. These countries account for over 30 million barrels of oil production per day.[77] The costs of environmental degradation in West Asia and

---

system does not give great importance to the *stare decisis*. In fact, the common law is a judge-made law. See further details in Section 4.2.1.

[70] Mark Fathi Massoud, 'How an Islamic State Rejected Islamic Law' (2018) 66, 3, *American Journal of Comparative Law*, 579–602 at 589.

[71] Otto Jan Michiel, *Sharia and National Law in Muslim Countries: Tensions and Opportunities for Dutch and EU Foreign Policy* (Leiden: Leiden University Press, 2018), 8. See also Massoud, 'How an Islamic State Rejected Islamic Law'.

[72] Leila Messaoudi, 'Grandeurs et limites du droit musulman au Maroc' (1995) 47, 1, *Revue internationale de droit comparé*, 146–54, at 149.

[73] Ibid., 150.

[74] Massoud, 'How an Islamic State Rejected Islamic Law'.

[75] See Chapter 3.

[76] Naser Haghamed, 'The Muslim World Has to Take Climate Action', *Al Jazeera*, November 4, 2016. Available at: www.aljazeera.com. For more details, see Damilola S. Olawuyi, 'Can MENA Extractive Industries Support the Global Energy Transition? Current Opportunities and Future Directions' (2020) *Extractive Industries and Society Journal*. Available at: https://doi.org/10.1016/j.exis2020.02.003

[77] Joseph Kaminski, 'The OIC and the Paris 2015 Climate Change Agreement: Islam and the Environment', in Leslie A. Pal and M. Evren Tok (eds.), *Global Governance and Muslim Organizations* (Cham: Springer, 2019), 190.

North Africa, for example, are estimated at between 2.1 and 7.4 percent of GDP in each country.[78] In the Gulf Arab states, per capita energy use is among the highest in the world. In 2014, for example, "six of the top 15 energy-consuming countries in the world were in the Gulf Arab states".[79] The Middle East would need to leave about 40 percent of its oil and 60 percent of its gas underground in order to comply with the objectives of the international climate regime and contribute to the limiting of global warming to below 1.5 degrees Celsius. But because Gulf states "hold around 30 percent of the world's proven oil reserves and 15 percent of the world's proven gas reserves, leaving the main source of income underground would be – economically and politically – a very difficult decarbonization option".[80]

However, all Muslim countries do not fit within this scenario. In fact, Muslim countries are predominantly poor countries with all the environmental concerns linked with poverty.[81] Indeed, "[s]ome of the most severe environmental problems in the world today are found in countries where the majority of inhabitants are Muslim".[82] In Indonesia, for example, it is estimated that coal-powered plants endanger the lives of 6,500 people every year.[83] Several Islamic countries are amongst the world's twenty most water-stressed states.[84] The annual internal water resources in the MENA region "amount to only 6 percent of its average annual precipitation, against a world average of 38 percent".[85] Moreover, severe ecosystem degradation due to overexploitation of natural resources is a common issue in many Islamic countries. For instance, "annual deforestation rates can be as high as 4 percent in the [MENA] region due to charcoal production for fuel and/or to profit from the Gum Arabic trade".[86] These threats

---

[78] Aicha Al Sarihi, 'Implications of Climate Policies for Gulf States Economic Diversification Strategies', The Arab Gulf States Institute in Washington, 9 July 2018. Available at: https://agsiw .org/implications-of-climate-policies-for-gulf-states-economic-diversification-strategies/

[79] Ibid.

[80] Ibid.

[81] For example, Yemen, Tajikistan, Ethiopia, Uzbekistan and Kyrgyzstan are rated among the poorest countries in the world. See for example: www.focus-economics.com/blog/the-poorest-countries-in-the-world

[82] Richard C. Foltz, 'Islamic Environmentalism in Theory and Practice', in Richard C. Foltz (ed.), *Worldviews, Religion, and the Environment: A Global Anthology* (Belmont, CA: Wadsworth, 2003), 358–67.

[83] Greenpeace Indonesia, 'Human Costs of Coal Power: How Coal-Fired Power Plants Threaten the Health of Indonesians', Greenpeace Report. Available at: www.business-humanrights.org/ en/indonesia-coal-fired-power-plants-threaten-peoples-health-greenpeace-report. See also Norah Bin Hamad, 'Foundations for Sustainable Development: Harmonizing Islam, Nature and Law' (SJD dissertation, New York: Pace University, 2017), 119.

[84] United Nations Development Programme (UNDP), 'Climate Change Adaptation in the Arab States, Best Practices and Lessons Learned' (2018). Available at: www.undp.org/content/dam/ undp/library/Climate%20and%20Disaster%20Resilience/Climate%20Change/Arab-States-CCA .pdf

[85] Ibid.

[86] Ibid.

are exacerbated by climate change impacts, which already cause the migration of thousands of people.[87]

Islamic countries should reinforce their environmental laws in order to tackle these issues. And because the legal systems in these countries are intertwined with religion, it is of paramount importance to reinforce the ecological religious–legal tools in order to ensure the enforcement of environmental law.

Fourth, in many Islamic countries, statutory environmental law is weak or not well enforced. In fact, despite the proliferation of environmental legal texts in many Islamic countries, most of them remain largely unenforced. For example, among major factors for the lack of environmental management in OIC countries we find: "(i) partial coverage of environmental issues in regulations and policies; (ii) limited availability of environmental data and their use for priority setting; (iii) low quality of environmental assessment systems; (iv) weak policy implementation".[88]

The non-enforcement of environmental law is not a phenomenon restricted to Muslim countries.[89] However, the particularity of Islamic countries is that they have a rich legal ecological heritage which is largely not explored nowadays. Yet this legacy would be likely to be effective.

In fact, as has been stated in the UNEP report on the environmental rule of law released in 2019: "[a] widespread problem with the initial framework laws is that many were based on laws of other countries and failed to represent the conditions, needs, and priorities of the countries into which they were imported".[90] Besides, the post-independence development policies often prioritize economic development rather than promoting environmental protection. Accordingly, "there is no stimulus

---

[87]  David L. Chandler, 'Persian Gulf Could Experience Deadly Heat', October 26, 2015. Available at: http://news.mit.edu/2015/study-persian-gulf-deadly-heat-1026

[88]  Other factors are: limited public information; and minimal consideration of environmental issues in sector ministries. Organisation of Islamic Cooperation, Statistical, Economic and Social Research and Training Centre for Islamic Countries, OIC Environmental Report, 2019, p. 11. Available at: www.sesric.org

[89]  UNEP, 'Environmental Rule of Law: First Global Report'. See also, for the case of Malaysia, Mohammad Noor, 'Environmental Law and Policy Practices in Malaysia: An Empirical Study' (2011) 5, 9, *Australian Journal of Basics and Applied Sciences*, 1248–60, at 1257. For the case of Morocco, see Samira Idllalène, 'La Charte marocaine de l'Environnement et du Développement Durable sera-t-elle une loi fondamentale?', *VertigO – la revue électronique en sciences de l'environnement*, Débats et Perspectives. Available at: http://vertigo.revues.org/9956. Similarly for the case of Kuwait, 'Despite government and other efforts, environmental degradation continues especially in biodiversity loss, water and air pollution and watershed destruction'. It also found that 'Legislations are still lacking' and that 'It is not lack of financial resources that inhibit progress, but rather the weakness of the relevant institutions and the lack of coordination among them, in addition to the lax application of internationally accepted environmental management standards'. Philip Tortell and Mai Al-Essa, 'Seeking Sustainability and Cost Efficiency: A UNDP Environment Programme for Kuwait' (2011), at 16. Available at: www.kw.undp.org

[90]  UNEP, 'Environmental Rule of Law: First Global Report'.

for reappraisal of the archaic colonial laws or the establishment of a systematic regime for environmental protection as a whole".[91]

Professor Abd-Ar-Rahman Othman Llewellyn considers that probably as a result of broader modernization paradigms, "[v]irtually all environmental legislation in Muslim countries is borrowed from the industrialized West, in spite of the many principles, policies, and precedents of Islamic law governing the protection and conservation of the environment and the use of natural resources. Much of this legislation remains inadequate and unenforced".[92]

Yet Muslim-majority countries represent a large part of the countries that ratified the United Nations Framework Convention on Climate Change[93] and the UNFCCC Paris Climate Agreement.[94] Most of these countries were listed as "non-Annex I" parties under the Convention, which means they have not been held to any mitigation commitments.[95] Thus, they have yet to contribute actively in the international climate change legal regime. Now, a majority of Muslim countries have presented their Intended Nationally Determined Contributions (INDCs), committing themselves to mitigation and adaptation efforts.[96] According to the Climate Action Tracker (CAT): "despite their efforts, when considering all that is needed to meet that rigorous standards set by the Paris Climate Agreement, many OIC member states' INDC plans (along with many non-OIC states') were still insufficient".[97] For example, the INDCs of Saudi Arabia, Turkey, Indonesia, Singapore and the UAE were rated as "insufficient", while Kazakhstan's INDC was rated as "medium", and Gambia and Morocco's INDCs were rated as "sufficient".[98]

---

[91] Ainul Jaria Bint Maidin, 'Challenges in Implementing and Enforcing Environmental Protection Measures in Malaysia', Malaysian Bar, November 17, 2005. Available at: www.malaysianbar.org.my/environmental_law/challenges_in_implementing_and_enforcing_environmental_protection_measures_in_malaysia_by_ainul_jaria_bt_maidin.html

[92] Llewellyn, 'The Basis for a Discipline of Islamic Environmental Law', 2. According to El-Ansary, 'For better or worse, secular approaches to environmental policy have dominated much of the Islamic world, at least since the colonial era' (in Waleed El-Ansary and David K. Linnan, *Muslim and Christian Understanding: Theory and Application of 'A Common Word'* (New York: Palgrave Macmillan, 2010), 151. Numanul Haq also states that 'we do see disappearing from the developing world practically all indigenous systems and institutions – a disappearance brought about in the recent past largely by direct European colonization, affected as a matter of deliberate colonial policy, and sometimes attended by fierce local resistance'. S. Nomanul Haq, 'Islam and Ecology: Toward Retrieval and Reconstruction', in Richard C. Foltz et al. (eds.), *Islam and Ecology: A Bestowed Trust* (Cambridge, MA: Harvard University Press, 2003).

[93] Available at: https://treaties.un.org/doc/Treaties/1994/03/19940321%2004-56%20AM/Ch_XXVII_07p.pdf

[94] Available at: https://treaties.un.org/doc/Treaties/2016/02/20160215%2006-03%20PM/Ch_XXVII-7-d.pdf

[95] Available at: https://unfccc.int/resource/bigpicture/

[96] Available at: www4.unfccc.int/sites/submissions/indc/Submission%20Pages/submissions.aspx

[97] Kaminski, 'The OIC and the Paris 2015 Climate Change Agreement', at 191.

[98] Ibid.

Muslim countries are also parties to most United Nations environmental conventions such as the Convention on Biological Diversity.[99] These international commitments did not prevent large biodiversity extinction, and all sorts of pollutions and climate change impacts, as mentioned.

I argue that because Muslim countries have a strong Islamic religious influence, there is an opportunity to orient decision-makers towards a fossil-free future that will protect the climate system. In fact, as "a way of life", *Sharia'* has a strong ecological dimension that is still subjugated in favor of the Western environmental legal model. Islamic environmental law is unknown to the majority of Muslims because in general the practice of Islam is limited to rituals or to other spheres of law (family law and land tenure more specifically) and does not involve environmental law. Therefore, the Islamic ecological heritage should be reinforced and reappropriated mainly through the law in addition to ethics, civic education and culture (Eco-Islam).[100] It is essential to enforce environmental law in order to counter the climate crisis and the loss of biodiversity. In his encyclical *"Laudato Si'"*,[101] Pope Francis, while addressing the role of religion in protecting the environment, emphasized in many parts of his discourse the importance of enforcing the law in order to protect natural resources. He also highlighted that the law should be more ethical in order to be effective for ecological purposes.[102]

The law is best enforced when it stems from the culture and beliefs of society. Islamic law is already intertwined with culture and society. If Islamic environmental law is applied through a flexible approach that corresponds to the actual needs of society, it will provide a clear answer to the issue of non-enforcement of environmental law in Muslim countries and will contribute to the global effort in this framework.

Fifth, comparatively, in the area of economics, Islamic law is growing in the banking system in many countries.[103] Following the first oil price shock of 1973–74,

---

[99] Available at: https://treaties.un.org/doc/Treaties/1992/06/19920605%2008-44%20PM/Ch_XXVII_08p.pdf

[100] As mentioned earlier, this aspect is already undertaken by many faith-based groups in Islamic countries and elsewhere. For a global overview, see Vincenti, '"Green" Islam and Social Movements for Sustainability'. See also Schwencke, 'Globalized Eco-Islam'.

[101] Pope Francis, *Laudato Si'* [Encyclical Letter on Care for Our Common Home] (May 24, 2015). Available at: www.vatican.va/content/francesco/fr/encyclicals/documents/papa-francesco_20150524_enciclica-laudato-si.html

[102] Anne Lucia Silecchia, '"Social Love" as a Vision for Environmental Law: Laudato Si' and the Rule of Law' (2016) 10, 3, *Liberty University Law Review*, 371. Available at: http://digitalcommons.liberty.edu/lu_law_review/vol10/iss3/5

[103] This revival has resulted from the emergence of a *Waqf* rehabilitation movement in the field of finance and banking. The countries that have adopted this tool in the field of finance include Saudi Arabia, Kuwait, Malaysia, Indonesia and the United Arab Emirates. Available at: www.weforum.org/agenda/2015/07/top-9-countries-islamic-finance/. The North African countries have also begun to welcome the products of Islamic banks very recently. Available at: www.africanews.com/2016/07/03/morocco-set-to-approve-10-islamic-banks-before-the-end-of-2016/

this revival was made possible by exploring the Islamic finance system that supported economic growth throughout the Muslim world during the Middle Ages.[104] Therefore, the global Islamic financial services industry now includes 284 institutions offering Islamic financial services operating in thirty-eight countries, both Muslim and non-Muslim.[105] In fact, Islamic finance is gaining momentum in the United States and Europe.[106] Its success is due to many factors, among them ethical aspects and the fact that the Islamic finance system is based on risk-sharing.

This trend could also be generalized to the protection of the environment. We can follow the same path by simply "greening" it. Some countries have already started to make this revival in the sphere of environmental protection.[107] Indeed, Islamic finance could be of great help to environmental law through some of its growing tools, such as the green *Sukuk*.[108]

Sixth, it is striking that the few Muslim countries where Islamic law is used for environmental protection (especially through charitable endowments, *Awqaf* or *Waqfs*) are, in general, countries with mixed legal systems with a common law component or at least countries that are former English colonies.[109] Among those countries, Pakistan[110] and Kuwait[111] are leading examples.[112] Comparatively, in

---

[104] Magda Ismail A. Mohsin, Hisham Dafterdar, Murat Cizakca, Syed Othman Alhabshi, Shaikh Hamzah Abdul Razak, Seyed Kazem Sadr, Thamina Anwar and Mohammed Obaidullah, *Financing the Development of Old Waqf Properties, Classical Principles and Innovative Practices around the World* (New York: Palgrave MacMillan, 2016). See also Mohammad Abdullah, 'Waqf, Sustainable Development Goals (SDGs) and Maqasidal-shariah' (2018) 45, 1, *International Journal of Social Economics*, 158–72.

[105] Wafik Grais and Matteo Pellegrini, 'Corporate Governance and Shariah Compliance in Institutions Offering Islamic Financial Services', World Bank Policy Research Working Paper 4054 (2006). Available at: https://openknowledge.worldbank.org/bitstream/handle/10986/8901/wps4054.pdf;seq

[106] Khan M. Mansoor and M. Ishaq Bhatti, 'Islamic Banking and Finance: On Its Way to Globalization' (2008) 34, 10, *Management Finance*, at 709.

[107] See further in Chapter 5.

[108] *Sukkuk* (plural of *Sakk*, bond) are instruments evidencing financial obligations. See further Section 5.2.2.

[109] Professor Al Suwaidi traced the evolution of the legal systems in the Gulf Arab states and how these countries decided at the end of English colonization to switch to other legal systems such as the civil law. This doesn't mean, however, that the legal system has completely got rid of the English legal legacy. We can sense this through the importance of case law in the former British colonies even if they claim to be civil law countries. In fact, the banking laws, for example, are also based on the common law system. Ahmed Al Suwaidi, 'Developments of the Legal Systems of the Gulf Arab States' (1993) 8, 4, *Arab Law Quarterly*, 289–301.

[110] The legal system in Pakistan 'is derived from the English model through the adoption of the laws and structures of British India, itself a codified legal system based on nineteenth century English law. As a result, the legal system and much of the substantive law of Pakistan is familiar to any Common Law lawyer'. Martin Lau, 'The Introduction to the Pakistani Legal System, with Special Reference to the Law of Contract' (1994) 3, *Yearbook of Islamic & Middle East Law*, at 3.

[111] Kuwait's legal system is a mix of British common law, French civil law, Egyptian civil law and Islamic law. Further information on Kuwait's legal system are available at: www.nationmaster.com/country-info/stats/Government/Legal-system

[112] See further Section 5.2.

Muslim countries where the legal system is a mix between *Sharia'* and civil law, *Sharia'* is not used for the protection of the environment. Indeed, in these countries environmental law is mostly statutory (Table 1.1).

One exception to this statement is Indonesia, a mixed legal system *Sharia'*/civil law/customary law, where the *Sharia'* is actively used for the protection of natural resources. However, *Sharia'*-based environmental law in Indonesia is intertwined with *Adat*, customary law. Professors Fachrudine Majeri Mangunjaya and Jeanne Elizabeth McKay summarized perfectly this idea while addressing the effectiveness of *Sharia'*-based environmental policies in Indonesia. They wrote:

> Efforts to protect or preserve Indonesia's natural environment are critically import-ant and will require a strong and innovative approach. Many conventional attempts in the past that have corresponded to government policies have, in general, followed a structural approach. This approach often represents a "top-down" pro-cess that is not socially inclusive. These policies may give the impression that local populations do not have the capacity to constructively engage in the process, particularly when the establishment of conservation areas requires the alteration of traditional rights (*"hak hak ulayat"* or *"tanah adat"*) that have been locally observed for generations.[113]

The aforementioned hypothesis based on the comparison between Muslim countries' legal systems is relevant when we observe the similarities between the common law and Islamic law instruments. These include Trust and *Waqf*, which are both charitable endowments with numerous applications.[114] Moreover, in Islamic finance the same trend is observed as the first countries that embraced Islamic finance, mainly through the *Waqf*, are also countries that have a mixed legal system *Sharia'*/common law.[115] This might be explained by the fact that countries with a mixed legal system based on common law and *Sharia'* (Islamic law) are "characterized by the flexibility of their legal system to make changes in their laws in response to the changing socioeconomic conditions and, therefore to develop the Islamic financial industry".[116] Therefore, these similarities can be usefully exploited in the framework of environmental law and natural resources conservation in Muslim countries.

---

[113] Fachruddin Majeri Mangunjaya and Jeanne Elizabeth McKay, 'Reviving an Islamic Approach for Environmental Conservation in Indonesia' (2012) 16, *Worldviews*, 286–305, at 287. See further Section 2.1.8 and in Chapter 5.

[114] See further Section 2.2.

[115] Rihab Grassa and Kaouthar Gazdar, 'Financial Development and Economic Growth in GCC Countries: A Comparative Study between Islamic and Conventional Finance' (2014) 41, 6, *International Journal of Social Economics*, 493–514 at 165. This paper compares the effects of Islamic financial development and conventional financial development on the economic growth for five GCC countries (Bahrain, Kuwait, Qatar Saudi Arabia and UAE). It demon-strates that Islamic banks appear a relevant determinant of economic growth in GCC countries. However, recently this trend has also been generalized to other countries with civil law systems.

[116] Ibid.

TABLE 1.1 Waqf *and the environment in Islamic countries' constitutions according to their legal systems*

| | Country | Legal system | Islamic supremacy clause | Environment in constitution | Waqf in constitution |
|---|---|---|---|---|---|
| Declared Islamic countries | Afghanistan | Muslim law | Preamble and Article 1 | Preamble and Article 15 | No |
| | Bahrain | *Sharia'*/civil law/ common law / customary law | Article 2: "*The religion of the State is Islam. The Islamic Shari'a is a principal source for legislation*" | Article 9 | Article 11 (public trust/ duty of care) |
| | Iran | *Sharia'*/civil law | Article 2 | Article 50 | No |
| | Mauritania | *Sharia'*/civil law | Preamble, Article 1 and Article 5 | Article 19. Article 57 on the legislation domain states that the law can be enacted on environmental matters | No |
| | Oman | *Sharia'*/common law/civil law | Article 2 | Article 12 (duty of care) | No |
| | Pakistan | Common law/ *Sharia'*/ customary law | Preamble and Article 2 | No (but right of life Article 9 was interpreted as implicitly including right to a healthy environment) | No |
| | Yemen | *Sharia'*/civil law/ common law/ customary law | Article 2 | Article 35 (duty of care) | Article 22 and Article 21 (Zakat – *Sharia'* tax article) |
| Countries declaring Islam as the religion of the state. | Algeria | Civil law/*Sharia'* | Preamble and Article 2 | No (except as included in the law domain Article 122–19) | No |
| | Bangladesh | *Sharia'*/common law | Part I, 2 A | Part II, 24: monuments) Article 15 (right to life) | No |

(continued)

TABLE 1.1 (*continued*)

| Country | Legal system | Islamic supremacy clause | Environment in constitution | Waqf in constitution |
|---|---|---|---|---|
| Egypt | *Sharia'*/civil law | Article 2 | Article 29/agriculture and environmental risk, Article 46 | Article 90 |
| Iraq | Civil law/*Sharia'* | Article 2 | Article 33 | Article 43 (included in the principle of freedom of religion) |
| Jordan | Civil law/*Sharia'*/customary law | Article 2 | No | Articles 105 and 107 (on *Sharia'* courts) |
| Kuwait | *Sharia'*/civil law/customary law | Article 2 | Article 21 | No |
| Libya | *Sharia'*/civil law | Article 1 | No | No |
| Malaysia | Muslim law/common law/customary law | Part I-3 | No | State list 9th schedule |
| Maldives | *Sharia'* | Chapter I-2 | Article 22 (duty of care), 23, 67h, 232) | No |
| Morocco | *Sharia'*/civil law | Preamble and Article 3 | Article 32 (right to a healthy environment), Article 34 (protection of the environment) and Article 72 (in the domain of the law) | No |
| Qatar | *Sharia'*/civil law/common law/customary law | Preamble and Article 2 | Article 33, Article 29 (duty of care) | No |

| | | | | |
|---|---|---|---|---|
| Tunisia | Civil law/*Sharia'*/customary law | Preamble and Article 1 | Articles 44 and 45 (duty of care) and Article 21 (right to life). Article 13 states that natural resources belong to the people of Tunisia and the state exercises sovereignty over them in the name of the people | No |
| United Arab Emirates. | *Sharia'*/customary law | Article 7 | Article 23 (for the economy) | No |
| Countries who are not declared as Muslim | | | | |
| India | Common law/Muslim law/customary law | Articles 48 A and 51 A.g | No | No |
| Indonesia | Civil law/Muslim law/customary law | Articles 28 H and 33 | No | No |
| Senegal | Civil law/*Sharia'*/customary law | Articles 8 and 25-1-2 | No | No |
| Singapore | Common law | No | Article 153 | No |

Source: adapted by author from https://constituteproject.org, www.cia.gov and www.nyulawglobal.org/globalex/

This leads to the seventh preliminary observation, which is: that the previous assumption is verified when one notices that the Trust, unlike *Waqf*, has experienced an extraordinary evolution in the protection of the environment in common law countries. As a result, in the former British colonies, the Trust-like *Waqf* has seen an ecological resurgence.

Although the *Waqf* system exists in Muslim-majority civil law countries as well, it is generally not automatically used for the protection of the environment. By contrast, in a few Muslim countries with a common law system and/or customary legal system, the revival of Islamic environmental law is an ongoing process.[117] In fact, those countries have already started to revive the *Waqf* for the protection of the environment. For example, they initiated an IUCN conference on this topic in 1994 following the previously mentioned 1983 IUCN paper by a group of Islamic scholars.[118]

Equivalent to the Trust, the *Waqf* (plural *Awqaf* or *Waqfs*) is a charitable Trust or pious endowment.[119] It is "a permanent dedication by a Muslim of any property for religious or charitable purposes, or for the benefit of the founder and his descendants, in such a way that the owner's right is extinguished, and the property is considered to belong to God".[120] The word *awqafa* is a verb literally meaning to arrest or to sequester. It is equivalent to the verb *habasa*, from which derives the synonym of the *Waqf* mostly used in North Africa, which is *hubs* or *habs*, plural *ahbas*.[121]

All over the Islamic world "from the Atlantic to the Pacific, magnificent works of architecture as well as wealth of services vitally important to the society have been financed and maintained for centuries through this system. It has been argued that many *Awqaf* had survived for considerably longer than half a millennium and some even for more than a millennium".[122] Thus, "it is not an exaggeration to claim that the *Waqf* [including environmental *Waqf*] has provided the foundation for much of what is considered 'Islamic civilization'".[123]

---

[117] See further in Chapter 4.

[118] A. Bagader et al., 'Environmental Protection in Islam' (Gland: Environmental Policy and Law Paper No. 20, 2d ed., IUCN, 1994). Available at: www.iucn.org/content/basic-paper-islamic-principles-conservation-natural-environment

[119] See Chapter 2.

[120] Jamila Hussain, *Islamic Law and Society – An Introduction*, cited by Raj Bhala. *Understanding Islamic Law (Shari'a)* (New York: LexisNexis, 2011), at 1115.

[121] The dictionary 'Lisàn al-'Arab' reveals, however, that during the early period of Islamic history these semantic differences were not drawn as sharply. As a result, it is not uncommon for modern historians of the *Waqf* to use the term 'habs' to refer to a pious endowment. Peter C. Hennigan, *The Birth of a Legal Institution: The Formation of the Waqf in Third-Century A.H. Hanafi Legal Discourse* (Leiden: Brill, 2004), xiii.

[122] Murat Cizakca, *A History of Philanthropic Foundations: The Islamic World from the Seventh Century to the Present* (Istanbul: Bogazici University Press, 2000).

[123] For example, in the first quarter of the last century, '5 to 7 percent of Palestinian land was considered *Waqf* including tens of villages. Some sources estimate that 15 percent of village land and 7 percent of town land was held in *Waqf* status. While there is less activity in the formation of a new *Waqf* today, existing institutions remain strong in Palestine'. Hennigan, *The*

The same observation can be made about the Trust. According to Professor Maitland, "[i]f we were asked what is the greatest and most distinctive achievement performed by Englishmen in the field of jurisprudence, I cannot think that we should have any better answer to give than this, namely the development from century to century of the trust idea".[124] The Trust is a fundamental common law concept. It describes "a relationship in which one person is the holder of the title to property, subject to an equitable obligation to keep or use the property for the benefit of another".[125]

Both the Trust and the *Waqf* can be used for the protection of natural resources. The *Waqf* can have many forms, among them protected areas (*Hima, Haram* or *Agdal*).[126] In fact, in the Ḥidjāz, the primitive *Waqf* is often called *Sadaqah muḥarrama*, which literally means forbidden charity.[127] The words *haram'* and *muharram* derive from the same root and have almost the same signification: that is, the idea of the forbidden, the sanctuary.[128]

However, in their origin, during the pre-Islamic era, *Harams* (or *arams*) were distinguished from *Himas*. While *Harams* were considered as "protected by a deity, and it maintained special rules and privileges" such as the banning of fighting, "which may explain their centrality in the development of Arabian trading",[129] the *Hima*, "by contrast, was an expanse of ground created by powerful nomadic lords to protect their flocks from the ill-effects of drought".[130] By creating the *Hima*, "the lords reserved to themselves, and their networks of relations and affiliates, the grazing and watering rights in certain rich pasture lands".[131]

---

*Birth of a Legal Institution*, xiii. For specific references to environmental *Waqf*, see Alan Mikhail, *Nature and Empire in Ottoman Egypt: An Environmental History* (Cambridge: Cambridge University Press, 2011), 44 and 94.

[124] Frederic William Maitland, *History of English Law*, 1968, p. 129 cited by Christopher G. Weeramantry, *Islamic Jurisprudence: An International Perspective* (New York: St. Martin, 1988), 74.

[125] George Gleason Bogert, *Handbook of the Law of Trusts* (Eagan, MN: West Publishing, 1921), 1.

[126] Hassan Jihadi, 'Agdal, ressemblance et divergence de deux législations, l'Agdal Amazigh et le Habous arabe' (in Arabic), in E. Ouaazzi and L. Aït Bahcine (eds.), *Droit et société au Maroc* (Rabat: Institut Royal de la Culture Amazigh, Série colloque et séminaires, no. 7, 2005), 259–65; A. A. Bagader, A. T. El-Chirazi El-Sabbagh, M. As-Sayyid Al-Glay and M. Y. Izz-Deen Samarrai (eds.), 'La protection de l'environnement en Islam', IUCN. 1994 (2d ed.), *Environmental Policy and Law Paper*, 20, p. 16. Available at: www.iucn.org/

[127] Translated from Claude Cahen, 'Réflexions sur le *waqf* ancien' (1961) 14, *Studia Islamica*, 37–56, at 56.

[128] In fact, *Haram* was, for example, used around the cities of Macca and al Madina according to a *Hadith* from the prophet Muhammad: 'It is sacred by virtue of the sanctity conferred on it by God until the day of resurrection. Its thorn trees shall not be cut down, its game shall not be disturbed ... and its fresh herbage shall not be cut'. *Haram* or *Harim* was also used for sources of water (seas and lakes, rivers, springs, wells, watercourses) where 'governing authorities have the right and obligation to prevent the violation of these zones'. Bagader et al., 'Environmental Protection in Islam'.

[129] J. Chelhod cited by Hennigan, *The Birth of a Legal Institution*, 63 (n. 61).

[130] Ibid.

[131] Ibid., 64.

*Himas* (or *agdals*) and harams of sacred places "often guarded by a few large families who sometimes had made adjustments to them, ... could prepare minds for the dissociation of property and usufruct, of the income [which is characteristic of the *Waqf*]".[132]

Islam prescribes the redistribution of wealth through various forms, including almsgiving, which is voluntary charity (*Sadaqah*) or compulsory payment of *Zakat*, which is mandatory charity (a sort of tax on fortune). *Waqf* falls into the category of voluntary charity.

The *Hima* is an early answer to the tragedy of the commons.[133] It is a tool for the protection of the pastoral and grazing lands within a seasonal system of closing access to these lands. *Hima* has been practiced for more than 1,400 years in the Arabian Peninsula.[134] "In pre-Islamic times, access to this place was declared forbidden by the individual or group who owned it. Later its meaning evolved to signify a rangeland reserve, a piece of land set aside seasonally to allow regener-ation".[135] The *Hima* has several synonyms in the Islamic world.[136] For example, in North Africa, *Agdal* derives from the verb *Gdl*, which in the Amazigh language means to close or to protect.[137]

The environmental *Waqf* and the *Hima* reflect the ecological dimension of *Sharia'* and, more broadly, traditions and culture in the Muslim world. So why is this dimension no longer exploited today? *Waqf* still exists in many Muslim-majority countries but it is mainly used for the construction of mosques, sometimes for schools and more rarely for the environment. But in general, the *Awqaf* (plural of *Waqf*) are not what they used to be, playing a central role in the life of the city; they have been relegated to a less important role. Nevertheless, as mentioned, in the last decade there has been a revival of *Waqf* in the field of economics in many countries.[138]

Born in England, the Trust was used "to convey the legal title to land to one person or group of person to the 'use' of another or others; the Common law would recognize the ownership only of the former person or persons, but the Court of

---

[132] Translated from Cahen, 'Réflexions sur le *waqf* ancien'.

[133] See Section 5.1.4.

[134] Hala Kilani, Assaad Serhal and Llewllyn Othman, 'Al-Hima: A Way of Life' (Beirut: IUCN, 2007), 1.

[135] Ibid.

[136] In the IUCN Regional Conservation Forum (RCF) in Iran in May 2007, the discussions focused on the potential of revival of traditional equitable approaches to nature conservation. All agreed that there are *Hima*-like systems across the region. In Sudan the word *mahmiyah* is used, in Iran *qorok* is used, in Yemen *mahjar* or *hujrah*, and *Agdal* in Algeria and Morocco. Kilani et al., 'Al-Hima: A Way of Life'.

[137] Idllalène, 'Le *habous*, instrument de protection de la biodiversité?'

[138] For a general updated overview, see: www.shariahfinancewatch.org/category/shariah-finance/. For a wide bibliography on the topic of Islamic finance until 2008, see: www.shariahfinancewatch.org/2008/02/25/bibliography-of-studies-on-islamic-finance-study-materials/. See Section 5.2.

Chancery (equity) would recognize the rights of those who held the 'use' interests",[139] and keep the property in trust for the heirs of the founder (settlor).

Charitable Trusts[140] were created because

> English feudal lords, fearing that the Church would soon rival their political power, enacted mortmain statutes which severely limited such devises. Almost immediately, however, a new form of endowment developed, designed to circumvent the restrictive mortmain acts. Rather than bequeathing property directly to a religious organization, benevolent testators began to convey their gifts to an individual in Trust for the use of the designated religious body.[141]

This system was developed by a man of the church, in this case the Chancellor. Chancery courts "balanced legal title against equitable rights, giving beneficiaries an interest in property donated for their use, and protecting them in the enjoyment of that interest".[142] It is part of the equity which is a branch of English law.

The Trust subsequently had various applications in land law, corporate law and also in environmental law, especially for the conservation of landscapes and natural sites. In England, Wales and Northern Ireland, the National Trust for Places of Historic Interest or Natural Beauty (National Trust), founded in 1895, is the most perfect application of charitable environmental Trusts. The National Trust is dedicated to the protection of historical places and spaces and it owns over 350 heritage properties.[143]

In the United States, the Trust has been even more successful in the field of environmental protection since it gave rise to a fairly well-developed doctrine, the Public Trust Doctrine (PTD). In fact, "[b]y analogy to the general law of Trusts, the government is regarded as Trustee, the public as the beneficiary of the Trust, and the natural resources as the corpus of the Trust, to be administered in the best interest of the beneficiary".[144] Originally applied to the *res communes* (navigable

---

[139] Paul G. Haskell, *Preface to the Law of Trusts* (Mineola, NY: Foundation Press, 1975), 4.

[140] Charitable Trusts have the same functions as private Trusts. However, there are two main differences. The first divergence is that in charitable Trusts the beneficiaries are in general not identified or identifiable. The second difference is the rule of perpetuity, which is automatic for the *Waqf* but not for private Trusts. For more details see Suzan N. Gary, 'History and Policy: Who Should Control Charitable Gifts?', in *Social Welfare Organisations: Better Alternatives to Charity?*, Conference Proceedings (New York: National Center on Philanthropy and the Law, 2016), 1–30. Available at: https://ncpl.law.nyu.edu/wp-content/uploads/2017/09/Revised-Gary-NYU-History-and-Policy-.pdf. For a comparison of the role of perpetuity between the private Trust and the *Waqf*, see Hamid Harasani, *Towards the Reforms of Private Waqfs: A Comparative Study of Islamic Waqf and English Trusts* (The Hague: Brill-Nijhoff, 2015), 88.

[141] Howard S. Miller, *The Legal Foundations of American Philanthropy 1176–1844* (Madison: State Historical Society of Wisconsin, Madison, 1961), ix.

[142] Ibid.

[143] The website of the National Trust contains information on its objectives and projects. Available at: www.nationaltrust.org.uk/our-cause

[144] James J. Lawler and William M. Parle, 'Expansion of the Public Trust Doctrine in Environmental Law: An Examination of Judicial Policy Making by State Courts' (1989) 70, 1, *Social Science Quarterly*, 135.

waters and submerged lands), the PTD soon became the most important concept in environmental law in the United States and was extended, after the seminal article by Joseph Sax in 1970,[145] to other natural resources. The PTD, "[f]unctioning as a public access doctrine ... imposes limits on governmental action and provides public access rights to trust resources".[146]

In sum, the PTD evolved from the Trust, which is very similar to the *Waqf*. Why then did the *Waqf* not evolve into an environmental theory as the Trust did? This book proposes an analysis of this phenomenon through the study of environmental instruments that can be and should be revived in order to protect the climate system more effectively. This analysis will be done through a comparative law lens. In fact, the success of the environmental Trust in common law countries could be inspiring for Muslim countries.

## 1.4 REINVIGORATING ISLAMIC ENVIRONMENTAL LAW AND BUILDING THE ATMOSPHERIC *WAQF* PARADIGM: LESSONS FROM COMPARATIVE LAW

While comparative law studies focus on comparisons between the Trust and the *Waqf*, especially between private Trusts and family *Awqaf* (plural of *Waqf*),[147] they have not yet expanded into the field of environmental law. Besides, even if scholars have been interested in the ecological potential of Islamic law, they have not explored the possible contribution of comparative law, especially at the level of major legal systems. A previous article attempted to remedy this gap by covering comparative law (*Sharia'* and common law, and incidentally civil law).[148] This book expands on the idea and suggests a new approach to environmental law in Muslim countries, taking into account the Islamic law sources and principles. Furthermore, this book suggests a roadmap for a doctrine based on Islamic environmental law, including not only the *Sharia'*, but also Muslim countries' ecological traditions. An important nascent literature focuses on this last aspect, especially on the *Hima* (protected areas) in the Middle East, and few are concerned with North Africa.[149]

---

[145] Joseph L. Sax, 'The Public Trust Doctrine in Natural Resource Law: Effective Judicial Intervention' (1970) 68, 3, *Michigan Law Review*, 471–566. For more details, see Chapter 4.

[146] Michael C. Blumm and Mary Christina Wood, *The Public Trust Doctrine in Environmental and Natural Resources Law* (Durham, NC: Carolina Academic Press, 2d ed., 2015).

[147] See for example Harasani, *Towards the Reforms of Private Waqfs*. See also Paul Stibbard, David Russel QC and Blake Bromeley, 'Understanding the Waqf in the World of the Trust' (2012) 18, 8, *Trust and Trustees*, 785–810; Jeffrey A. Schoenblum, 'The Role of Legal Doctrine in the Decline of the Islamic Waqf: A Comparison with the Trust' (1999) 32, *Vanderbilt Journal of Transnational Law*, 1191–203; Lionel Smith (ed.), *The Worlds of the Trust* (New York: Cambridge University Press, 2013).

[148] Except, as mentioned, my previous attempt to delve into the topic in an article I wrote in 2012. See note 79.

[149] One of the more complete studies on the topic focuses on the Middle East. See, for example, Kamal Kakish, 'Facilitating a Hima Resurgence: Understanding the Links between Land

But the legal potential of these protected areas is not yet sufficiently explored; in particular, their relationship with statutory law is not sufficiently emphasized.

It is legitimate to ask if Islamic law is able to protect the climate system and whether the potential ecological tools of Islamic law are likely to evolve like those of the common law. It is also legitimate to question the possible shortfalls of this contribution. Indeed, the question that arises here is whether Islamic environmental law, and specifically instruments such as the *Waqf* or the *Hima*, are capable of experiencing the same evolution as the Trust did in the field of common law. It is interesting to note that one of the major reasons why Joseph Sax, the father of the environmental Public Trust Doctrine, was interested in the Trust was that at the time it was difficult for individuals to gain access to justice in order to defend environmental rights.

The parallel with Islamic countries is therefore in many ways compelling: first, because of the similarities between the Islamic law (*Sharia'*), especially the *Waqf*, and the common law; second, because in several Muslim countries environmental law is generally not enforced; and third, the common law has evolved in the field of the environment by applying similar tools to the ones used in Islamic law and could thus help to inspire a reframing of this law.

The aim of this comparison is to make a call for a revival of Islamic environmental law as a framework for an "Atmospheric *Waqf* Doctrine or paradigm",[150] drawing from the experience of the environmental Trust in the common law countries, in particular from the evolution of the PTD in the United States and in many other countries around the world.[151]

It is worth mentioning that this call is not nostalgia for the past. As Professor Richard Foltz stated: "going back to some imagined past seems impossible, and its un-fulfillable promise misleading, if not dangerous ... rather, we should acknowledge that among all the possible interpretations available to us, it is the ecofriendly, nonhierarchical ones that we desperately need to articulate".[152] In fact, this call starts from a logical observation of the reality: Islamic law has a strong application in many socioeconomic fields but is still not effectively concerned, in the majority of Muslim countries, with environmental protection. Besides, statutory environmental law is

---

Governance and Tenure Security West Asia–North', West Asia–North Africa Institute, WANA, 2016. Available at: http://wanainstitute.org/sites/default/files/publications/Facilitating%20a%20Hima%20Resurgence.pdf

[150] In common law countries, the notion of doctrine refers essentially to case law. In this book, the environmental *Waqf* doctrine is broadly defined as a tool for litigation (case law) but also as a theoretical conception of the law. That is why Atmospheric *Waqf* doctrine and Atmospheric *Waqf* paradigm will be used interchangeably in this book. In fact the aim of the Atmospheric *Waqf* paradigm is to constitute the foundations of the law in Muslim countries including those that are not applying the common law.

[151] See further in Section 4.2.

[152] Richard Foltz, Frederick Mathewson Denny and Azizan Haji Baharuddin (eds.), *Islam and Ecology: A Bestowed Trust* (Cambridge, MA: Harvard University Press, 2003), 250.

not enforced in these countries.[153] Yet an environmental component is present at the core of Islamic law. This environmental component resembles the Trust in the common law that is still evolving for ecological purposes.

Furthermore, it can be argued that the similarity between *Waqf* and the Trust militates in favor of the revival of the Islamic environmental law not only in Islamic law countries but also in other countries. The comparative law approach is enriching in this regard. In fact, the Trust, which is the essence of the common law, has evolved dramatically in the field of environmental protection.[154] This evolution is still ongoing. Therefore, it is legitimate to ask whether it is possible to use the *Waqf* in this area as well. Indeed, if the *Waqf* has so many similarities with the Trust, what are the impediments to its evolution in the field of the environment? Is this evolution desirable? Is it possible? If so, what could be its ingredients?

The main purpose of this book is to analyze the ecological potential of Islamic law, especially the *Waqf* and its derivatives, through the lens of comparative law in order to call for a revival of Islamic environmental law and to suggest a roadmap for this revival.

This book addresses the main issues noted, which are: an overview of the place of Islamic law in the global movement of Spiritual Ecology, especially in its implementation in Muslim countries. In order to do so, I first explain what are the sources of Islamic environmental law, and then analyze two major environmental instruments under Islamic law, namely the *Waqf* and the *Hima* (or *Agdal*) (Chapter 2). The third chapter addresses the reasons why Islamic environmental law has fallen into disuse. The chapter largely borrows from existing work on the subject of the *Waqf* and also from a few studies on the customary environmental law in Muslim countries, as customary rules are often intertwined with religious rules in these countries. The fourth chapter focuses on the main comparisons between the Trust and the *Waqf* and explains how the Trust in common law countries has evolved in the field of the environment. It particularly addresses evolution from the concept of the Trust to the principle of the Public Trust Doctrine and how this principle served as the main argument in the Atmospheric Trust litigation, for example.

Chapter 5 explores the potential for growth of environmental law in Muslim countries. It delves into Islamic law principles embedded in the institutions of *Waqf* and *Hima/Agdal* by comparing them to modern environmental law principles in order to argue for the importance of their revival. Then it analyzes some avenues to be explored in the field of Islamic environmental law as a framework for the Atmospheric *Waqf* Doctrine.

---

[153] UNEP, 'Environmental Rule of Law: First Global Report'.
[154] See Chapter 4.

# What Is "Islamic Environmental Law"?

The Islamic tradition places great emphasis upon the centrality of the Holy Law, or shariah, in the good life. At the same time, it affirms with equal emphasis that the Holy Law is not given to man ready-made, to be passively received and applied; rather, it is to be actively constructed on the basis of those sacred texts which are its acknowledged sources.

Bernard Weiss[1]

For many Muslim thinkers, "Islamic Environmental Law" is self-evident.[2] However, to an environmental law scholar, talking about Islamic environmental law may seem a bit premature. As such, there is no branch or discipline, properly speaking, called Islamic environmental law. However, there are a few *Sharia'* rules that have some potential to be used for the protection of the environment.

Several Muslim legal environmental scholars have dedicated at least one article to Islamic environmental ethics.[3] But most of these studies rarely go beyond explaining the ecological significance of scriptures. Besides, to speak of a legal branch dedicated to Islam and the environment requires several conditions that are not yet met in Muslim countries today.[4]

As a source of the legal system, it can therefore be argued that Islamic environmental law is an ongoing independent legal branch. We find here and there a few

---

[1] Bernard Weiss, 'Interpretation in Islamic Law: The Theory of Ijtihad' (1978) 26, 2, *American Journal of Comparative Law*, 199–212, at 199.

[2] At the first UN Faith for Earth Dialogue during the UN Environment Assembly in March 2019 in Nairobi, I started my presentation by asking the following question: Have you already heard about Islamic environmental law? The only people who answered 'yes' were the recognized personalities in the world of Eco-Islam and the representative of ISESCO.

[3] See for example Mohamed Ali Mekouar, 'Islam et environnement: une éthique pour la conservation', in M. A. Mekouar (ed.), *Etudes en droit de l'environnement* (Rabat: Okad, 1988), 32–50.

[4] The first basic condition is to have a political will to effectively use the legal rule.

uses of *Sharia'* for environmental purposes.[5] This effort has been undertaken mainly by environmental activists.[6] Besides, a fragmented literature on Islamic environmentalism is also being developed by scholars in biology, economics and philosophy, as mentioned in Chapter 1. However, governments are slow to respond to those requirements. In fact, in Muslim countries, environmental law adopts the Western legal model.

But if Islamic environmental law is difficult to identify today, there is no doubt it once existed.[7] It is therefore interesting to examine how this law can be revived, because law – the set of legal rules that govern society – is designed to evolve. The need for an effective legal approach to protect the climate system is felt more than ever. Therefore, it is important to explore the potential of any branch of the law, especially if it has an ecological background. The call for the revival of Islamic environmental law begins with a look back at history and the *Sharia'* (Islamic law) as the common ground.

Islamic environmental law derives from the sources of Islamic law and focuses on the protection of natural resources using special tools such as a *"Waqf"* (which is basically an endowment made by a Muslim to a religious, educational or charitable cause) or a *"Hima"* (protected area).[8]

As was mentioned in the previous chapter, in Islamic society the *Sharia'* "is perceived altogether differently". It means, literally, the Way, the path to water, the source of life.[9] The *Sharia'*

> embraces in its scope every human act, including religious devotion and purely ethical issues, as well as the various fields of law known to the modern world, such as constitutional and international law, family law, penal law, law of contracts, property law, and indeed, environmental law. Each act is examined to determine how much good and harm it may lead to, not only in the material realm of the present world, but also in the spiritual realm of the hereafter.[10]

For example, commercial law prohibits usury because it is considered as not ethical. This principle is still adopted today in Muslim countries even if its application sometimes contradicts other modern legal rules.[11]

---

[5]  See Section 2.2 and also Chapter 5.
[6]  See further in Chapter 5.
[7]  See further in Chapter 5.
[8]  Professor Llewellyn cited other tools such as the *Iqta, Ijara, Ihtikar* or *Hisba*. Llewellyn, 'The Basis for a Discipline of Islamic Environmental Law', 185–247. The *Fatwas* (Islamic legal opinions) are also technical legal tools that can be used in the framework of Islamic environmental law. For more details see Chapter 5.
[9]  Ibid., 187.
[10]  Ibid.
[11]  Paraphrased from Azziman, 'La tradition juridique islamique dans l'évolution du droit privé marocain', 251–72.

In Islamic countries, Islamic law is proclaimed as a source of the legal system in the constitution (the "Islamic Supremacy clause").[12] Several countries declare themselves as Islamic countries (Afghanistan, Iran, Mauritania, Oman, Pakistan and Yemen).[13]

In general, Islamic law nowadays mainly concerns only family law and sometimes the land legal regime, while commercial law, urban planning and criminal law, for example, follow a modern legal regime based on the Western legal model.[14] This widespread phenomenon across the Muslim world "has a profound effect on the Muslim and European assumptions of what *Sharia'* is and can be".[15] Indeed, it helped to convey the image of a rigid and static law.[16] Yet, after a look back to history, we realize that Islamic law has been particularly fruitful in its adaptation to different real situations, as the analysis of two institutions of *Waqf* and *Hima* will demonstrate.[17]

In fact, Islamic law has a strong environmental cutting-edge component. This component appears through the sources of the *Sharia'* (Section 2.1) and through specific environmental legal tools (Section 2.2).

## 2.1 THE SOURCES OF ISLAMIC ENVIRONMENTAL LAW

This section describes the main sources of Islamic law that are used or could potentially be used to call for the revival of Islamic environmental law. Those sources encompass the Qur'an and the Hadith but also other complementary sources.

Islamic law derives mainly from the Qur'an, the Sunnah or the Hadith (acts and sayings of the prophet Muhammad), the *Ijma'* (consensus of Muslim jurists or *Fuqahas*) and the *Qiyas* (analogy).[18] These last two sources are part of the *Fiqh* or

---

[12] Michiel, *Sharia and National Law in Muslim Countries*, 8. See also Ahmed Dawood and Tom Ginsburg, 'Constitutional Islamization and Human Rights: The Surprising Origin and Spread of Islamic Supremacy in Constitutions', University of Chicago Public Law & Legal Theory Working Paper, No. 477 (2014); Massoud, 'How an Islamic State Rejected Islamic Law'. See also Schehrazade S. Rehman and Hossein Askari, 'How Islamic Are Islamic Countries?' (2010) 10, 2, *Global Economy Journal*. Available at: www.worldscientific.com/doi/abs/10.2202/1524-5861.1614

[13] For example, Islamic Republic of Mauritania, Islamic Republic of Afghanistan, Islamic Republic of Iran. This doesn't show, however, the degree of implementation of *Sharia'* as a state religion. For example, Saudi Arabia is one of the countries that applies *Sharia'* in the whole legal system (including in criminal law) but does not declare itself as an Islamic country (the Kingdom of Saudi Arabia).

[14] Michiel, *Sharia and National Law in Muslim Countries*.

[15] Anver M. Emon , 'Shari'a and the Modern State', in Anver M. Emon, Mark Ellis and Benjamin Glahn (eds.), *Islamic Law and International Human Rights Law: Searching for Common Ground* (London: Oxford University Press, 2012), 67.

[16] Ibid., 65.

[17] Ibid. See also Weeramantry, *Islamic Jurisprudence: An International Perspective*, 74.

[18] For a general overview of Islamic law sources, see Schacht, *An Introduction to Islamic Law*. See also Christopher C. Weeramantry, *Islamic Jurisprudence: An International Perspective*; and Wael B. Hallaq, *An Introduction to Islamic Law* (New York: Cambridge University Press, 2009).

FIGURE 2.1 The sources of Islamic environmental law

Islamic science (also known as *Ilm Usul Al Fiqh*) developed on the basis of the Qur'an and the Sunnah or Hadith.

*Qiyas* is applied in the framework of the *Ijtihad* (independent legal reasoning). *Ijtihad* also seeks to apply general principles such as the concept of *Al Maslaha* (public good or benefit or public welfare) or *Istihsan* (seeking benefits) which are parts of the higher objectives of Islamic law (*Maqasid al sharia'*). These are mainly to protect faith, freedom of belief and worship.[19] *Ijma', Qiyas, Ijtihad, Istislah* and *Istihsan* are considered as complementary sources of Islamic law besides the *urf* (customs) (Figure 2.1).

### 2.1.1 *The Qur'an: The Principal Source of Islamic Environmental Law*

The Qur'an is the main source of Islamic law. All schools of Islamic law agree with the principles of the Qur'an, even though they can have different interpretations of its verses.[20]

---

[19] Raysuni, 'Theory of the Higher Objectives'.
[20] The Islamic legal schools (*madahib*) in Sunni Islam are Hanafi, Maliki, Shafi'i and Hanbali. In Shi'a Islam, they are Imamite, Ismailite, Zaidite. See Hallaq, *An Introduction to Islamic Law*, 31. See also for a brief overview: Aaron W. Hugues, 'Why Is Islam So Different in Different Countries?', *The Conversation*, February 18, 2016. Available at: https://theconversation.com/why-is-islam-so-different-in-different-countries-51804

The purpose of the Qur'an is "to awaken in man the higher consciousness of his manifold relations with God and universe".[21] Many verses of the Qur'an contain the idea of the protection of the environment.[22] For example: "you can see no fault in His creation" (Qur'an, Surah Al-Mulk, 67:3).[23] In fact, in the Qur'an nature is a sign (*aya*) or verse. Aya means both the Qur'anic verses (as statement from God) and nature as a sign of God.[24] The Qur'an also states: "Corruption has appeared on land and sea by what people's own hands have wrought, that He may let them taste some consequences of their deeds, so that they may turn back" (Qur'an, Surah Ar-Rum, 30: 41).

The Qur'an contains numerous Surahs (verses) on the protection of animals, trees and water.[25] Some scholars interpret the verse entitled "the Smoke" as bearing an ecological dimension. It is considered by them as a warning of punishment that "is likely to come about as a result of mankind's ill treatment of nature".[26]

In total, "675 verses in 84 chapters, throughout the 30 parts of the Qur'an, have environmental content relating to the core components of the environments: human beings, water, air, land, plant, animals, and other natural resources".[27] According to the Qur'an, natural resources are part of the global community of creation.[28] The principle of *Khilafa* (viceregency or trusteeship) confirms the responsibility of human beings for the protection of the environment with which they have been entrusted.[29]

The Qur'an states that there is "a due measure (*qadr*) to things, and a balance (*mizan*) in the cosmos, and humanity is transcendentally committed not to disturb

[21] Sir Muhammad Iqbal, *Payam-i-mashriq* (Sheikh Ghulam Ali, 1958), cited by Özdemir, *The Ethical Dimension of Human Attitude towards Nature*, 1124.

[22] Khalid, 'Islam and the Environment'. See also Mohammad Hashim Kamali, *Principles of Islamic Jurisprudence* (Cambridge: Islamic Texts Society, 2004); and Zeki Saritoprak, 'Qur'an', in Bron R. Taylor and Jeffrey Kaplan (eds.), *Encyclopedia of Religion and Nature* (New York: Thoemmes Continuum, 2008), 1321. For a detailed global overview, see Ghazi Bin Muhammad, Ahmed Aftab and Reza Shah-Kazemi, 'The Holy Qur'an and the Environment' (Amman: Royal Aal al Bayt Institute for Islamic Tought, 2010).

[23] The Qur'an also states: 'He created everything and determined it most exactly' (Surah Al-Furqan, 25:2) and 'It is He Who appointed the sun to give radiance and the moon to give light, assigning it in phases ... Allah did not create these things except with truth. We make the signs clear for people who know' (Qur'an, Surah Yunus, 10:5).

[24] Saritoprak, 'Qur'an', 1321.

[25] Ibid.

[26] E. Kula, 'Islam and Environmental Conservation' (2001) 28, 1, *Environmental Conservation*, at 4. For example, one of the *Ayah* of this verse states: 'Then watch for the day when the sky will bring a visible smoke' (Qur'an 44:10). The verse continues: 'But mark them on the day when the Heaven shall give out a palpable smoke; which shall enshroud mankind which will be afflictive moment; They cry, our Lord relieve us from this torment, see! We are believers. But how did warning avail them, when an undoubted apostle had come to them: and they turned their back on him' (Qur'an, Al Dukhan, 44-10-20).

[27] Abdelzaher et al., 'Eco-Islam'.

[28] Özdemir, 'Toward an Understanding of Environmental Ethics', 7.

[29] See Chapter 5.

or violate this *qadr* and *mizan*".[30] Generally, "[t]he Qur'anic prohibition of corruption in the earth wastage or excess and destruction mandates the use of techniques which maximize the conservation and beneficial use of resources".[31] In fact, all types of pollution are prohibited by the Qur'an.[32]

The ecological considerations in the Qur'an and in the Sunnah are fairly well documented and thus will not be reproduced in detail here.[33] However, it is important to mention here that the Qur'an is a source of the legal system in Muslim countries (Table 1.1). That means that its verses could be used as legal arguments in court or while enacting new laws. Therefore, they can also serve in the framework of environmental law. This has already been done in the aforementioned *Fatwas* (Islamic legal rulings or opinions) issued by the Council of Islamic Scholars in Indonesia (Majliss Ulama Indonesia) and Perlis Fatwa Committee in Malaysia, such as the *Fatwa* prohibiting the traffic of endangered species (Table 2.1).[34]

The Qur'an verses have also been used as an argument in Islamic international declarations related to the protection of the environment, such as the Islamic Declaration on Nature, the Islamic Declaration on Sustainable Development and the Islamic Declaration on Global Climate Change.[35]

These declarations emphasize quotes from the Qur'an in order to call for the protection of natural resources. The Islamic Declaration on Global Climate Change, for example, "[I]interspersed with quotes from the Qur'an, ... sets out demands on political and business leaders, as well as ordinary Muslims".[36] The declaration ends appropriately with the verse "Do not strut arrogantly upon the earth. You will never split the earth apart, nor will you ever rival the mountain's stature" (Qur'an, 17:37). This call for a paradigm shift through the verses of the

[30]  Haq, 'Islam and Ecology', 127.
[31]  Llewellyn, 'The Basis for a Discipline of Islamic Environmental Law', 40.
[32]  Taylor and Kaplan, *Encyclopedia of Religion and Nature*, 1332.
[33]  For a summary of the Qur'an's verses dedicated to the environment, see the Islamic Declaration on Global Climate Change. Available at: www.arrcc.org.au/islamic_declaration. For a general overview of the connection between Islam and the environment, see Fazlun Khalid, 'Exploring Environmental Ethics in Islam: Insights from the Qur'an and the Practice of Prophet Muhammad', in John Hart (ed.), *The Wiley Blackwell Companion to Religion and Ecology* (Oxford: Wiley Blackwell, 2017), 130–45. See also Foltz et al., *Islam and Ecology: A Bestowed Trust*. For further readings, see also: Taylor and Kaplan, *The Encyclopedia of Religion and Nature*, 1321; and Bin Hamad, 'Foundations for Sustainable Development'.
[34]  *Fatwa* number 04/2014 on Protection of Endangered Species to Maintain the Balanced Ecosystems. The text of the fatwa is available at: https://assets.documentcloud.org/documents/1049328/indonesias-wildlife-trafficking-fatwafull-text.pdf. See further Chapters 1 and 5.
[35]  The Islamic Declaration on Sustainable Development is available at: www.isesco.org/. The Islamic Declaration on Global Climate Change is available at: www.arrcc.org.au/islamic_ declaration
[36]  Megan Darby, 'Muslim Leaders Tell Petropowers to Lead on Climate Change', *Climate Change News*, 2015. Available at: www.climatechangenews.com/2015/08/18/muslim-leaders-call-on-faithful-to-tackle-climate-change/

TABLE 2.1 *Environmental* Fatwas *in the world*

| *Fatwa* date | Country | *Fatwa* topic | Text or information source |
|---|---|---|---|
| 1992 | Yemen | Against Killing Animals | www.arcworld.org www.almotamar.net/ |
| 2002 | Qatar - Worldwide | Islam and the Environment | www.islamweb.net |
| 2006 | MUI Indonesia | Forest Fires and Smog (Kalimantan) | www.arcworld.org http://sipongi.menlhk.go.id/ cms/images/files/10246.pdf |
| 2011 | MUI Indonesia | Environmentally Friendly Mining Practices | https://mui.or.id/ |
| 2014 | MUI Indonesia | Wildlife Conservation for the Preservation of Ecosystem Balance | www.arcworld.org |
| 2014 | MUI Indonesia | Waste Management for the Prevention of Environmental Degradation | https://mui.or.id/ |
| 2014 | Terengganu's Mufti Department – Malaysia | Against Wildlife Poaching | www.arcworld.org www.nst.com.my |
| 2015 | MUI Indonesia | The Utilization of *Zakat* Wealth, *Infaq, Sadaqah,* and *Waqf* for the Construction of Clean Water and Sanitation Facilities for Communities | https://mui.or.id/ |
| 2015 | Dar *Al-Iftaa* Egypt | On Killing stray animals | www.dar-alifta.org |
| 2016 | MUI Indonesia | Regarding the Law on the Burning of Forests and Land, and the Control Thereof | www.arcworld.org |
| 2016 | Dar Al-Iftaa Egypt | A Ruling on Dumping Garbage and Dead Animals in the Nile and Canals? | www.dar-alifta.org |
| 2016 | Malaysia | Pollution of the Environment (*Fatwa Pencemaran Alam Sekitar*) | https://mufti.perlis.gov.my/ index.php/himpunan-fatwa-negeri/113-fatwa-pencemaran-alam-sekitar |

Source: author.

Qur'an embraces "the notion that we are now entering an 'Anthropocene' (an 'age of humans') in which the vaunted pride of human irresponsibility towards the environment is plain for all to see".[37] As was mentioned earlier, this declaration

[37] Chaplin, 'The Global Greening of Religion', 3.

echoes Pope Francis's Encyclical *Laudato Si'* and was adopted in a critical moment, as a lead-up to the Paris Climate Summit.[38]

Similarly, in Egypt, environmental activists prepared two booklets they handed to the Commission in charge of drafting the new constitution. The booklets contain the main Qur'an Surahs and Hadith on animal welfare.[39]

### 2.1.2 *The Sunnah or Hadith: The Interpreting Rules of Islamic Environmental Law*

The Sunnah or Hadith – all the acts and sayings of the prophet Muhammad – is the second source of *Sharia'*.[40] Although not all Hadiths are verified and should not be considered as such (*sahih* or true), it is important to emphasize that according to the tradition of the prophet Muhammad, the protection of animals and natural resources generally is central to the Sunnah.[41]

According to the Hadith, man will be rewarded for his efforts to develop the land in a manner that benefits Allah's creation. In fact, working the land diligently is considered as an act of worship. Imam Al-Bukhari reports that, "Anyone who plants a tree or sows a field and a human, bird or animal eats from it, it shall be counted as charity from him".[42] It is interesting to note that "in *Ṣaḥīḥ al-Bukhārī*, considered the most authentic of the six canonical authoritative collections of *'aḥādīt h* (*Al-Kutub as-Sittah*), there is an entire 'Book of Agriculture' that deals with many different environment-related issues, including regular admonitions to properly cultivate the land and to be charitable in the distribution of its resources".[43]

According to Professor Ibrahim Özdemir, the prophet Muhammad can be considered as the first example of the Qur'anic viceregency.[44] Indeed, the prophet "attached great importance, in his own practice and saying (hadiths), not only to public worship, civil law, and social etiquette, but also to planting trees, preserving forests, and conserving the environment".[45]

---

[38] See further Chapter 5.

[39] For more details, see Kristen A. Stilt, 'Constitutional Innovation and Animal Protection in Egypt' (2017) 43, 4, *Law and Social Enquiry*, 1364–90.

[40] Hadith means the sayings of the prophet Muhammad. Sunna means the acts of the prophet. They are often used interchangeably because they both form the second source of *Sharia'* (Islamic law). In this book, I will use those terms, paying attention, when necessary, to the nuances between Hadith and Sunna.

[41] See further Section 5.1.5. Hadiths are grouped in collections by authoritative Muslim scholars. But all these collections are not considered authentic. Among the collections of Hadith considered authentic, there are the collections (called Sahih or True) by Imam Al-Boukhari and by Imam Muslim.

[42] Available at: https://sunnah.com/bukhari/41

[43] Kaminski, 'The OIC and the Paris 2015 Climate Change Agreement', at 174.

[44] Özdemir, *The Ethical Dimension of Human Attitude towards Nature*, 1124.

[45] Ibid. According to Hadith and Fiqh, discharging sewage into streams and rivers is prohibited, all potentially contaminating activities around water wells are proscribed and no animals

In early sayings of the prophet (Hadiths), what is now known as *Waqf* was referred to as "continuous charity" (*Sadaqa jariyeh*). During the time of the prophet, properties such as mosques, water bores, land and horses were made *Waqf* for charitable purposes.[46] Therefore, the prophet established the *Waqf* as an Islamic legal tool as well as the *Hima* and *Harim* (or *Haram*).[47] These two related notions were developed by Muslim scholars, "who articulated them particularly in their environmental dimensions, designing some places as protected sanctuaries". Thus, *Hima* and *Harim* (sanctuary) "developed into legislative principles of land equity on one hand; and of environmental ethics on the other, and were subsequently incorporated into the larger body of the Islamic legal code".[48] This has been made possible also through the complementary sources of *Sharia'*. In fact, these sources have played an important role in extending the implementation of this law.

Besides the Qur'an and Hadith or Sunna, the Islamic scholars (*Fuqahas*) have developed an extensive work of interpretation of these sources (*Fiqh*) by using tools such as *Ijma'*, *Qyas*, *Istihsan* and *Istislah* or *Al Maslaha* or even the customary law (*Urf*). Furthermore, judges have been able to implement these rules in the daily life of Muslims. This leads to a consistent Islamic legal legacy that could be used towards the protection of the environment today.

### 2.1.3 Ijma': *The Necessary Consensus of* Ulamas

*Ijma'* is a source of *Sharia'* that derives from the consensus of legal scholars (*Fuqahas* or *Ulamas*). It thus necessitates that the legal scholars had agreed on an interpretation of the Qur'an or the Sunna. *Ijma'* was developed after the death of the prophet Muhammad (632 AD) and within the proliferation of different schools of Islamic law. *Ijma'* is still in use today in the *Ulama's* organizations. In *Fiqh* (jurisprudence or Islamic science) books, scholars still refer to the *Sharia'* case-books.[49] Thus, *Ijma'* can either help in the evolution of the *Sharia'* or can make it more conservative.[50]

---

should be kept in close proximity to them. Besides, the prophet advised in numerous Hadiths to protect the existing trees and that Muslims should plant new trees for charitable purposes. Moreover, according to the Hadith and Sunna, '[a]n Islamic city should have a green belt where planting of crops, hay making, tree felling and hunting of animals or birds, should be forbidden, but the faithful could use the area for recreational purposes'. Kula, 'Islam and Environmental Conservation', at 5.

[46] Ann Black, Hossein Esmaeili and Nadirsyah Hosen, *Modern Perspectives on Islamic Law* (Cheltenham: Edward Elgar, 2013).

[47] See Chapter 1 and the glossary.

[48] Haq, 'Islam and Ecology', at 149.

[49] Such as the Imam Shatibi's book on Maqasid Al-Sharia'. See, for example, Raysuni, 'Theory of the Higher Objectives'.

[50] Ibid.

In the framework of environment protection, *Ijma'* could concern different aspects of environmental law.[51] The aforementioned Islamic Declaration on Nature, the Islamic Sustainable Development Declaration and the Islamic Declaration on Global Climate Change can be considered as examples of the consensus by the Islamic scholars in favor of the global treaties on the environment and could represent a starting point for the *Ijma'*. The role of faith-based groups in steering the *Ijma'* for ecological purposes is also critical.

Some Islamic environmental rules are the product of *Ijma'*.[52] Consequently, it is normal to "expect some strands of environmental ethics to vary across geographic, socio-economic, and cultural communities".[53] To be valid, *Ijma'* has to be accomplished by a *Mujtahid* who should be qualified with full knowledge of the Qur'an and the Sunnah and to perform the technics of the *Qiyas* (analogy).[54]

### 2.1.4 Ijtihad: *The Evolutionary Principle for Islamic Environmental Law*

*Ijtihad* literally means effort. Its first sense is "to infer with a high degree of probability the rules of the *Shari'ah* from the textual sources (i.e., the Qur'an and Hadith). ... The second sense ... is the implementation of the science of *usul al-fiqh* and applying it to particular situations and issues, that is, the formulation of a legal opinion or judgment (*hukm shar'i*)".[55]

*Ijtihad* is "the Islamic way to legislate; it is a legislative initiative based on the interpretation of the sources of Islamic law. This grounding in the sources is what maintains the 'Islamicity' of the legislated law, and therefore this is what ensures that Muslims continue to live by the 'divine' law".[56]

*Ijtihad* makes it possible to adapt religion to the evolution of society. It "is vital because it insures the continuous development of Islamic law. Legal texts are finite, and novel circumstances are infinite".[57]

One of the environmental applications of *Ijtihad* is "the ruling that on a small stream with insufficient water, the senior irrigation rights of upstream users are subject to prior appropriation. Security is thereby provided for the investment of

---

[51] El-Ansary and Linnan, *Muslim and Christian Understanding*, 289.
[52] It is possible to consider the *Fatwas* pronounced by the Majlis Ulamas Indonesia, for example, as a sort of *Ijma'*. For more details on the *Ijma'* and its different types, see Schacht, *An Introduction to Islamic Law*.
[53] James L. Wescoat Jr., 'Islam and Environmental Ethics', in Bron Raymond Taylor and Jeffrey Kaplan (eds.), *The Encyclopedia of Religion and Nature* (New York: Thoemmes Continuum, 2005), 866–68, at 867.
[54] Bhala, 'Understanding Islamic Law (Shari'a)', at 314.
[55] Feisal Abdul Rauf, *Islam: A Sacred Law* (Brattleboro, VT: Qiblah Books, 2000), 35–36. See further on the use of Qiyas Section 2.1.5.
[56] Harasani, *Towards the Reforms of Private Waqfs*, 20.
[57] Ibid., 18.

energy, time and money in revival of dead lands, by the empathic protection of the previously established irrigation rights".[58]

Up until the middle of the ninth century (850s), *Ijtihad* was used intensively by the Islamic religious and legal scholars (*Ulama* and/or *Fuqaha*). Yet, according to several scholars, the gate of *Ijtihad* was closed around the ninth or tenth century.[59] This is explained by the fact that the "Islamic legal system had developed and passed its formative stage, and with that the role of the jurist had evolved from systemising and rendering a methodological order to the legal system, to working from within a systemised and methodological legal system".[60] The consequences were the intensification of black-letter law and a decrease in creative holistic legal thought.[61]

After the tenth century, the role of Muslim jurists was confined to commentary on the works of past masters. But it attained on occasion a remarkable degree of casuistry.[62] The important Islamic jurisprudence books compiled after the tenth century, like *Tamhid* and *Istithkar* by Ibn Abd Albarri (eleventh century), *Majmu* by Alnawawi's (thirteenth century) and *Fatawas* by Ibn Taymiya (thirteenth and fourteenth centuries) are the proof that the gate of *Ijtihad* was not completely closed.[63] *Ijtihad* can, in fact, still rely on numerous techniques like the *Qiyas* and *Istihsan*. These are still in use today for comparison in the framework of *Maqasid Sharia'*.

### 2.1.5 *Qiyas (Analogy): A Tool for Comparison*

*Qiyas* literally means measurement. It is a logical method to interpret the main sources of the *Sharia'* (the Qur'an and the Hadith) by using different tools.[64] It allows Muslim jurists to find solutions to new problems which are not necessarily cited either in the Qur'an or in the Hadith (or Sunnah). For example, applying the *Fiqh* (Islamic science) principle, "the repelling of evil takes precedence over the acquisition of benefits", can lead to the closure of a polluting industry regardless of the economic loss.[65] In the same way, the *Fiqh* principles are used by the aforementioned environmental *Fatwas* in order to ask the government to protect natural resources and the climate system.[66]

---

[58] Llewellyn, 'The Basis for a Discipline of Islamic Environmental Law', 38.
[59] Schacht, *An Introduction to Islamic Law*, 69. See also Wael B. Hallaq, 'Was the Gate of Ijtihad Closed?' (1984) 16, 1, *International Journal of Middle East Studies*, 3–41.
[60] Harasani, *Towards the Reforms of Private Waqfs*, 24–25.
[61] Ibid., 26.
[62] Ibid., 33.
[63] Ibid., 25.
[64] Ibid., 320.
[65] Llewellyn, 'The Basis for a Discipline of Islamic Environmental Law', 42.
[66] See further Chapter 5.

A specific legal training is required to be able to perform the *Qiyas*:

> Only a scholar deeply learned in all the nuances of the law through many years of training was equal to the task. Such a scholar was known as a *mujtahid*, one capable of exertion or initiative in thought about the law. Such exertion or initiative was known by the name of *Ijtihad*. *Ijtihad* provided Islamic law with a means of adaptation to the changing needs of a rapidly expanding and developing society.[67]

*Qiyas* relies on two kinds of similarities between cases: "[t]he original case must be factually similar to the new situation. The legal reasoning (*'illa*) underlying each must also correspond".[68]

The rules governing the *Qiyas* have been rigorously developed by jurists in the field of the right to water, whether for humans or for animals.[69] From there, nothing prevents their implementation today in the framework of environmental law. In fact, "any action with a view to protecting the planet and environment is also a step towards achieving the objective (*Maqasid*) of Sharia".[70] For that purpose, jurists also developed other sources for Islamic law, namely the *Istihsan* and the *Istislah* (or *Al Mashala*). *Istihsan* could, for example, be used as a legal technique for seeking a healthy environment.

### 2.1.6 *The Juristic Preference:* Istihsan, *a Tool for Seeking a Better Environment*

*Istihsan* is "the determination of a solution to a legal case based on either (1) a direct provision in the [Qur'an], sunna, or consensus [*Ijma'*], or (2) reasoning by analogy [*Qyas*] from one of these three sources".[71] *Istihsan* or juristic preference means literally "seeking for good". It is a method for extracting the *ratio legis* from the texts of the law. As such, it is a flexible and thus debated source of Islamic law.[72] It expresses the "idea that equity and justice, as defined by God, must factor into the formulation and interpretation of law".[73]

*Istihsan* was called "a 'hidden' *Qiyas* by the Islamic jurists as opposed to an 'apparent' *Qiyas* which required a strict application of the law".[74] The following is a classical illustration of *Istihsan* cited by Muslim scholars (*Fuqahas*):

---

[67] Weeramantry, *Islamic Jurisprudence: An International Perspective*, 41.
[68] Bhala, *Understanding Islamic Law*, 314.
[69] Wescoat, 'Islam and Environmental Ethics', 867. See further in Section 5.5.
[70] Mohammed Obaidullah, 'Managing Climate Change: Role of Islamic Finance' (2018) 26, 1, *Islamic Economic Studies*, at 33.
[71] John Makdisi, 'Legal Logic and Equity in Islamic Law' (1985) 33, 1, *American Journal of Comparative Law*, at 73.
[72] The Shafii school, for example, rejects *Istihsan* as a tool of *Fiqh*.
[73] Bhala, *Understanding Islamic Law*, at 340.
[74] Makdisi, 'Legal Logic and Equity in Islamic Law', at 73.

Under a rule of principle, the remaining water in which a wild carnivorous animal has drunk is impure. By *Qiyas*, it looks like the rest of the water that feeds on a predatory carnivorous bird is also impure. Indeed, as the flesh of the wild animal is impure, a closer examination allows [us] to say that the water in which the animal has drunk is also impure. But as the bird does not drink water with its tongue (impure according to the rule of principle because it is a wild animal) but with its beak formed of bone. The water in which this bird has purpose is therefore not impure. This is a "hidden" reason that would destroy the apparent reason of the previous analogy. The purity of the water would then be admitted in the second case by *Istihsan*, that is to say by hidden *Qiyas*.[75]

Again, *Istihsan*, like *Qiyas*, needs to be applied by a competent scholar. According to Imam Al Ghazali, the *mujtahid* (who is exercising *Ijtihad*) has to find an indication (*dalil*) from the Qur'an or the Sunnah even though it opposes a particular reasoning by analogy.[76]

Several scholars have argued that *Istihsan* functioned as a means of bringing customary (or, in this case, "foreign" cultural practices) into the *Sharia'* in conjunction with the public interest rule (*Al Maslaha*).[77] As such it can be used today in order to revive the environmental *Waqf*.

### 2.1.7 Al Maslaha (*Public Benefit*): *The Vehicle of the Atmospheric* Waqf *Paradigm*

*Al Maslaha* (the public benefit or interest) or *Istislah* (seeking what is correct) is also a debated source of Islamic law.[78] It is used when there is no indication of right or wrong in the sources of Islamic law. *Al Maslaha* is part of the general purposes of *Sharia'* (*Maqasid*). It is inherited from premodern jurists, and has increasingly been appropriated by reformists seeking to adapt *Sharia'* to modern contexts".[79] In fact, "the concept of *maslaha* can serve as a vehicle for legal change".[80] It is thus paramount to rely on it in order to promote Islamic environmental law and to build the Atmospheric *Waqf* Doctrine.

The degree of legal change that could lead to the application of the *Al Maslaha* rule depends "primarily on the purpose *maslaha* serves within a jurist's overall conception of the law".[81] In this regard, in applying *Al Maslaha* the jurists should

---

[75] Ibid.
[76] Ibid., at 73.
[77] Kamali, *Principles of Islamic Jurisprudence*. See also Hennigan, *The Birth of a Legal Institution*, 69; and Hallaq, 'Was the Gate of Ijtihad Closed?'
[78] It is rejected by the Maliki school but is accepted with conditions by the other schools.
[79] Nathan J. Brown and Mara Revkin, 'Islamic Law and the Constitution', in Emon M. Anver and Ahmed Rumee (eds.), *The Oxford Handbook of Islamic Law* (Oxford: Oxford University Press, 2018), 34.
[80] Felicitas Opwis, 'Maṣlaḥa in Contemporary Islamic Legal Theory' (2005) 12, 2, *Islamic Law and Society* at 183.
[81] Ibid.

take into account the big picture, including developments in international environmental law.[82]

The lawgiver ultimately uses the *Al Maslaha* or *Istislah* "to create a set of considerations that not only prevents harm, but also secures benefits, for society, that are consistent with the objectives of the *Sharia'a* (i.e., religion, life, intellect lineage and property)".[83]

However, applying the *Al Maslaha* rule should fit within three main conditions agreed upon by scholars:

1 The *Maslaha* must be genuine, as opposed to just plausible.[84]
2 The proposed policy must be generally beneficial. It should confer a benefit or prevent a harm to people as a whole, not to a specific group of people.
3 The policy must not conflict with a principle that is already part of the explicit text of the Qur'an or Sunnah, or established by consensus (*Ijma'*).[85]

These conditions can be verified while making the reforms to environmental law in Islamic countries. The purpose of environmental law is to prevent and limit pollution, the loss of biodiversity and to ensure a safe climate system. Those objectives fit well with the *Al Maslaha* rule. Consequently, any rule that can help to realize *Al Maslaha* can be considered as in Islamic environmental law. Creating a paradigm shift is consistent with the first condition of *Al Maslaha*. A *Fatwa* that prohibits the killing of wild animals (because they have an ecological function and because they are protected by international law) is, in fact, acting according to a genuine *Maslaha*. This rule is also compatible with the second condition. Finally, it does not conflict with the Qur'an or the Sunna. On the contrary, it conforms to those two sources of Islamic law, especially to verses and Hadiths on the protection of natural resources and care towards animals.[86] This example could be extrapolated to many other areas of environmental law, such as the "Atmospheric *Waqf*".[87]

Basically, *Waqf* was a customary law institution. Its evolution is thus possible. It is also necessary.

## 2.1.8 Al Urf (Customary Law): Back to the Waqf Roots

Since its origins, Islamic law has not made a complete break with the previous Arabian customs. On the contrary, many of the previous Arab institutions had a new

---

[82] See further Section 5.1.
[83] Bhala, *Understanding Islamic Law*, at 341.
[84] Thus, '[p]oorly reasoned conclusions simply would be, and indeed were, rejected by the scholars. The constraint on the use of individual reasoning was disapproval, and thereby the preclusion of a proposition from gaining support to achieve the status of a consensus (*ijma'*)'.
[85] Bhala, *Understanding Islamic Law*, at 342.
[86] See further Sections 2.1.1 and 2.1.2. See also Section 5.1.5.
[87] See further Chapter 5.

revival under Islamic law.[88] *Urf* or customs are thus one of the sources of *Sharia'*. However, Islam "overruled the oppressive and corrupt practices of the [Arabian] society. Islam also attempted to amend and regulate some of the Arab customary laws with a view to bringing them into line with the principles of the *Sharia'h*".[89]

For example, the *Himas* (protected areas) and *Waqf* (charitable endowments) predated Islam. According to Professor Claude Cahen, the *harams* (or *harims*) and the *Himas* of the Jàhilì Arabs (period before Islam) had possibly provided a legal and conceptual inspiration for the first Islamic pious endowments.[90] In fact, *Waqf* and *Hima* were used for the protection of natural resources for centuries before Islam. As such, the *Hima* evolved more than 1,400 years ago in the pre-Islamic Arabian Peninsula.[91] It seems, indeed, that "pre-Islamic pagan shrines [also] provided a prototype for the Islamic *Waqf*".[92]

From the fourteenth to the late nineteenth century, jurists of Islamic law "[w]hen revising or disregarding established and accepted rulings, ... had to refer to subsidiary legal principles, such as juristic preference (istihsan) and custom ('urf)".[93] They established special rules for it. Thus, in order to be considered as such, the *Urf* should obey to certain conditions:

- First of all it should be ethically correct.
- Secondly, it should have the ingredients of a legal rule (the binding effect).

Customary law can add a flexible aspect to Islamic environmental law, which could evolve by taking into account the social roots. The combination of *Al Maslaha*, *Qias* and *Al Urf* offers multiple opportunities for the revival of this law.

For example, as mentioned earlier, Indonesia offers an interesting illustration of the combination of customary law and *Sharia'* in the field of environmental protection. *Adat* (customs), are used in the framework of Eco-Islam as a basis for numerous *Fatwas* elaborated by Muslim scholars. The "success" of Islamic environmental law in this country is an essential milestone, as Indonesia is one of the pioneer countries in establishing green *Fatwas*. Indonesia is the country where the majority of Muslims live. According to Professors Mangunjaya and McKay, the *Minang* community in Indonesia

---

[88] Madelein Fletcher, 'How Can We Understand Islamic Law Today?' (2006) 17, 2, *Islam and Christian–Muslim Relations*, 159–72 at 159 and 162.

[89] Kamali, *Principles of Islamic Jurisprudence*, 249. See also Fletcher, 'How Can We Understand Islamic Law Today?', 163. Professor Fletcher cited the customs according to which Arabs buried girls when they were born and emphasized how these customs had been banned by Islamic law since the advent of Islam in the Arab peninsula.

[90] Translated from Cahen, 'Réflexions sur le *waqf* ancien', at 56. See also Hennigan, *The Birth of a Legal Institution*, 64.

[91] Kakish, 'Facilitating a Hima Resurgence'.

[92] Hennigan, *The Birth of a Legal Institution*, 64.

[93] Opwis, 'Maṣlaḥa in Contemporary Islamic Legal Theory', at 190.

have a rich heritage of religious and cultural traditions, or *adat*, which still have a great influence on daily life. The tight bond between *adat* and Islam is encapsulated in a popular Minangkabau saying, *"adat basandi syara', syara' basandi kitabullah,"* which means that all rules and regulations within the community should be based on Islamic religious law and the Qur'an. This provided a valuable opportunity to initiate a faith-based approach to conservation.[94]

For example, in Indonesia, the *Nagari* is similar to *Hima* in the Middle East and *Agdal* in North Africa. These protected areas are an illustration of how Islamic and customary legal rules can be intertwined and conserved through continuous practices across centuries. Yet these traditional areas should constitute the foundations of modern protected areas in order to build upon their spiritual and social values.

Besides, while *Nagari* have served as a basis for a faith-based approach to conservation, this possibility is not exploited in other Islamic countries. Yet this approach, reinforced in the framework of Eco-Islam, creates incentives for Islamic environmental law in Indonesia and neighboring countries.[95]

The next section will address both how *Hima* and *Waqf* contributed to protect the environmental in Islamic society and how they can therefore be reinvigorated in the framework of Islamic environmental law and Atmospheric *Waqf* Doctrine.

## 2.2 ISLAMIC ENVIRONMENTAL LAW INSTRUMENTS: THE INGREDIENTS OF THE ATMOSPHERIC WAQF DOCTRINE/PARADIGM

The history of Islamic law reveals the use of several tools for the protection of the environment.[96] Some tools are general in scope while others are specifically dedicated to the protection of natural resources.

The main general tool that has been applied to environmental protection is the *Waqf*. As a flexible legal tool, the *Waqf* perfectly meets the requirements of the protection of environment. Thus, alongside the *Waqf* of the mosques, it was not unusual to witness *Awqaf* dedicated to the protection of animals, especially birds or old horses.[97]

*Hima, Agdal, Nagari* (numerous names for the same reality) is more specifically dedicated to the protection of lands as an answer to the tragedy of the commons.[98]

---

[94] Mangunjaya and McKay, 'Reviving an Islamic Approach for Environmental Conservation in Indonesia', at 299.

[95] See further Chapter 5.

[96] See note 7 above.

[97] See Chapters 3 and 4.

[98] In this study, I mostly use the terms *Hima* and/or *Agdal* to talk about protected areas in customary and Islamic law. In fact, each country gives different names to these protected areas. See, for example, Kilani et al., 'Al-Hima, a Way of Life'. See further Section 5.1.4.

*Waqf* and *Hima* are interwoven in the legal system in many Islamic countries. Their combination offers multiple opportunities for the protection of natural resources.[99] In fact, *Hima* may derive from the *Waqf*, which is a landmark general tool for environmental protection under the *Sharia'*.

### 2.2.1 Waqf *as a Landmark General Tool for Environmental Protection in Islamic Law*

Although it has no source in the Qur'an, the *Waqf* was developed by the *Fiqh* (Islamic sciences or jurisprudence) based on the *Urf* and the Hadith and few general verses of the Qur'an relating to charity.[100] In this regard, *Fiqh* used *Qiyas* and *Istihsan* in order to develop the *Waqf* legal theory.

Most of the *Fiqh* books refer to the Hadith of the prophet concerning a question asked by the Khalif Omar Ibn Al Khattab about land he wished to use for the purposes of charity. The prophet advised him to sequester the substance and give the usufruct.[101] The *Waqf* is "an institutional arrangement whereby the founder endows his property in favour of some particular persons or objects. Such property is perpetually reserved for the stated objectives and cannot be alienated by inheritance, sale, gift or otherwise".[102]

Professor Kolowski gave a complete definition of the *Waqf* as:

Waqf and its plural form, awqaf, are derived from the Arabic root verb, waqafa, which has the basic meaning of "to stop" or "to hold".

When the word is employed in a legal sense with regard to a piece of land or a building, it signifies that henceforth that "property" is "stopped".

In theory, it can never again change hands by inheritance, sale or seizure.

An individual creating a waqf, known in Arabic as the "waqef" or "waqif", divests him or her self of the formal rights of possession, but retains the power to appoint a custodian: "mutawalli" (literally "one who is trusted"), who manages the property dedicated. Founders of awqaf also have the power to distribute the income which that property generates for any purpose they wish, provided that the purpose is meritorious by "Islamic" standards.[103]

---

[99] See Chapter 1.

[100] For example, 'They will ask thee as to what they should spend on others. Say: 'Whatever of your wealth you spend, shall (first) be for your parents, and for the near of kin, and the orphans, and the needy, and the wayfarer; and whatever good you do, verily, God has full knowledge thereof'' (Qur'an, Sourat Al Baqarah: 2-215).

[101] In this Hadith, Khalif Umar Ibn Al-Khattab asked the prophet Muhammad for advice about land he owned in Khaybar. The prophet advised him to make the property inalienable and give the proceeds to charity.

[102] Muhammad Zubair Abbasi, 'Shari'a under the English Legal System in British India: Awqāf (Endowments) in the Making of Anglo-Muhammadan Law' (PhD thesis, Oxford University School of Law, 2013), 124.

[103] Gregory C. Kozlowski, *Muslim Endowments and Society in British India* (Cambridge: Cambridge University Press, 1985), 1.

The *Fiqh* also used the *Qiyas* (analogy) in the interpretation of the Surah Al Imran, verse 92: "By no means shall ye attain righteousness unless ye give (freely) of that which ye love; and whatever ye give, of a truth God knoweth it well".

Combining those two main sources with other Surahs and Hadiths on the protection of natural resources, it could be concluded that the *Sharia'* establishes the legal foundations for the environmental *Waqf.*

It is noteworthy that *Waqf* is distinguished from *Zakat*, which is an income transfer entitlement as a right of the poor on the wealth and income of the rich, while *Waqf* is a voluntary act and thus falls under non-entitlement transfers.[104] There are two types of *Awqaf*: the family *Waqf* (also called private *Waqf*) dedicated to the descendants of the donor and their children until their death, and the public *Waqf* dedicated to the whole community. The *Waqf* formula may specify the beneficiaries of the *Waqf* or not. Thus, the *Waqf* can name the heirs of the founder as the beneficiaries or adopt a general formula that includes all the donor's descendants.[105]

The *Waqf* can fall under several legal categories in Islamic law: charity, gifts, and inheritance. Muslim jurists often devoted a separate book on *Waqf* in their treatises on Islamic law. The legal regime of the *Waqf* is also intimately related to the property right in those books.[106]

The *Waqf* is constituted by three major components: the founder (the *Waqef*) who institutes the *Waqf*, the manager (called *Mutawalli or Nazir*) who administers the *Waqf* and the beneficiary (*Mawquf 'alayh or Mawquf liajilih'*), who can be either a member of the *Waqef* family or the general community of Muslims (Figure 2.2). The judge controls the *Waqf* and examines how it is managed.

Even if it is a family *Waqf*, the *Waqf* is finally dedicated to the poor after the death of the last member of the *Waqef* family. The manager (*Mutawalli or Nazir*) has an obligation towards the *Waqef* to diligently administer the *Waqf* assets. As in contracts in comparative law, the *Waqf* is subject to conditions of validity which sometimes change according to the school of law or the doctrine concerned.[107] In general, for it to be valid, the *Waqf* must be perpetual, irrevocable, unconditional and inalienable.

---

[104] Ahmed Habib, 'Role of Zakat and Awqaf in Poverty Alleviation' (Jeddah: Islamic Research and Training Institute, Occasional Paper 8, 2004), 63. Available at: http://ieaoi.ir/files/site1/pages/ketab/english_book/201.pdf

[105] The nominative familiar *Waqf* is allowed to include the female descendants of the *Waqef*, who could not benefit from a large part of the inheritance otherwise. The *Waqf* thus managed to escape the strict rules of inheritance as conceived in the Qur'an. As a result, there was considerable debate about the validity of this kind of *Waqf*.

[106] Maya Shatzmiller, 'Islamic Institutions and Property Rights: The Case of the 'Public Good' Waqf' (2001) 44, 1, *Journal of the Economic and Social History of the Orient*, 44–74. See also Kozlowski, *Muslim Endowments and Society in British India*, 12.

[107] For example, the rule of perpetuity is a *sine qua non* condition for the validity of *Waqf* in all law schools except for the Maliki doctrine which allows the *Waqf* to be non-permanent.

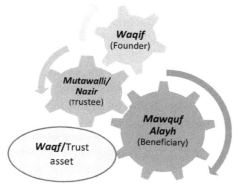

FIGURE 2.2 Functioning modes of *Waqf* and Trust

The schools of law are not always in agreement as to the possibility of alienating the property of the *Waqf*. Some are permissive when the *Waqf* assets fall into ruin and allow them to be sold or exchanged according to strict conditions, such as the use of the new property for the same purposes as the original.[108] The books of *Fiqh* also discussed the possibility of applying the *Waqf* to movable property. This application made it possible to develop a whole section of the law of cash *Waqf*.[109]

*Awqaf* (plural of *Waqf*) for public utilities also provided the services of drinking and cleaning water. Water systems

> consisting of independent wells were established especially on the highway and wells and springs with small canals and ponds set up mostly in villages and small cities. Underground-canal-based water systems were built in the major cities such as Damscus, Qayrawan, Fez and Cordova. Certain cities (like Damascus and Fez) also had sophisticated underground sewage systems built as Waqf for the city's inhabitants.[110]

---

[108] Muhammad Zubair Abbasi, 'The Classical Islamic Law of Waqf: A Concise Introduction' (2012) 26, 2, *Arab Law Quarterly*, 121–53.

[109] Ahmad Mahadi, 'Cash Waqf: Historical Evolution, Nature and Role as an Alternative to Riba-Based Financing for the Grass Root' (2015) 4, 1, *Journal of Islamic Finance*, 63–74. Available at: https://journal.wahedinvest.com/an-introduction-to-cash-waqf/. Cash *Waqf* means that a person (a company or any institution) sets aside an amount of money and its usufruct is dedicated in perpetuity to the welfare of the society: 'it aimed at mobilizing public funds to be pooled as a *Waqf* asset (financial capital/endowment) and managed in such a way that it can generate income stream besides maintaining its initial value to grow, or at least to preserve its perpetuity. The income generated from investing the funds will be distributed to the beneficiaries. Cash *Waqf* can play an important role in providing public services needed by the community'. Cash *Waqf* originates from *Waqf* on jewelry created by wealthy pious women on the Arab peninsula in order to provide loans for other women, especially for young brides.

[110] Monzer Kahf, 'Shari'ah and Historical Aspects of Zakah and Awqaf', cited by Habib, 'Role of Zakat and Awqaf in Poverty Alleviation', 34.

Waqf is in fact a major welfare services tool in the Islamic world.[111] Its applications encompassed water supply, gardens, animal welfare, schools and hospitals, etc.

According to this brief overview of the legal status of *Waqf*, it is possible to understand how environmental *Waqf* worked in the past. Indeed, it was, for example, an application of the principles of the public *Waqf* to animal species, in particular to birds. This kind of *Waqf* finds its *Sharia'* legitimacy in another Hadith of the prophet, which validates charity for animals. This Hadith reported: "The people asked, 'O Allah's Apostle! Is there a reward for us in serving the animals?' The prophet said, '[Yes] there is a reward for serving any animate [living being]'".[112]

Nevertheless, some scholars specify that the beneficiary (*Mawquf alay'h*) must be capable of owning property.[113] This statement seems to contradict the *Waqf* of animals unless it is admitted that these animals are likely to have rights. This issue has not been sufficiently developed by the *Fiqh*, as was the case, for example, for the cash *Waqf*. This debate would certainly have taken place if the protection of animals raised the same problems as today.[114]

Besides, environmental *Waqf* would have been much more developed today if *Ijtihad* (legal reasoning) had been actively used as a source of law.[115] It is, for example, possible that the beneficiaries be specified in the *Waqf* deed that they can be integrated into the *Waqf* and what is important is that they can be either humans or animals. From there, it is not excluded that the *Waqf* can also be dedicated to *Himas*. Indeed, it was sufficient that an owner declares his land *Waqf* and the sequestration is for the regrowth of the vegetation.

### 2.2.2  *Protected Areas: A Specific Tool for the Protection of Natural Resources under Islamic Law*

Like the *Waqf*, *Hima*, *Nagari*, *Agdal* and many other protected areas under Islamic law, can have a charity component. Like the *Waqf*, *Hima* is a "way of life".[116] It encompasses ecological, social and economic aspects. *Hima* is the area of defense of forests and pastoral environments, with an obvious ecological character that also reflects its cultural value.[117]

---

[111] See Chapter 1 and see further Chapter 5.

[112] Sahih Al Boukhari. Available at: https://sunnah.com/bukhari/41

[113] Abbasi, 'Shari'a under the English Legal System in British India'.

[114] See further in Chapter 5.

[115] See further on *Ijtihad* above Section 2.1 'Sources of Islamic Environmental Law' and Chapter 4.

[116] Kilani et al., 'Al-Hima: A Way of Life'.

[117] Hsain Ilahiane, 'The Berber Agdal Institution: Indigenous Range Management in the Atlas Mountains' (1999) 38, 1, *Ethnology*, 21–45. See also, Laurent Auclair, Patrick Baudot, Didier Genin, Bruno Romangy and Romain Simenel, 'Patrimony for Resilience: Evidence from the Forest Agdal in the Moroccan High Atlas Mountains' (2011) 16, 4, *Ecology and Society*, at 24.

As mentioned earlier, *Hima* and the *Waqf* share numerous features. In fact, the *Waqf* is also used to institute the *Hima*.[118] Following the advent of Islam, "religious values and norms were incorporated into the *Hima* system. The function of the *Hima* changed and became property dedicated to the wellbeing of the community around it".[119] Scholars agree that the prophet Muhammad transformed the *Hima* from a private enclave into a public asset, "distributing its shares to all members of the community, consistent with their religious duty as stewards (*Khulafa*) of God's natural world".[120]

The foundation of *Hima* under Islamic law could thus be found in the *Sunnah*, as the prophet had made the area around Medina and Macca a sanctuary (*Harim* or *Haram*) where hunting and destruction of plants were forbidden.[121] The califs (*Khulafa*) who succeeded the prophet "established additional *himas* for the cavalry, the camels allocated for charity, and the livestock of the poor".[122]

According to the Calif Omar Ibn Alkhattab: "All property belongs to God and all creatures are but servants of God. By God, if it did not bear upon the cause of God, I would not have reserved a hand's span of the land".[123]

In the first years of Islam, there was a strong central administration to manage the *Hima*. After that, these lands were managed by the tribes until the twentieth century. The delegation of authority to manage the *Hima* to the tribes "is grounded in the practice of the prophet Muhammad, and under the circumstances [it] was probably the most effective way to secure the common good at the local level".[124]

One of the first *Himas* under Islamic law (*Hima* al-Naqi') was instituted by the prophet near Al Madina.[125] It was created so that the first Muslim cavalry could benefit from the land's resources when they moved from one city to another. In the sanctuaries around the cities of Mecca and Al Madina hunting was prohibited within four miles of the city. Similarly, the destruction of plants within twelve miles was also illegal.[126] These areas were thus "considered 'safe zones', protected from overgrazing and hunting".[127]

The *Hima* "was passed from generation to generation and was practiced spontaneously and almost unconsciously".[128] Its equivalent in North Africa, the *Agdal*, is still considered more as a customary law institution than as a religious institution.

---

[118] See further in Chapter 1.

[119] Gari Lutfallah, 'A History of the Hima Conservation System' (2006) 12, *Environment and History*, at 213. Available at: https://muslimheritage.com/ecology-muslim-heritage-history-hima-conserv-syst/#sec_5

[120] Kakish, 'Facilitating a Hima Resurgence'.

[121] Lutfallah, 'A History of the Hima Conservation System', at 216.

[122] Llewellyn, 'The Basis for a Discipline of Islamic Environmental Law', 212.

[123] Lutfallah, 'A History of the Hima Conservation System', at 216.

[124] Kilani et al., 'Al-Hima: A Way of Life', 5.

[125] See Chapter 1, note 115.

[126] Kakish, 'Facilitating a Hima Resurgence', 5.

[127] Ibid.

[128] Ibid.

However, it is controlled by the religious power within the tribe.[129] As was mentioned earlier, this same aspect could also be noticed for customary/Islamic protected areas called *nagari*, in Indonesia. In fact, the *Hima* (or *Agdal or nagari*) is "the most widespread traditional land management system in [Muslim countries]".[130] It is managed by the tribe or village in accordance with its specific purposes and the specific characteristics of the site.[131] In some *Himas* grazing is prohibited, while others are used as protected woodlands or rangelands.

For example, in Arabia, five types of *Hima* have existed:

1. A *Hima* for forest trees (where woodcutting is prohibited or limited), 2. Hima in which grazing was prohibited, 3. Hima in which grazing was limited to certain seasons (such as the one for beekeeping during flowering period); 4. Hima restricted to certain species and numbers of livestock; and 5. Hima managed for the welfare of a particular community which occasionally suffered from drought or other natural disasters.[132]

To be valid under Islamic law, *Hima* has to meet four conditions:[133]

- It has to be constituted by a legitimate Islamic authority.
- It has to be dedicated to the purpose of public welfare.
- Its scope should not be too large or deprive the local community of indispensable resources.
- Its overriding aim must be the economic and environmental benefit of the community.

Like the *Hima*, *Agdal* provides a "holistic conceptual framework integrating ecosystems and resources, knowledge and practices, rules and institutions, representations and beliefs, within a territory".[134] As a resource management system, *Agdal* "offers ecological responses to environmental constraints which show common features with the contemporary new opportunistic range management at disequilibrium approach".[135]

*Hima* and *Agdal* and many other protected areas under Islamic and customary law still exist today. However, they have lost much of their power as specific tools for the protection of natural resources because of historical and political dynamics.[136] In many countries, *Himas* and *Agdals* were supplanted by the modern protected areas and sometimes simply integrated according to a new reconfiguration into new legal texts.

---

[129] Ilahiane, 'The Berber Agdal Institution', at 27, Auclair et al., 'Patrimony for Resilience'.
[130] Kakish, 'Facilitating a Hima Resurgence', 5.
[131] Ibid.
[132] Lutfallah, 'A History of the Hima Conseration System', 156. See further Section 5.3.
[133] Ibid., 216.
[134] Auclair et al., 'Patrimony for Resilience', at 4.
[135] Ibid.
[136] See Chapter 3.

The same reasons also explain why environmental *Waqf* has been frozen for decades. The inertia that affects these two institutions *Hima* (*Agdal*) and *Waqf* (to different degrees, of course) are the major impediments to Islamic environmental law.[137] These impediments can also be explained by the lack of connection between scholars in environmental sciences (including legal sciences) and scholars in Islamic sciences. This resulted in the dormancy of Islamic environmental law. Hence, the sources of environmental law are not sought in Islamic law. On the contrary they are still turning their backs on an important and rich legal heritage.

The next chapter will focus on some of the factors which are likely to lie behind the dormancy of Islamic environmental law.

---

[137] *Hima* did not experience the same fate as the environmental *Waqf*. In fact, a few *Himas* still exist in some Muslim countries because they are intertwined with indigenous customs.

# 3

# The Dormancy of Islamic Environmental Law

Rather than focusing entirely on traditional forms of charity, many of the new organizations introduced concepts into their organizational communication such as sustainable development, human rights, capacity building, and empowerment. This discursive shift was also reflected at state level.[1]

In spite of its important historical role, Islamic law dedicated to the protection of natural resources is not in effect in the majority of Muslim countries. In fact, although the tools exist in common Muslim law, they are not used for ecological purposes. For example, *Waqf*, as a provider of social welfare services, is still in use for the construction of mosques or schools in several Muslim countries, but in the majority of those countries it does not cover the ecological aspects. Yet environment is one of the major public welfare services that is urgently needed in these countries. Professor Othman Llewellyn underlined this aspect more than ten years ago. He observed that "[t]he analysis of the current environmental policy in countries where Islam is claimed as a basis for legislation by the government in power shows that instruments like the Waqf or Harim [the equivalent of Hima] are not cited as legal environmental potential instruments in those laws".[2] However, many Muslim countries recognize a constitutional value in the protection of the environment and often include Islamic principles in the preambles of environmental charters[3] (Table 1.1).

It should be noted here that the dormancy of Islamic environmental law is not of the same order as the lack of enforcement of "modern" environmental law. Indeed, the non-implementation of Islamic environmental law is due to the fact that it has fallen into disuse, whereas the non-enforcement of modern environmental law for a

---

[1]  Harmsen, cited by Dietrich Jung, Marie Juul Petersen and Sara Lei Sparre, *Politics of Modern Muslim Subjectivities, Islam, Youth, and Social Activism in the Middle East* (Basingstoke: Palgrave MacMillan, 2014), 66.

[2]  Llewellyn, 'The Basis for a Discipline of Islamic Environmental Law', 186.

[3]  This is the case for example of Saudi Arabia, Malaysia, Iran, Kuwait, Morocco.

variety of other reasons.[4] The reasons why Islamic environmental law instruments have fallen into disuse are historical, political, economic and social.

Historical and political reasons seemingly start with the fall of the Ottoman Empire and the birth of modern states with the nationalization of natural resources. Another possible factor is the separation between the stakeholders responsible for the management of natural resources on one hand and those who govern Islamic affairs on the other (Section 3.1).

On the socioeconomic level, it must be noted that Islam, although it is the very foundation of the state and the constitution, and in spite of being strong in other aspects of social life, is not always systematically translated into civic behavior.[5]

The economic factors behind the dormancy of Islamic environmental law could be summarized as the adoption of the capitalistic model based on consumerism (Section 3.2).

## 3.1 HISTORICAL AND POLITICAL FACTORS

Despite their overwhelming achievements, for centuries the fate of *Awqaf* "was closely linked to the fates of the states under which they functioned".[6] *Waqf* "experienced dramatic ups and downs: the period of establishment and growth was often followed by one of decline and neglect until with a new state emerging, renewal and prosperity once again prevailed".[7] However, according to studies, the real decline of *Waqf* and *Hima* (and then of potential Islamic environmental tools) started in the nineteenth and twentieth centuries, mostly after colonization.[8]

The first attempt at a massive centralization of the *Waqf* system was made by the decree of the Fatimid Caliph Al-Mu'izz in 369 after Hijra (AH), which ordered all the *Waqf* assets to be handed over to the Public Treasury, *Bayt al-mal*.[9] After that, the process of centralization was not linear, but what makes the reforms of the nineteenth and twentieth centuries important is that they have lasted.[10] Since then, "the *Waqfs* all over the Islamic world remain firmly centralized and controlled by the state",[11] as was also the case for the *Hima*.[12] This change is due to the

---

[4]  UNEP, 'Environmental Rule of Law: First Global Report'.
[5]  See further Section 3.2 'Socioeconomic Factors'.
[6]  On the historical and political factors in the decline of the *Waqfs*, see Cizakca, *A History of Philanthropic Foundations*. See also David S. Powers, 'Orientalism, Colonialism, and Legal History: The Attack on Muslim Family Endowments in Algeria and India' (1989) 31, 3, *Comparative Studies in Society and History*, 535–71. See also Murat Cizakca, 'Awqaf in History and Its Implications for Modern Islamic Economics' (1998) 6, 1, *Islamic Economic Studies*, 43–70 at 44.
[7]  Cizakca, *A History of Philanthropic Foundations*.
[8]  Kilani et al., 'Al-Hima: A Way of Life'; Cizakca, *A History of Philanthropic Foundations*, 1.
[9]  Cizakca, *A History of Philanthropic Foundations*, 71.
[10]  Ibid., 75.
[11]  Ibid.
[12]  Kilani et al., 'Al-Hima: A Way of Life'.

transformation in the functions of the Islamic state itself. Indeed, from distributive and accommodative functions, the state has evolved into a more controlling entity.[13]

The second historical and political factor that led to the decline of the *Waqf* is, according to authors, the impact of the colonization of Muslim countries by European countries. This decline naturally limited the contribution of *Waqf* to protection of the environment. According to Professor Murat Cizakca, "colonists wanted to acquire land in the countries that they controlled. Since *Waqf* land could not be sold or acquired, this institution emerged as the greatest impediment to colonial ambitions".[14] Consequently, in many Islamic countries, *Waqf* properties were transformed into state property (public domain).[15]

Besides this, the rejection of the *Awqaf* by the colonizer also likely stems from the fact that a corresponding role has been reserved for the charitable institutions in Europe. According to Professor Paul Stibbard and colleagues, the abuse of *Awqaf* in the Ottoman Empire and their exploitation by the British in colonial India "have real parallels to the dissolution of the monasteries and chantry endowments by the Tudor monarchs in their struggle to win the allegiance of their people away from the Pope".[16]

The first consequence of the centralization of *Awqaf* is that their management depended on the scrupulousness of the officials responsible for collecting their income. Second, the *Waqf* system was suddenly obliged to give money to the state. But it is only following the Tanzimat, during the 1830s, that the greatest blow to the Ottoman *Waqf* system began.[17]

The intervention of the state is also a factor that limited the *Ijtihad* from which the law of *Waqf* stems. It is easy to imagine that any innovative improvements of *Waqfs* were then made difficult. However, according to Professor Hamid Harasani, "the fact that state control has relegated the position of Islamic law does not mean that Islamic jurists should 'stagnate' and allow Ijtihād to 'stagnate'".[18] For some scholars, *Ijtihad* has never really ceased to function.[19] Nevertheless, concerning the environmental *Waqf*, it seems that nothing has been added by scholars so far. In fact, the number of *Awqaf* that encompass the environmental aspect has declined.

The decline of environmental *Waqf* can also be explained by the separation of the ministerial departments responsible on the one hand for the protection of the

---

[13] Cizakca, *A History of Philanthropic Foundations*, 75–76.
[14] Ibid., 78.
[15] Tahar Khalfoune, 'Le Habous, le domaine public et le trust' (2005) 57, 2, *Revue internationale de droit comparé*, 441–70. Professor Tahar Khalfoune brings the example of Algeria where the government had integrated *Waqfs* into the public domain, which took all its specificity away from this institution.
[16] Stibbard et al., 'Understanding the Waqf in the World of the Trust', at 791.
[17] Ibid., 84. See also Cizakca, 'A History of Philanthropic Foundations', 74–75.
[18] Harasani, *Towards the Reforms of Private Waqfs*, 26.
[19] See for example, Wael B. Hallaq, 'Was the Gate of Ijtihad Closed?' (1984) 16, 1, *International Journal of Middle East Studies*, 3–41.

environment and on the other hand for Islamic affairs. Now managed by the state, *Awqaf* have become the responsibility of dedicated ministries that often replaced the managers of the *Waqf* (*Mutawalli, Nazir*). Yet these departments have no connection with the ministries of the environment. As a matter of fact, environmental departments have emerged in Muslim countries on the aftermath of the decline of the *Awqaf*.

Furthermore, founding legal texts rarely treat *Waqf* as a basis, even if these texts include the Islamic supremacy clause (see Table 1.1). Besides, *Waqf* is not incorporated in environmental legal texts. Consequently, environmental instruments created in the framework of these texts are superimposed, in the best scenarios, onto preexisting environmental institutions based on Islamic or customary law. But more often they replace them. For example, environmental law does not cite *Hima* as a potential instrument for natural resources conservation or for climate system protection, in spite of their huge potential in this regard. In fact, "[f]or communities who have attempted to maintain their traditional lifestyles [through the *Hima* model], the introduction of complex frameworks and regulations concerning land ownership and urban planning have had negative impacts".[20] Consequently, in some cases, those communities have been dispossessed of their land rights, while in others they have been alienated from decision-making processes around land and its use.

In both cases, this situation negatively affected communities' sense of responsibility for their land. Consequently, "while the tradition of the *Hima* still exists in different forms and under various names, these land management systems are increasingly at risk, with declining numbers of young people involved in rangeland agricultural and pastoral activities".[21]

Moreover, from the period of banning the *Himas* to the creation of new protected areas based on international standards, there was "severe destruction of the plant cover through overgrazing and felling of trees as well as over-hunting of wild animals".[22] Therefore, the lack of regulation in some countries (as is the case in several Jordanian rangelands), is one of the reasons for the *Himas'* decline, which led to an uncontrolled increase in grazing.[23]

For example, in Saudi Arabia, from three thousand *Himas* existing in the 1950s, few dozen remained in the 2000s. Four old "*Himas*" are managed by the Ministry of Agriculture and others by local communities.[24] In Saudi Arabia, "the government took over responsibility for the management and security of rural lands resulting in a decline in local decision-making and participation in the management of *Himas*".[25]

---

[20] Kakish, 'Facilitating a Hima Resurgence', 7.
[21] Ibid., 72.
[22] Kilani et al., 'Al-Hima: A Way of Life'. See also Llewellyn, 'The Basis for a Discipline of Islamic Environmental Law'.
[23] Kakish, 'Facilitating a Hima Resurgence', 12.
[24] Ibid.
[25] Ibid., 6.

In North Africa, *Agdals* started to lose their autonomy because they became "increasingly linked to the national institutions from which they are claiming support and arbitration".[26]

As for the *Awqaf*, their general decline has also led to their disintegration in terms of environmental protection.[27] For that reason, it is no exaggeration to admit that the creation of environmental ministries in Muslim countries has contributed to the non-enforcement of Islamic and customary environmental law. The lack of knowledge by those who are designated to manage those ministries regarding the ecological potential of Islamic law contributed to this ineffectiveness.[28] Besides, the Muslim scholars (*Fuqaha*) who potentially have knowledge of Islamic environmental law ignore environmental sciences and "modern" environmental law principles.

Consequently, having no local model to follow, legal texts elaborated by these ministries followed the Western legal model as relayed by international organizations. Experts recruited to write these legal texts lacked knowledge of local realities and the history of local law. In the best scenarios, a few environmental laws, especially on water and forest management, encompassed a few "transitory provisions" stating that local traditions on natural resource management should be taken into account. This often leads to conflicts between these two legal systems.[29]

It must be acknowledged that the drafting of environmental legal texts by borrowing from the *Sharia'* and customary law is not an easy task. This requires a thorough knowledge of Islamic law and customary law, and collaborative work between the *Fuqaha*, legal and scientific scholars.

Furthermore, according to Professor Seyyed Hossein Nasr, "the autocratic, and in some cases dictatorial, nature of regimes in many Islamic countries makes an environmental movement based on Islamic principles [and thus an Islamic environmental law] a threatening undertaking if it challenges government policies and plans – many of them are dangerous from the environmental point of view".[30]

---

[26] Auclair et al., 'Patrimony for Resilience', at 10.

[27] Lutfallah, 'A History of the Hima Conservation System', 213. Available at: https://muslimheritage.com/ecology-muslim-heritage-history-hima-conserv-syst/#sec_5. See also Kilani et al., 'Al-Hima: A Way of Life'; and Kakish, 'Facilitating a Hima Resurgence'.

[28] Llewellyn, 'The Basis for a Discipline of Islamic Environmental Law', at 236.

[29] For example, in Nigeria, customary water law is not explicitly mentioned by the Water Resources Decree of 1993. This text 'vests the right to the use and control of surface and groundwater in the federal government for watercourses in more than one state'. Marco Ramazotti, 'Customary Water Rights and Contemporary Water Legislation, Mapping Out the Interface', FAO Legal Papers, 76, December 2008. Some authors argue that there is a 'resistance' of customary law in some Muslim countries. See, for example, Aboulkacem El Khatir, 'Droit coutumier amazigh face aux processus d'institution et d'imposition de la législation nationale au Maroc' (undated). Available at: www.ilo.org/wcmsp5/groups/public/—ed_norm/—normes/documents/publication/wcms_100800.pdf

[30] Seyyed Hossein Nasr, 'Islam, the Contemporary Islamic World, and the Environmental Crisis', in Richard Foltz, Frederick Denny and Azizan Baharuddin (eds.), *Islam and Ecology: A Bestowed Trust* (Cambridge, MA: Harvard University Press, 2003), 85–105, at 91.

This trend seems to have changed, at least in the MENA region. Especially in the aftermath of the tragedy of September 11, 2001, likely perpetuated by a terrorist group (Al Qaida) claiming its affiliation to Islam, governments in Muslim countries have become more aware of the necessity to promote a positive image of Islamic practices. This included a new concern for environmental faith-based groups. Professor Béchir Chourou summarizes this aspect:

> governments in the Maghreb have attempted to appeal to people's attachment to Islam to convince them to show greater respect for nature and the environment. However, this approach does not necessarily stem from any deep concern for the environment or a desire to enlist popular support for measures designed to protect the environment. Rather, it is part of campaigns waged in the Maghreb to stem the rise of Islamist/Fundamentalist movements in the region and that include such measures as increasing the number of new mosques built, or giving greater visibility to the celebration of religious holidays, or making it easier for citizens to meet their religious obligations (Hajj, Ramadan. . .). The overall message that governments want to convey is that people do not need the Fundamentalists to promote and protect their Muslim identity. In fact, most messages that governments attempt to transmit are couched in religious language, including respecting the environment and . . . being faithful and obedient to one's ruler.[31]

In both these previous scenarios, governments do not seem to be interested in environmental ethics "for its own sake". This could also explain why Islamic environmental law is not generally adopted in Muslim countries. Nevertheless, this trend might change in the framework of Islamic finance encouraged by these same countries, especially because there are many synergies between these two branches of Islamic law.[32]

In fact, as mentioned earlier, it is possible for Islamic environmental law to go along with the revival of Islamic finance by simply greening it.[33] Indeed, Islamic finance is gaining impetus in several countries and even in non-Muslim countries. This revival happened after a long period of stagnation. Accordingly, socioeconomic factors also played an important role in the decline of Islamic rules dedicated to the protection of natural resources.

## 3.2 SOCIOECONOMIC FACTORS

The decline of Islamic environmental law is linked to the fall of some important Islamic law institutions such as the *Waqf* due to the "changing typologies of wealth

---

[31] Béchir Chourou, 'Environmental Challenges and Risks in North Africa. Human Security in the Arab World: A Perspective from the Maghreb', in H. G. Brauch et al. (eds.), *Coping with Global Environmental Change, Disasters and Security*, Hexagon Series on Human and Environmental Security and Peace, vol. 5 (Berlin: Springer, 2011).

[32] See further Section 3.2.

[33] This is already happening in several Muslim countries. See further Section 5.2.

and socio-economic conditions".[34] According to Professor Jeffrey Schoenblum, among reasons explaining the fall of the *Waqf* is the fact that legislation addressing the *Waqf* "has tended more to its overregulation or outright prohibition, sometimes accompanied by expropriation of property currently held in existing Awqaf".[35]

It is particularly interesting to observe that while some religious practices are still strong in Muslim society – for example, the poor-tax (*Zakat*) and fasting (Ramadan) – environmental ethics is almost absent in the practice of religion in the Islamic world today. In fact, in countries ruled by the *Sharia*' there are "appalling cases of environmental abuse, over-indulgent lifestyles and waste".[36]

Professor Seyyed Hossein Nasr summarizes the idea of the ineffectiveness of Islamic view of the natural environment:

> One must therefore ask what the obstacles are to knowing and then implementing Islamic teachings concerning the natural environment. This question becomes particularly pertinent if one remembers that through nearly the whole Islamic world, the religion of Islam is still strong. The mosques are full, and on Fridays thousands upon thousands listen to preachers discussing various issues. Books and media programs dealing with Islam have a vast readership and audience. To answer this question, we must turn to deeper causes that concern not the religion of Islam, which places so much responsibility on human beings in their relation to nature, but the external obstacles that prevent these teachings ... from being propagated and implemented in a society in which the voice of religion is still very strong and where all ethics, whether they be personal, social, or environmental, have a religious foundation.[37]

This paradox is particularly well illustrated during the month of Ramadan, also reputed as the month of wasteful consumption. Among the examples of a wasteful economy is the case of Saudi Arabia, where the government encouraged large-scale wheat production in the desert by using expensive groundwater in an arid environment.[38]

In sum, the reasons for the non-enforcement of Islamic environmental legal rules, are: first, they are not well known. The environmental ethics of Islam is not taught, as is the case for other Islamic practices (such as prayers, fasting and pilgrimage). Therefore, it does not appear as compelling as other religious practices. Spirituality is in general limited to dogma rather than expanded to the other aspects of ethics. Second, as in other countries all over the world, the consumerist economic model is predominant in Muslim societies. This, of course, pushes environmental consider-ations into the background. Consequently, one of the first issues addressed by the "Spiritual Ecology" movement is precisely this one and how societies can move

---

[34]  Schoenblum, 'The Role of Legal Doctrine in the Decline of the Islamic Waqf', at 1192.
[35]  Ibid., at 1193. And see Harasani, *Towards the Reforms of Private Waqfs*, 73.
[36]  Kula, 'Islam and Environmental Conservation', at 6.
[37]  Nasr, 'Islam, the Contemporary Islamic World, and the Environmental Crisis', 87
[38]  Kula, 'Islam and Environmental Conservation', at 6. See also Saniotis, 'Muslims and Ecology'.

from this model to a more ethical one based on frugality. We find an echo of this idea in all Islamic declarations related to the protection of the environment adopted since the 1980s.[39]

To sum up, Professor Seyyed Hossein Nasr cited eight obstacles to realizing and implementing the Islamic view of the natural environment.[40] Besides the rapid transformation of Islamic societies due mainly to the use of modern technology, Professor Nasr advanced the factors of massive migration from the countryside to the cities, the Westernization of Islamic societies and the adoption of imported solutions to environmental problems.

Moreover, the Islamic law scholars, *Ulamas*, are not well prepared to handle the task of environmental awareness, mainly because this topic did not become crucial until recently. In fact, environmental issues are increasingly complex and even if they are well aware of the basic traditional knowledge regarding Islamic environmental law, the *Ulamas* generally lack knowledge of the current environmental issues and are more focused in their sermons on the rudiments of daily life.

This trend is now changing. Each year, the ministries of environment of Islamic countries organize conferences to debate about how Islamic ethics and law can contribute to addressing the current environmental issues.[41] Besides, in a few countries *Ulamas* are part of the Spiritual Ecology movement (Eco-Islam). This could lead to a grassroots movement that will impact the enacting and enforcement of Islamic legal rules for the protection of the environment.[42] In some countries, the religious sermons (*Khutbahs*) given by *Ulamas* include more and more ecological principles. They can even have a strong social impact. This is the case, for example, in Singapore.[43]

Neither the *Waqf* nor the *Hima* are today expressly considered potential environmental legal instruments in the statutory law in Muslim countries. Environmental legal texts are drafted following Western legal models even if they are in general preceded by preambles that acknowledge the Islamic supremacy rule.[44]

Historical, political and economic factors explain why Islamic environmental law is not functional in the majority of Muslim countries today. First of all, the ecological potential of *Waqf* has been frozen because the institution of *Waqf* has ceased to be managed by civil society and came under the responsibility of the state. This resulted in mismanagement and stagnation of the *Awqaf* in general. Second, the traditional modes of natural resources conservation were artificially transformed

---

[39] See Chapter 1 (Section 1.1 'Background') and Chapter 5.

[40] Nasr, 'Islam, the Contemporary Islamic World, and the Environmental Crisis', 87–93.

[41] See the meetings of environmental ministries of Muslim countries. Available at the ISESCO website: www.isesco.org.ma/

[42] For more details, see Chapter 4.

[43] In Singapore, *Khutbahs* are produced by the Office of the Mufti in Majliss Ugama Islam Singapura (MUIS). These *Fatwas* are available in several langages (English, Malay and Tamil). For more details see Ramlan, 'Religious Law for the Environment'.

[44] See further Section 5.2.

by colonization, and then by the new independent states, through the superposition of new models of natural resources governance. Thirdly, the ecological potential of Islamic law was eroded by the new economic model.

Overall, one of the most important impediments to the evolution of Islamic environmental law is the dormancy of *Ijtihad* as a source of Islamic law and policy. Yet *Ijtihad*, by using *Qiyas* (analogy), *Istihsan* or *Istislah* (public good), as mentioned in the previous chapter, is able to lead to an evolution of the Islamic environmental law and should be undertaken by Islamic legal scholars and environmentalists. One of the available tools *Ijtihad* can use is comparative law. Indeed, while the environmental *Waqf* have stagnated in the Islamic world, a similar institution, the Trust, has seen a continuous boom in common law countries. Therefore, the ecological potential of the *Waqf* can be reinvigorated by looking to the experience of the ecological Trust. The following chapter will focus on this prospect.

# 4

# A Fruitful Comparison with the Common Law

The public trust doctrine can be traced back to Roman civil law, but its principles are grounded in English common law.[1]

Michael C. Blumm and Mary Christina Wood

Why is it useful to compare Islamic environmental law with environmental common law?

First, it should be noted that the comparison between Islamic law and common law is not a completely new exercise. We have already seen how some authors have sought to find a common denominator between the Trust and the *Waqf*, for example.[2] However, the comparison between these two institutions has not yet been analyzed by scholars in the context of environmental law,[3] although this analysis is useful in more ways than one.

Second, the two systems of law (common law and Islamic law) have several similarities. Indeed, if the Trust is at the core of the common law, its equivalent, the *Waqf*, is at the core of Islamic law.[4]

Third, the comparison with common law is all the more useful in that it could help in finding new avenues of evolution for the environmental *Waqf* insofar as common law has succeeded in evolving Trusts in the field of environmental law. This evolution is still happening.

---

[1] Blumm and Wood, *The Public Trust Doctrine in Environmental and Natural Resources Law*, 389.

[2] See Chapter 1. Weeramantry, *Islamic Jurisprudence: An International Perspective*. See also Monica M. Gaudiosi, 'The Influence of the Islamic Law of Waqf on the Development of the Trust in England: The Case of Merton College' (1988) 136, 4, *University of Pennsylvania Law Review*, 1231–61. For a general overview see Gilbert Paul Verbit, *The Origins of the Trust* (Bloomington, IN: Xlibris Corporation, 2002).

[3] Except, as far as I know, my previous attempt to address this question: Idllalène, 'Le *habous*, instrument de protection de la biodiversité?'

[4] See Chapter 1.

Besides, as mentioned, it is interesting to observe that the few Muslim countries that are using the *Waqf* for environmental purposes today are mostly mixed *Sharia'/* common law countries or are at least former British colonies.[5] Muslim countries not using the environmental potential of the *Waqf* are in general *Sharia'/*civil law countries. This could be explained by the facility for the *Waqf* to evolve in a common law context because of its numerous synergies with the Trust (Section 4.1). These synergies should be exploited in order to ensure the revival of Islamic environmental law inasmuch as the Trust is continuing to evolve into a doctrine called the Public Trust Doctrine (Section 4.2).

## 4.1 EXPLOITING THE NUMEROUS SIMILARITIES BETWEEN THE TRUST AND THE WAQF

The principle of *Waqf* is universal. We find this principle under different names in many cultures and civilizations. This is what likely explains that narratives on the origins of the *Waqf* are not all uniform.[6] As mentioned in Chapter 1, some authors contend that the *Waqf* imitated the Trust, while others argue that the Trust was inspired by the *Waqf*. The global idea of the *Waqf* is the transmission of property from one person to another for the benefit of a third entity. The principle is distinguished from the usufruct.

Without delving into the arguments of each proponent, what is interesting to take from this academic debate is that historians agree there are multiple similarities between the *Waqf* and the Trust. According to Professor Vesey-FitzGerald, "many of the apparent borrowings between Islamic law and pre-existing Near Eastern practices may have resulted from human beings' similar responses to societal needs".[7] In fact, during the Middle Ages "the Islamic system appears to have marched on parallel lines with the canon law of the Christian Church", but "most of these parallels are due to what [David de] Santillana calls 'L'identité essentielle de l'âme humaine'".[8]

This "essential identity of the human soul" is also used today as an argument for the "Nature's Trust" paradigm that serves as a way to push the limits of the Public Trust Doctrine as conceived in the common law.[9] Professor Mary Christina Wood argues that this doctrine "retrieves essential human wisdom deposited by the ancients".[10] Therefore, if the Trust and the *Waqf* found "one soul", then they are likely both able to evolve in a similar way. It is legitimate to call for an expansion of the limits of the *Waqf* as well.

---

[5]  See Tables 1.1 and 4.2.
[6]  See Section 1.1.1.
[7]  S. G. Vesey-FitzGerald, 'The Alleged Debt of Islamic to Roman Law' (1951) 67, *Law Quarterly Review*, 81–102, esp. 83. Cited in Hennigan, *The Birth of a Legal Institution*, 61.
[8]  Vesey-FitzGerald, 'The Alleged Debt of Islamic to Roman Law'.
[9]  Mary Christina Wood, *Nature's Trust: Environmental Law for a New Ecological Age* (New York: Cambridge University Press, 2014), 16.
[10]  Ibid., 261.

The similarities between common law and Islamic law are such that in some common law states where a minority of Muslims live there is no hesitation in recognizing the *Waqf* as a Trust and vice versa. This is the case in South Africa, where "Muslims have established their *Awqaf* [plural of *Waqf*] under the South African Law of Trusts. The hundreds of mosques and madrasahs built all over South Africa are all managed under this law which is the closest approximation to an Islamic Waqf law"[11] (Table 4.1).

This is also the case in the mixed Islamic law and common law countries. For instance, in Malaysia, "people wanting to create a family *Waqf* usually choose to set up a common law Trust with family members as Trustees. However, they refer to it as a *Waqf* even though it is at law a Trust".[12]

The same thing occurs in the Straits Settlements. According to Professor Lionel Smith, "[c]onsidering the basic similarities between the English trust and the waqf, it was not surprising that Arab inhabitants of the Straits Settlements felt confident in establishing an Islamic institution within English legal jurisdictions which, after all, already possessed a similar establishment".[13]

In fact, the similarities between the *Waqf* and the Trust can be summarized in four points: the religious foundations, the similar functioning modes and purposes and the inalienability rule (Table 4.2).

### 4.1.1 *The Religious Foundations*

Even if it has no direct legal basis in the Qur'an, *Waqf* derives from doctrine of the Islamic jurists (*Fuqahas*) who refer to the Hadith of the prophet. Hence, "[t]he great attraction of the *Waqf* to devout Muslims is the theological basis of the instrument".[14] The same can be said for the *Hima*. Other Hadiths are cited as its Islamic legal foundation.[15]

Besides, no one can question the religious origins of the Trust. Originating from England, the Trust derives from Equity, which is a source of English law resulting from the decisions of the chancellor, who was generally an ecclesiastic.[16] In fact,

---

[11] Cizakca, *A History of Philanthropic Foundations*, 13–14.

[12] Stibbard et al., 'Understanding the Waqf in the World of the Trust', at 800.

[13] Smith, *The Worlds of the Trust*, 172.

[14] Stibbard et al., 'Understanding the Waqf in the World of the Trust', 810.

[15] See further details in Section 2.2.2.

[16] The common law system has two sources: case law (also broadly called common law) and equity. Trusts are parts of the equity. For further details see: Philip S. James, *Introduction to English Law* (London: Butterworths, 1979), 30 and 496. See also Frederick G. Kempin Jr., *Historical Introduction to Anglo-American Law in a Nutshell* (St. Paul, MN: West Publishing Co., 3d ed., 1990), 18. For an overview of the history of the trust, see for example William Searle Holdsworth, Arthur L. Goodhart, Harold Greville Hanbury and John McDonald Burke, *A History of English Law* (London: Methuen, 1903), 238. See also S. F. C. Milsom, *Historical Foundations of the Common Law* (London: Butterworths, 1969), 74 and following (on the rises of equity) and 169 (on the origins of the trusts).

TABLE 4.1 *Waqf laws and their potential application to the protection of the environment*

| Country | Waqf law | Definition of Waqf | Definition of the beneficiary |
|---|---|---|---|
| Bahrain | Decision of the Council of Ministers No. 11, 1991 on the internal list of the Councils of awqag (Sunnyia and Jaafaryia) | No definition | "The Awqaf Council supervises the affairs of the Awqaf, administers them, exploits them, disburses their revenues, preserves their properties and reconstructs them in accordance with the concept of drafting Waqfs and Waqif expressions and in accordance with the provisions of Islamic Sharia and in accordance with the final decisions issued by the competent Sharia court"[a] |
| Bangladesh | The Waqfs Ordinance, 1962 (East Pakistan Ordinance)[b] (Ordinance No. I of 1962) | (10) "Waqf" means the permanent dedication by a person professing Islam of any movable or immovable property for any purpose recognized by Muslim law as pious, religious or charitable, and includes any other endowment or grant for the aforesaid purposes, a Waqf by user, and a Waqf created by a non-Muslim" | (2) "beneficiary" means any person entitled to receive any pecuniary or other material benefits from a Waqf and includes any institution, such as mosque, shrine, dargah, khanquah, school, madrasah, idgah or graveyard entitled to receive any such benefits" |
| Indonesia | Republic of Indonesia Act Number 41 of 2004 regarding *Waqf* | | a. workshop facilities and activities; b. education and health facilities and activities; c. support to the poor, abandoned children, orphans, and scholarships; |

| Country | Law | Definition |
| --- | --- | --- |
| | | d. development and improvement of the people's economy; <br> e. other general welfare improvement that are not contrary to sharia, laws and regulations (Article 22) |
| Iran | Civil Code of the Islamic Republic of Iran | Article 55 "An Endowment consists in the surrender of a property, and the devotion of its profits to some purpose" <br> Article 66 "An endowment for an unlawful purpose is null and void" <br> Article 74 "In the case of an endowment for the public use, if the donor also becomes entitled to benefit under the endowment he is permitted to benefit" |
| Malaysia | Johor Enactment (Selangor, Negeri Sembilan, Melaka and Terengganu states) <br> The Federal Territories Act, Kelantan and Pahang enactments | "[A]ny permanent gift of properties or part thereof by its owner for religious purposes in accordance with Hukum Syara [*Sharia*]" <br> Public *Waqf* is "a dedication in perpetuity of the capital and income of property for religious and charitable purposes" <br> "[A]ny property from which its benefit or interest may be enjoyed for any charitable purpose whether as wakaf 'am or wakaf khas in accordance with Hukum Syarak" |
| Mauritania | Obligations and Contracts Law 89-126 of September 14, 1989 (amended by law No. 2001-31 on February 7, 2001) | "The *Waqf* is valid for natural and moral persons and for those present and who will be born as descendants of so-and-so, and those who are determined as children of so-and-not, like the poor" (Article 817)[c] |

*(continued)*

TABLE 4.1 (*continued*)

| Country | *Waqf* law | Definition of *Waqf* | Definition of the beneficiary |
|---|---|---|---|
| Morocco | Dahir No. 236.09.1 of 8 Rabia I 1431 (February 23, 2010) concerning the Awqaf Code | *Waqf* is "all property that is locked up as a permanent or temporary asset, and its benefit is allocated to a public or private charity. It is established by contract, by will, or by force of law. The Waqf is either public, familial, or joint" (Article 1)[d] | The Waqf is valid for any entity that can benefit from it. (Article 11) "The Mawquf alayh [beneficiary] may be present at the time the Waqf is established, or it may be found in the future" (Article 13)[e] |
| Qatar | Law No. (8) of 1996 regarding the *Waqf* | Article 1: "[W]aqf is the confinement of a specific asset that can be used, while remaining in the same res, on a lawful purpose"[g] | "The types of Waqf are: 1 – A Waqf the benefit of which is allocated to the righteous authority from the beginning" (Article 3)[h] |
| Saudi Arabia | Royal Decree No. (M / 11) and date: 2/26/ 1437 AH General Authority of Awqaf | Public *Waqf*: "conditional endowment on specific public grounds, in particular or in general" (Article 1) | "Al Mawquf Alayh: The beneficiary of the Waqf according to the condition of the Waqf" (Article 1) |
| Senegal | Law No. 2015-11 of May 6, 2015 on Waqf | Public *Waqf*: "any *Waqf* property managed by a public person and whose enjoyment is allocated first or last to charitable and benevolent works as well as to the carrying out of a work of general interest" | Beneficiary: "any natural or legal person capable of receiving the usufruct of the Waqf property" |
| United Arab Emirates | Federal Law No. (5) of 2018 | | "Mawquf Alayh: who is entitled to benefit from the Waqf, whether he is a natural or legal person, initiative, project or others" (Article 1) |

| Yemen | Republican Order No. 23 of 1992 concerning the legal *Waqf* Law No. 32, 2008 amending the Republican Order No. 23 of 1992 concerning the legal *Waqf* | "A *Waqf* is the imprisonment of money and the donation of its benefit or fruit as a matter of sake in perpetuity" (Article 3). The public *Waqf* "is what stood on public and private entities" (Article 4) |
| Singapore | Administration of Muslim Law Act (Chapter 3) Act 27 of 1966, revised October 31, 2009 | "'[W]akaf' means the permanent dedication by a Muslim of any movable or immovable property for any purpose recognized by the Muslim law as pious, religious or charitable" |
| Turkey | Foundations Law No. 5737, February 20, 2008 | "b) the purpose of the Foundation [*Waqf*]; It must be lawful, specific, understandable and continuous" "[W]akaf 'am' means a dedication in perpetuity of the capital and income of property for pious, religious or charitable purposes recognized by the Muslim law and the property so dedicated" Article 21 Private foundation forests may be planted. Chapter 3 (Foundation's cultural and natural assets) |

*Notes*: ᵃ Translated from Arabic. Available at: www.sunniwaqf.com/.
ᵇ Available at: http://bdlaws.minlaw.gov.bd/act-326/section-6747.html.
ᶜ Translation added.
ᵈ Translation added.
ᵉ Translation added.
ᶠ The original version is available at: www.almeezan.qa.
ᵍ Translation added.
ʰ Translation added.
ⁱ Available at: www.jo.gouv.sn/.
ʲ Translated from: www.yemen-nic.info.

TABLE 4.2 *Comparison between the* Waqf *and the Trust*

|  | Waqf | Trust |
| --- | --- | --- |
| Functioning mode | *Waqif – Mutawallee – Mawquf alayh* | Founder – trustee – beneficiary |
| Religious foundation and purpose | Charity – religion – ethics | Possible but not automatic |
| Perpetuity | A *sine qua non* rule | Possible (charitable Trusts) |
| Flexibility | Adjustments are possible | Adjustments are possible in some Trusts |
| Inalienability | A *sine qua non* rule | Possible (charitable Trusts) |
| Dedication to nature | Possible (*Waqf* for animals) | Possible (National Trusts in England) |
| Application in finance (funding) | Possible | Possible |

Source: author.

"even though the so-called '*jus* commune' never conquered mainstream English law, it left its mark on exceptional jurisdictions such as the ecclesiastical courts and, later, on equity and admiralty law".[17]

According to Honorable Judge Weeramantry, the *Waqf* predated the Trust, whose origins go back to friars of St. Francis. In his view, "[a]mong the reasons for such a conclusion are that the Islamic charitable Trust antedated by several centuries the doctrine of uses and Trusts in English law and that Trusts or uses were first introduced in England in the thirteenth century by Franciscan friars".[18] It is, according to him, an old doctrine that the inventors of "the use" were "the clergy" or "the monks". He states: "[w]e should be nearer the truth if we said that, to all seeming, the first persons who, in England, employed 'the use' on a large scale were, not the clergy, nor the monks, but the friars of St Francis".[19] This opinion is shared by other scholars, such as Professors Gaudiosi and Makdisi.[20] However, other authors claim that the foreign origins of the *Waqf* centered on two Byzantine and Roman institutions – the *res sacra* and *piae causae*.[21] The similarities between the

---

[17] Legrand, *Le droit comparé*, 232 (translation added).
[18] Weeramantry, *Islamic Jurisprudence: An International Perspective*, 73.
[19] Ibid.
[20] Gaudiosi, 'The Influence of the Islamic Law of Waqf on the Development of the Trust in England'; John A. Makdisi, 'The Islamic Origins of the Common Law' (1999) 77, 2, *North Carolina Law Review*, 1635–739. Available at: https://scholarship.law.unc.edu/nclr/vol77/iss5/2
[21] See for example Patricia Crone, *Roman, Provincial and Islamic Law: The Origins of the Islamic Patronate* (London: Cambridge University Press, 1987). According to Professor Peter Hennigan 'Like the Waqf khairi, the *res sacra* consisted of property consecrated for religious purpose – usually the construction of a temple – that became inalienable. The *piae causa* also shares a number of features with the Islamic Waqf. Both are inalienable properties managed by administrators, and supervised by religious functionaries – the bishop for the *piae causae* and

*piae causa* and the *Waqf* Khayri (charitable *Waqf*) led the historian John Robert Barnes to conclude that scholars should look to Byzantium for the origins of the *Waqf*.[22] This academic debate acknowledges clearly the similarities between the trust and the *Waqf* to the point they are considered as the same institution.

In the modern era, British authorities in Muslim colonies actively gathered knowledge about the *Waqf* and its multiple forms in order to administer local endowments in the colonies.[23] Consequently,

> [b]y the first half of the twentieth century, British colonial authorities had amassed crucial knowledge on a wide range of *Awqaf*, such as family endowments, mosques, schools, burial grounds, shrines and tombs which were located within British spheres of influence including British India, Palestine, Iraq, Egypt, Mecca, Madina and Syria. Correspondences on *Awqaf* by colonial officials were widely circulated amongst the Colonial Office, the India Office and the various offices in particular colonies.[24]

This effort was enabled by the fact that *Waqf* has numerous similarities with the Trust, which is well known to British authorities. The Mohammadan law in India and Pakistan, for example, looks like a mixture of the two.

In the United States, charitable Trusts illustrate the religious origins of the Trust. According to Professors Hare and Blossey "it can be instructive to imagine public Trusts as broadly analogous to private or charitable Trusts".[25] The Public Trust Doctrine (PTD) carries this religious origin.[26]

As mentioned in the first chapter, the PTD "[a]ligned with religious Trust convictions, ... holds whispers of epochal resonation as it stirs humanity to confront the crisis of ecology".[27] The *amicus curiae briefs* presented by religious groups in the public Trust litigation offer an occasion to express the spiritual characteristic of the PTD. In that sense, the NGO Our Children's Trust used the encyclical message *Laudato Si'* in its legal arguments in *Kelsey Cascadia, Rose Juliana, et al.* v. *USA*,

---

the qadi for the Waqf. More significantly, the charitable purposes of the *piae causae* parallel those of the Waqf – relief for the poor, the ransom of captives, and the construction of churches, hospitals, hospices for travelers, orphanages, and almshouses'. Hennigan, *The Birth of a Legal Institution*, 53. For further details on this debate, see Wael B. Hallaq, 'The Use and Abuse of Evidence: The Question of Provincial and Roman Influences on Early Islamic Law' (1990), 110, 1, *Journal of the American Oriental Society*, 79–91. For a general overview, see Hennigan, *The Birth of a Legal Institution*, 47 and following.

    Cited by Hennigan, 'The Birth of a Legal Institution', 50.

[22] John Robert Barnes, 'Introduction to Religious Foundations in the Ottoman Empire', cited by Hennigan, *The Birth of a Legal Institution*, 53.

[23] Smith, *The Worlds of the Trust*.

[24] Ibid., 170.

[25] Darragh Hare and Bernd Blossey, 'Principles of Public Trust Thinking' (2014) 19, 5, *Human Dimensions of Wildlife*, 397–406 at 402.

[26] See Section 4.1.2.

[27] Wood, *Nature's Trust*, 281.

et al. (hereafter *Juliana et al. v. United States*) lawsuit.[28] These *amicus curiae briefs* also advance the PTD argument and help to expand the principle of Trust on natural resources.[29]

Besides, even if the protection of the environment is not perceived as charitable in the statutory law, the development of the law for the protection of animals offers a precursor example of charitable environmental Trusts.[30] Similar to Islamic law, this dedication to animals resembles the *Awqaf* for animals seen in the history of Islamic law.[31] As mentioned, Islamic law also governs protected areas in some countries (the *Hima*), which can derive from the *Waqf*.[32]

In addition to their similar origins, Trusts and *Waqf* have the same functioning modes.

### 4.1.2 *Similar Functioning Modes*

According to Professor Gilbert Paul Verbit, "[a] Waqf is a transfer from A to B for the benefit of C. That is to say, it fits into the classic pattern of the Trust where B is a fiduciary who manages the property for the benefit of C. Using common law terminology C can encompass a variety of present and future interests".[33]

In fact, both the Trust and the *Waqf* are constituted of three main components: the settlor or the founder (*Al waqef*) who instituted the *Waqf* or the Trust, the trustee (*Mutawalli/Nazir*) who manages the *Waqf* and the beneficiary (*Al Mawquf Alay'h*). Besides, both the Trust and the *Waqf* are founded on assets, the object of the Trust, which are the property of the *Al Waqef* (or the founder, settlor of the Trust – *Al Mawquf bih*) (Figure 2.2 and Table 4.1).

Furthermore, both the Trust and the *Waqf* are based on the idea of separating the legal and beneficial ownership of a given property. In fact, "the ownership of the property by the Waqf was no longer held by the founder, nor was it acquired beneficially by any other person. This is similar to the Trust concept of separating legal and beneficial title in that the property is held for the purposes of the Waqf".[34]

The similarities between the *Waqf* and the Trust as to their functioning modes are such that Article 2 of the Hague Convention encompasses them both. "A Waqf would seem to be a Trust within the meaning of Article 2, and, as reciprocity is not required under the Hague Convention, in Convention countries their status should not be in serious doubt if the Convention has been adopted without qualification."[35]

---

[28] Ibid., 375.

[29] Ibid., 52.

[30] Karl S. Coplan, 'Public Trust Limits on Greenhouse Gas Trading Schemes: A Sustainable Middle Ground?' (2010) 35, 2, *Columbia Journal of Environmental Law*, 287–336.

[31] See Section 5.1.5.

[32] Lutfallah, 'A History of the Hima Conservation System'.

[33] Verbit, *The Origins of the Trust*, 117.

[34] Stibbard et al., 'Understanding the Waqf in the World of the Trust', at 786.

[35] Ibid., 808.

The functioning scheme of the Trust is also at the core of the PTD. In fact, this doctrine is grounded in the common law set up on the Trust principle.[36] The idea of fiduciary duty is entrenched within the functioning method of the Trust.[37] It permitted its evolution towards the PTD. This same idea also exists within the *Waqf*.[38]

In *Juliana et al. v. United States* the court upheld that: "Defendants have failed in their duty of care to safeguard the interests of Plaintiffs as the present and future beneficiaries of the public trust. Such abdication of duty abrogates the ability of succeeding members of the Executive Branch and Congress to provide for the survival and welfare of our citizens and to promote the endurance of our nation".[39] This case is one example among many others that are using the principle of the Trust, especially the idea of the fiduciary duty or "duty of care", in order to ask the government and companies to be accountable for failure to take care of the Trust asset.

While the Trust principle can also be found in Islamic law under the *Waqf* institution, it is not yet used in environmental law. However, similarities between the Trust and the *Waqf* appear also through the rule of inalienability.

### 4.1.3 *The Inalienability of the Assets*

The inalienability rule means that the *Waqf* assets could not be sold or gifted or inherited.[40] This same rule exists within the Trust. However, in the Trust the rule of inalienability is not absolute, except for some charitable Trusts.[41]

Concerning the PTD, the inalienability rule is one of its main components. In fact, the PTD has made inalienability its defense against not only the appropriation of public resources (water, sea, soil under the sea, air), but also against the abuses of natural resources as a whole.

Indeed, the Atmospheric Trust litigation is a result of this extension. In the US District Court Order *Juliana et al. v. United States*, "[t]he complaint alleges defendants violated their duties as trustees by failing to protect the atmosphere, water, seas, seashores, and wildlife".[42]

If, in the PTD, the inalienability applies to resources regarded as inherently public under the law (the equivalent of the public domain in Roman law), this is

---

[36] See Section 4.2.1 for more details on how the Trust has evolved to the Public Trust Doctrine.
[37] Daniel Clarry, 'Fiduciary Ownership and Trusts in a Comparative Perspective' (2014) 63, 4, *International and Comparative Law Quarterly*, 901–33.
[38] See Section 5.1.2.
[39] *Juliana et al. v. United States et al.*, 9th Circuit Court, 2015. Available at: www.supremecourt .gov/
[40] Black et al., *Modern Perspectives on Islamic Law*, 207.
[41] Alastair Hudson, *Equity and Trusts* (London: Cavendish Publishing, 4th ed., 2005), 862.
[42] *Juliana et al. v. United States et al.*, 9th Circuit Court, 2015. Available at: http:// climatecasechart.com/case/juliana-v-united-states/

not the case in the charitable Trust or *Waqf*, which can render any property inalienable as long as it is "immobilized" as a *Waqf* or Trust asset. Thus the *Waqf* can have as its object land, a school or books, or any other objects, which become assigned to the public interest (*Al Maslaha*). Therefore, the inalienability rule is able to secure the *Waqf* and its beneficiaries, whether they are humans or animals or even nature at large. As an example, *Hima* can be a *Waqf* asset dedicated to the benefit of the tribe or even to the benefit of an environmental *Maslaha* such as ecosystem services or the balance in the climate system. The tribe can in fact be at the same time the founder of the *Waqf* and the beneficiary.

While Islamic law recognizes God's ownership of the *Waqf*, the Public Trust Doctrine considers inalienability as the corollary of common use. In fact, "the conviction that some resources are inherently public means that Trustees or government agencies cannot abandon, sell, transfer, delegate, or alienate them".[43] Although it is the subject of various interpretations in the schools of Islamic law,[44] but also in the common law, the rule of inalienability offers a guarantee for the protection of natural resources as the object of the Trust or the *Waqf*. Indeed, exempted from the covetousness of private appropriation, the object of the *Waqf* or the Trust is preserved.

In the British colonies, the *Waqf*

> was in effect a species of Trust ... being a dedication or consecration of property either in express terms, or by implication for any charitable or religious object or to secure any benefit to human beings. The establishment of a *Waqf* was comparable to establishing a Trust in England. In order to establish a Waqf, the settlor would sequester the property such that it became perpetually inalienable, and appoint a Trustee to manage the property.[45]

The rule of inalienability in both the Trust and *Waqf* is also dedicated to similar objectives.


### 4.1.4 *Similar Purposes*

The most common purpose of the Trust and the *Waqf* is their dedication to the public interest for present and future generations. Both the Trust and the *Waqf* are designed to meet the public interest, including charitable purposes. Nevertheless, while the charitable objective is automatic for the *Waqf*, it is not for the Trust. In particular, the protection of natural resources is recognized as a purpose of the charitable Trust.[46]

---

[43] Hare and Blossey, 'Principles of Public Trust Thinking', 399.
[44] Some schools of law *madahib*, enable the exchange of the *Waqf's* assets. See Smith, *The Worlds of the Trust*.
[45] Ibid., 171.
[46] See for example Gary, 'History and Policy'.

However, concerning the PTD, the wide interpretation of the concept of public interest has allowed major developments in the sphere of environmental law. In fact, "the public Trust doctrine is rooted in the precept that some resources are so central to the well-being of the community that they must be protected by distinctive, judge-made principles".[47]

More than that, the Public Trust Doctrine could be extended to those who are "yet to be born".[48] This same purpose is also at the core of the *Waqf*. The common formula of private *Waqf*, for example, is: "for the benefit of our sons and children and the members of our family from generation to generation and, in their absence, for the benefit of the poor".[49]

This resemblance between the Trust and the *Waqf* recalls what Professor Cattan wrote when comparing Trusts and *Waqf* and admits that they both encompass:

> [t]he same legal device of divestment or renunciation of ownership of property and the appropriation of its usufruct (the right to use an asset owned by another) for a time or in perpetuity, in favor of successive beneficiaries, not all of whom are in existence at the time of the original settlement, but who are designated by or are capable of identification according to the wishes of the settlor.[50]

However, in practical terms, the difference between *Waqf* and the Trust concerning their dedication to future generations lies in the fact that in contrast to the *Waqf*, the dedication to future generations is emphasized in the public Trust litigation.[51] All over the world, this litigation is gaining momentum precisely because it highlights the interests of future generations. It started in the Philippines with the lawsuit *Oposa* v. *Factoran*. This is one of the principal aspects of the divergence between the Trust and the *Waqf* in 1993.[52]

The next section will focus on the evolution of the Trust in the framework of environmental law.

## 4.2 THE FABULOUS DESTINY OF ENVIRONMENTAL TRUSTS (FROM THE TRUST TO THE PUBLIC TRUST DOCTRINE)

The success of the Trust in the framework of the protection of natural resources and its evolution in the United States and all over the world can be explained first of all

---

[47] Charles F. Wilkinson, 'The Public Trust Doctrine in Public Land Law' (1980) 14, *University California Davis Law Review*, 269–16, at 315. Available at: https://scholar.law.colorado.edu/articles/1081

[48] Timothy Patrick Brady, '"But Most of It Belongs to Those Yet to Be Born": The Public Trust Doctrine. NEPA and the Stewardship Ethic' (1990) 17, 3, 5 *Boston College Environmental Affairs Law Review*, 621–46.

[49] Verbit, *The Origins of the Trust*, 129.

[50] Cited by Paul Brennan, 'Perpetual and Inalienable Islamic Endowments: A Practical Introduction' (2017). Available at: www.academia.edu/32035700/WAQF_perpetual_and_inalienable_Islamic_endowments. See further in Section 5.1.

[51] See further details in Section 5.1.

[52] See further in 4.2.2

by history, secondly by the flexibility of the Trust and thirdly by the efforts undertaken by judges and scholars.

Imported to the United States, the Trust was able to evolve in a country where
everything had to be built.[53] Thus it was able not only to operate as a charitable
Trust, as in England, but also by imbuing with the law of the public domain as
conceived in the *Corpus Iuris Civilis* of Justinian.[54] This gave rise to the concept of
the public Trust and then to the Public Trust Doctrine. Judges and scholars have
played a decisive role in the evolution of this doctrine.[55] According to Professor
James Huffman, "Nature's Trust" or "ecological Trust" are the new concepts that try
to expand the Public Trust Doctrine in the field of environmental law.[56]

The Trust is indeed an interesting overarching principle for the protection of
natural resources. The PTD has allowed evolution of both Trust law and environmental law in the United States and beyond. The evolution was first carried out
between the Trust and the PTD, and then within the PTD itself.

### 4.2.1 *From the Classical Trust to the Public Trust Doctrine*

The Trust has existed since the thirteenth century in England. The subsequent
evolution of the Trust "is characterized by its accommodation to a diversity of
purposes to the point that it is presently the most universal institution, for, next to
the contract, it is employed for the greatest variety of purposes".[57]

The protection of natural resources through charitable Trusts is one of these
purposes. In the United States, apart from charitable Trusts, the Trust also evolved
through the PTD. In fact, "[d]espite its common law origins in England, during the
last two centuries it was American courts that fleshed out the PTD".[58]

From a comparative law point of view, the PTD brings together two different legal
concepts: the notion of the public domain (according to civil law) and the concept
of the Trust. The public domain finds its equivalent in American law in the notion

---

[53]   But with major changes to the procedure. US charitable Trusts seem to be more flexible than
English charitable Trusts. Miller, *The Legal Foundations of American Philanthropy*, ix.

[54]   *Corpus Iuris Civilis* is the compilation of civil law by the Imperator Justinian between 528 and
523. Justinian, Institutes, Proemium, 2,1,4. (T. Sandars trans., 4th ed., 1867). Available at: https://
supreme.justia.com/cases/federal/us/146/387/

[55]   Most of the credit for the revival of the public trust in US environmental law is due to the work
of Professor Joseph Sax. For a complete bibliography of the PTD, see Blumm and Wood, *The
Public Trust Doctrine in Environmental and Natural Resources Law*.

[56]   James L. Huffman, 'Why Liberating the Public Trust Doctrine Is Bad for the Public' (2015) 45,
2, *Environmental Law*, 337–77. While criticizing the doctrine, Professor Huffman brought
interesting insights on the connection between the common law and the civil law with the
Public Trust Doctrine and he describes how scholars such as Professors Wood and Blumm are
trying to expand it to cover the environment.

[57]   Ignacio Arroyo Martinez, 'Trust and the Civil Law' (1982) 42, 5, *Louisiana Law Review*,
1709–20, at 1714.

[58]   Bradley Freedman and Emily Shirley, 'England and the Public Trust Doctrine' (2014) 8,
*Journal of Planning and Environmental Law*, 839–48 at 843.

of the public Trust. The public Trust (or "public domain" according to civil law) was originally considered as the submerged lands and navigable waterways. Generally speaking, "Public Trust lands ... are those lands below navigable waters, with the upper boundary being the ordinary high water mark. Tidelands, shorelands of navigable lakes and rivers, as well as the lands beneath the oceans, lakes and rivers, are usually considered public Trust lands".[59]

The Public Trust Doctrine provides that the public Trust (lands, water and living resources) "are held by the state in Trust for the benefit of all the people, and establishes the right of the public to fully enjoy public trust lands, waters and living resources for a wide variety of recognized public uses".[60] The Public Trust Doctrine "is applicable whenever navigable waters or the lands beneath are altered, developed, conveyed, or otherwise managed or preserved. It applies whether the Trust lands are publicly or privately owned. It also sets limitations on the states, the public, and private owners, as well as establishing duties and responsibilities of the states when managing these public trust assets".[61] The PTD provides government with both the authority and the duty to act as trustee to conserve these resources for the benefit of current and future generations.[62]

The first landmark case concerning the PTD, *Arnold* v. *Mundy* (1821), was a lawsuit brought by a property owner against an individual for harvesting oysters from submerged lands. The Supreme Court of New Jersey declared that the state must protect common use rights to "navigation, fishing, fowling, sustenance and all the other uses of (navigable water) and its products".

The court upheld that:

By the law of nature, which is the only true foundation of all the social rights; that by the civil law, which formerly governed almost the whole civilized world, and which is still the foundation of the poli[c]y of almost every nation in Europe; that by the common law of England, of which our ancestors boasted, and to which it were well if we ourselves paid a more sacred regard; I say I am of opinion, that by all these, the navigable rivers ... are common to all the citizens, and that each has a right to use them according to his necessities, subject only to the laws which regulate that use; that the property, indeed, strictly speaking, is vested in the sovereign, but it is vested in him not for his own use, but for the use of the citizen, that is, for his direct and immediate enjoyment.[63]

---

[59] Blumm and Wood, *The Public Trust Doctrine in Environmental and Natural Resources Law*, 13.

[60] Ibid., 12.

[61] Mary Turnipseed, Raphael Sagarin, Peter Barnes, Michael C. Blumm, Patrick Parenteau and Peter H. Sand, 'Reinvigorating the Public Trust Doctrine: Expert Opinion on the Potential of a Public Trust Mandate in U.S. and International Environmental Law' (2010) 52, 5, *Environment: Science and Policy for Sustainable Development*, 6–14, at 8.

[62] Ibid.

[63] *Arnold* v. *Mundy*, 6 N.J.L. 1 (N.J. 1821). See Blumm and Wood, *The Public Trust Doctrine in Environmental and Natural Resources Law*, 57.

This is the same definition of the public domain that is found, with varying degrees of detail,[64] in civil law countries and is taken from the *Corpus Iuris Civilis*: "By the law of nature these things are common to all mankind – the air, running water, the sea, and consequently the shores of the sea. No one, therefore, is forbidden to approach the seashore, provided that he respects habitations, monuments, and the buildings, which are not, like the sea, subject only to the law of nations".[65]

Thus, like the public domain under the civil law system, the public Trust is inalienable, imprescriptible and dedicated to the use of the public. But what distinguishes the public Trust from the public domain, as known in the civil law system, is precisely that under the common law it is automatically linked to the idea of the Trust. For example, in *Illinois Central Railroad Co. v. Illinois* (1892), the Supreme Court of the United States upheld that "[t]he title to the lands under the navigable waters of Lake Michigan … is a title held in Trust for the people of the State that they may enjoy the navigation of the waters, carry on commerce over them, and have liberty of fishing therein freed from the obstruction or interference of private parties … The control of the State for the purposes of the Trusts can never be lost".[66]

In fact, the Trust referred to in this case "is a real Trust in the legal sense of the word. There are Trust assets, generally in the form of navigable waters, the lands beneath these waters, the living resources therein, and the public property interests in these trust assets".[67]

What characterizes the Trust compared to the public domain in civil law is precisely the idea of the fiduciary obligation which is absent within the public domain concept.[68] For instance, "[t]rustees may not sit idle and allow damage to

---

[64] For example, in France (a civil law country), the public domain encompasses maritime public domain and rivers public domain. See Code général de la propriété des personnes publiques. Available at: www.legifrance.gouv.fr. It is interesting to note that many Islamic countries (which also adopt the civil law system) keep the same definition of public domain.

[65] Justinian, Institutes J. INST., Proemium, 2,1,4. (T. Sandars trans., 4th ed., 1867). The same definition is also adopted by the Magna Carta through two specific rules relating to weirs and riverbeds (chapters 16 and 23). Chapter 16 provides: 'No riverbanks shall be placed in defense from henceforth except such as were placed in the time of King Henry, our grandfather, by the same places and the same bounds as they were wont to be in his time'. Chapter 23 provides: 'All weirs for the future shall be utterly put down on the Thames and Medway and throughout all England, except upon the seashore'. For more details, see N. J. Hulley, 'New Zealand's Public Trust Doctrine', LLM Research Paper, Victoria University of Wellington (2018), 20.

[66] *Illinois Central Railroad Co. v. Illinois* (1892). Supreme Court Case 146 US 387. Available at: http://cdn.loc.gov/service/ll/usrep/usrep146/usrep146387/usrep146387.pdf

[67] David C. Slade, *Putting the Public Trust Doctrine to Work* (Washington, DC: Coastal States Organization, 2d ed., 1997), cited by Blumm and Wood, *The Public Trust Doctrine in Environmental and Natural Resources Law*, 11.

[68] Khalfoune, 'Le Habous, le domaine public et le trust', at 459. According to Professor Tahar Khalfoune, 'the habous [or Waqf] has its own legal existence, independent of the beneficiaries or managers of its property [and this in contrast to the public domain]; it acts through its manager and its legal personality is recognized only to allow it to be managed for a purpose of general interest' (translation added).

occur to the Trust". Hence, "the governmental trustee bears a strict fiduciary obligation to protect the people's Trust assets from damage".[69]

Moreover, what distinguishes the PTD from the public domain regime, and brings it closer to the Trust system as conceived in common law, is the way in which the public Trust is divided into *jus publicum* and *jus privatum*. *Jus publicum* is the dominant title of the public Trust land, while *jus privatum* is its subservient title. "The *jus publicum*, simply described as the bundle of Trust rights of the public to fully use and enjoy Trust lands and waters for commerce, navigation, fishing, bathing and other related public purposes. The subservient title is the *jus privatum*, or the private proprietary rights in the use and possession of Trust lands."[70] We do not find such a subdivision within the notion of public domain in the civil law.

According to Professor James L. Huffman: "Roman law was innocent of the idea of Trusts, had no idea at all of a 'public' (in the sense we use the term) as the beneficiary of such a Trust, allowed no legal remedies whatever against state allotment of land".[71] If the Roman law has anything to do with it, the tracks have long since disappeared.[72]

This is why the Public Trust Doctrine does not exist in countries with a civil law system, although they have the equivalent of the notion of the public Trust ("*domaine public*"). What the PTD adds is exactly what constitutes the essence of common law, namely the Trust – in other words, the three-pillar structure of the public Trust (Figure 2.2).[73] This is what explains why it was mainly common law countries that embraced the PTD. Indeed, "[s]everal countries, such as Australia, Eritrea, India, Pakistan, South Africa, Sri Lanka, Tanzania and Uganda, invoke public trust responsibilities in some part of their legal system".[74]

The idea of the Trust is therefore at the core of the PTD. In fact, "[t]he large body of law concerning private and charitable Trusts provides clear, tested guidelines to the Trustees and beneficiaries of natural resources Trusts. These guidelines are attractive for sustainable resource management under a public Trust framework".[75] The law on conventional Trusts, including charitable Trusts, is thus likely to enrich and expand the PTD.[76]

---

[69] Wood, *Nature's Trust*, 168.
[70] Slade, *Putting the Public Trust Doctrine to Work*, cited by Blumm and Wood, *The Public Trust Doctrine in Environmental and Natural Resources Law*, 15.
[71] Huffman, 'Why Liberating the Public Trust Doctrine is Bad for the Public', 343.
[72] Ibid.
[73] See Section 4.1.2 for further details.
[74] Turnipseed et al., 'Reinvigorating the Public Trust Doctrine', at 11.
[75] Raphael D. Sagarin and Mary Turnipseed, 'The Public Trust Doctrine: Where Ecology Meets Natural Resources Management' (2012) 37, *Annual Review of Environmental Resources*, 473–97 at 486.
[76] Ibid., at 484 and following.

As a case law-based system, common law has expanded the scope of the PTD. Courts have done so in order to include elements that are not cited in the classical definition of the public Trust, such as wetlands, groundwater, dry sand beaches, wildlife and the air. We have therefore moved from the traditional public Trust to an ecological public Trust.[77]

Overall, the extensions of the PTD have occurred in five major sub-doctrinal areas: (1) application of the doctrine to waters which are not navigable by commercial vessels; (2) expansion of public rights to include recreational use and environmental protection; (3) extension of judicial oversight of legislative and administrative decisions beyond "substantive evidence" or "rational basis" review, extending the courts' ability to reverse legislative and administrative decisions; (4) extension of the doctrine to provide a right of public access to privately owned resources; and (5) extension of the doctrine to nonaquatic resources.[78]

The legal arguments used to realize this extension are various. But, in general, they all rely on a broad interpretation by the judges of two main concepts: the "public concern" and the "fiduciary duty" of the trustee. For example, in *National Audubon Society v. Superior Court*, the Supreme Court of California ruled that: "[t]he public Trust is ... an affirmation of the duty of the state to protect the common heritage of streams, lakes, marshlands and tidelands".[79]

This evolution had already been predicted by Professor Joseph Sax, who declared: "Certainly the phrase 'public trust' does not contain any magic such that special obligations can be said to arise merely from its incantation ... But that the doctrine contains the seeds of ideas whose importance is only beginning to be perceived, and that doctrine might usefully promote needed legal development, can hardly be doubted".[80] This development, which is well documented,[81] gave rise to Atmospheric Trust litigation by arguing that air is also a common good that the states are bound to protect.[82]

The Atmospheric Trust litigation started by claiming the right to a healthier environment for future generations, who are represented by a guardian. This formula had worldwide success.

---

[77] Robin Kundis Craig, 'Adapting to Climate Change: The Potential of State Common Law Public Trust Doctrines' (2010) 34, *Vermont Law Review*, 781–853. See also Mary Christina Wood, 'Advancing the Sovereign Trust of Government to Safeguard the Environment for Present and Future Generations (Part I): Ecological Realism and the Need for a Paradigm Shift' (2009) 39, 43, *Environmental Law*, 78–84.

[78] Lawler and Parle, 'Expansion of the Public Trust Doctrine in Environmental Law', at 70.

[79] Cited by Sagarin and Turnipseed, 'The Public Trust Doctrine', at 476.

[80] Sax, 'The Public Trust Doctrine in Natural Resource Law', at 485.

[81] Ibid. See also Blumm and Wood, *The Public Trust Doctrine in Environmental and Natural Resources Law*, 407.

[82] Mary Christina Wood, 'Atmospheric Trust Litigation: Securing a Constitutional Right to a Stable Climate System' (2018) 29, 2, *Colorado Natural Resources, Energy & Environmental Law Review*, 331–39.

### 4.2.2 *Atmospheric Trust Litigation: The Claim for a Trust for Future Generations*

One of the first cases to have advanced this argument was *Oposa* v. *Facotran* in the Philippines. In this lawsuit, petitioners, a group of thirty-nine minors, represented by their parents, brought a suit against the government, which issued licenses to timber companies to cut the aggregate area of 3.89 million hectares for commercial logging purposes. The petitioners claimed that they "represent their generation as well as generations yet unborn" and advanced their right to a healthy environment which is recognized by the constitution of the Philippines.[83]

The Philippine Supreme Court upheld that "the adverse effects, disastrous consequences, serious injury and irreparable damage of this continued trend of deforestation to the plaintiff minors' generation and to generations yet unborn are evident and incontrovertible. As a matter of fact, the environmental damages ... are already being felt, experienced and suffered by the generation of plaintiff adults".[84]

In *Juliana et al.* v. *United States*, plaintiffs allege that: "because CO2 persists in the atmosphere, future emissions will lead to severe impacts on children and future generations and the current level of CO2 has already taken our country into the 'danger zone'".[85] They further allege that "defendants have violated a public trust doctrine, secured by the Ninth Amendment, by denying future generations essential natural resources". Amongst the plaintiffs, "Future Generations" are represented by their guardian, Dr. James Hansen. They claim to "retain the legal right to inherit well-stewarded public Trust resources and to protection of their future lives, liberties, and property – all of which are imminently threatened by the actions of Defendants". As a guardian, Dr. Hansen stands in this case "both to demand effective governmental action to protect these fundamental rights and, until that is done, a cessation of governmental action that exacerbates the imposed risk" (§ 92).[86]

In *Urgenda* v. *The Netherlands*, the Hague district court stated that: "Contrary to what the State argued in its oral arguments, Urgenda's interest was made sufficiently clear in its extensively explicated assertions that there is a real threat of dangerous climate change, not only today but certainly also in the near future".[87] The court referred to the UN Framework Climate Change Convention (UNFCCC), especially provisions related to future generation (Preamble and Articles 2 and 3).

The Court of Appeal stated in October 2018 that the District Court's ruling in the *Urgenda* case in 2015 should stand. That means that the Dutch government has to

---

[83] *Oposa* v. *Factoran*, Supreme Court Manila, Philippines, 1993. Available at: www.elaw.org/content/philippines-oposa-et-al-v-fulgencio-s-factoran-jr-et-al-gr-no-101083

[84] Ibid.

[85] Paragraph 1.

[86] *Juliana* v. *United States*, 9th Circuit Court, 2015. Available at: http://climatecasechart.com/case/juliana-v-united-states/

[87] https://elaw.org/nl.urgenda.15

substantially reduce its emissions by the end of 2020, in accordance with the judge's decision. Consequently, the court recognized the validity of Urgenda's claims that the state had violated the constitutional requirements to protect "the living environment" for "present and future generations" (Article 21 of the Dutch State Constitution).

In this regard, the court noted that:

> In defending the right of not just the current but also the future generations to availability of natural resources and a safe and healthy living environment, it also strives for the interest of a sustainable society. This interest of a sustainable society is also formulated in the legal standard invoked by Urgenda for the protection against activities which, in its view, are not "sustainable" and threaten to lead to serious threats to ecosystems and human societies. (§ 4.8)[88]

A major milestone case of climate change litigation occurred in a Muslim-majority country: Pakistan. It considers the right to a safe and healthy climate a human right. In the landmark case *Legahri* v. *Federal Park* in Pakistan, the Supreme Court largely interpreted the word "life" under Article 9 of the constitution, which can be extended if read with Article 14 of the constitution to "all amenities and facilities which a person born in a free country, is entitled to enjoy with dignity, legally and constitutionally".[89] It is noteworthy that the judiciary in this country does not distinguish the PTD from the right to life.

Comparatively, such an evolution of the Trust is difficult to conceive in countries based on civil law because the legal arguments used to make the expansion of the PTD are not all available under the civil law system. On one hand, if the first argument exists more or less under civil law, that is the concept of "public Trust" (or public domain), the second argument is absent under the civil law system. Indeed, the civil law judge cannot greatly extend what was strictly defined under the statutory law, that is, the notion of public domain. The common law system is more a judge-made law than the civil law system.[90] On the other hand, the notion of fiduciary duty used to allow the extension of the PTD does not exist under the civil law system.[91]

---

[88] In fact, the dedication to future generations is an illustration of the principle of sustainability. See further Section 5.1.

[89] Jacqueline Peel and Hari M. Osofsky, 'A Right Turn in Climate Change Litigation?' (2018) 7, 1, *Transnational Environmental Law*, 37–67 at 52.

[90] Sellers, 'An Introduction to the Rule of Law in Comparative Perspective'. See also: Legrand, *Le droit comparé*; and Seon Bong Yu, 'The Role of the Judge in the Common Law and Civil Law Systems: The Cases of the United States and European Countries' (1999) 2, 2, *International Area Review*, 35–46.

[91] However, according to Professor Lionel Smith, '[F]iduciary ownership is not unthinkable within a Romano-Germanic system. The French fiducie, which has recently appeared in the Code Napoléon as a nominate institution as a result of the enactment of the Law of 19 February 2007, seems to stand as an example within statutory law of just this sort of recognition'. Smith, *The Worlds of the Trust*, 22. This will nevertheless necessitate profound legal adjustments that are not necessary under Islamic law. In fact, the trust principle exists under Islamic law.

Nevertheless, comparative law studies underline that this difference is now changing and that there is more and more convergence between the two legal systems concerning the role of judges.[92] More specifically, judges play a crucial role in the evolution of environmental law in several countries, including civil law countries. This is what appears within the Atmospheric Trust litigation which is expanding to civil law countries such as the Netherlands, as we have seen, and France in the framework of "the Case of the Century" (*Affaire du siècle*). In this lawsuit, four NGOs are suing the French government in order to ask it to conform to the Paris Climate Agreement.[93]

The Paris agreement was a turning point in the development of the atmospheric litigation inasmuch as it creates obligations enforceable against the states. However, the litigation cannot all be labeled "Atmospheric Trust litigations" precisely because they do not use the "Trust argument". In fact, the arguments used in "the Case of the Century" in France, for example, are mostly drawn from the civil liability legal regime and human rights, as embedded in the constitution.

Comparatively, in Islamic countries, where the *Waqf*, similar to the Trust, is grounded in the legal system, such an evolution is totally possible and could be made, theoretically, much more easily. The *Waqf* shares characteristics with the Trust. The fiduciary obligation is at the core of the *Waqf*. The idea of a public Trust is embedded within the notion of *Khilafa* and illustrated in the institution of *Hima*, for example.[94]

In sum, if the PTD has undergone this evolution, it is because it has succeeded in using the Trust as an overarching principle and has evolved the very notion of the public Trust by detaching itself from the strict definition of its elements.

### 4.2.3 An Overarching Principle: The "Trust in the Higher Sense"

Even if the Trust is at the heart of the PTD, it does not need to be instituted as in the conventional Trust. In the PTD, the Trust exists rather as the spirit of the law. There is a "common core of principles ... forming the foundation for how the Doctrine is applied in each state".[95]

The PTD "exists regardless of whether or not it is written down".[96] It represents the "chalkboard on which the Constitution is written, [Thus] it is more appropriate to consider the Constitution as rooted in the public Trust doctrine rather than think

---

[92] See note 79 above.

[93] The Paris Agreement is available at: https://unfccc.int/sites/default/files/english_paris_agreement.pdf. Details on the Case of the Century, the lawsuit brought in France by four NGOs, are available at: https://laffairedusiecle.net/the-case-of-the-century-additional-pleading/

[94] See further Chapter 5.

[95] Blumm and Wood, *The Public Trust Doctrine in Environmental and Natural Resources Law*, 12.

[96] Gerald Torres and Nathan Bellinger, 'The Public Trust: The Law's DNA' (2014) 4, 2, *Cornell Law Faculty Publications*, 218–317. Available at: http://scholarship.law.cornell.edu/facpub/1213

of the public Trust doctrine as rooted in the Constitution".[97] In fact, the PTD "functions in a quasi-constitutional way: it establishes overarching fiduciary principles regarding Trust resources that may not be overridden by legislative or executive action".[98]

It is therefore a guiding principle which is supposed to orient the action of the government. In *Kinloch* v. *Secretary of State for India*, the judge stated that: "[a] 'higher sense' of Trust inhered in the Crown's control of a phosphate-rich island colony which had an Ordinance providing a commissioner would establish the formula for paying mining royalties".[99]

In sum, "the Trust's continuing background presence is felt through the field" in the PTD.[100] Consequently, the PTD can prevail over the legislation.[101] As stated by Professor Timothy Patrick Brady, the PTD "is a result of the law acting in an anticipatory fashion".[102] The PTD can deal either with the silence or with the technicality of the legal texts and with their complexity, which sometimes leads to the opposite results.[103] In fact, "[i]ncreasingly modern agencies fail to protect public resources, and citizens look to the PTD to provide more effective action by requiring fiduciary action".[104] For example, the Atmospheric Trust litigation "seeks to force government action to curtail carbon pollution, since the Clean Air Act has largely failed".[105]

It is because it was elevated as an overarching principle that the PTD has expanded in common law countries. Thus, its new extension in England, for example, does not require major modifications to the law. As Professors Freedman and Shirley stated: "it is logical to conclude that there is a cause of action somewhere in English law based on violation of the Public Trust. It must simply be discovered".[106] Even if its relations with the English law are quite distant, the PTD represents, as mentioned earlier, the extension of the English Trusts.

Paraphrasing the cited authors, we could also argue that the PTD must simply be discovered within Islamic law. This would seem to be the case because we have seen so many similarities that exist between the English Trusts and the *Waqf*.[107]

Professor Sax's argument for broader recognition of the PTD stemmed from his belief that, looking around at the paucity of options for concerned citizens, "[o]f all

---

[97] Ibid., 294.
[98] Ibid., at 303.
[99] Freedman and Shirley, 'England and the Public Trust Doctrine', at 841.
[100] Plater et al. cited by Sagarin and Turnipseed, 'The Public Trust Doctrine', 490.
[101] Wood, *Nature's Trust*, at 14.
[102] Brady, 'But Most of It Belongs to Those Yet to Be Born', 631.
[103] Wood, *Nature's Trust*, at 65.
[104] Blumm and Wood, *The Public Trust Doctrine in Environmental and Natural Resources Law*, 8.
[105] Mary Christina Wood and Dan Galpern, 'Atmospheric Recovery Litigation: Making the Fossil Fuel Industry Pay to Restore a Viable Climate System' (2015) 45, *Environmental Law*, 259.
[106] Freedman and Shirley, 'England and the Public Trust Doctrine', 848.
[107] See Sections 4.1.1–4.1.4.

the concepts known to American law, only the [PTD] seems to have the breadth and substantive content which might make it useful as a tool of general application for citizens seeking to develop a comprehensive legal approach to resource management problems".[108]

The same argument could also be used for the *Waqf*. The following chapter offers a few suggestions on how the *Waqf* could be used more efficiently as a response to the challenging environmental threats. It sets forth the arguments for an Atmospheric *Waqf* Doctrine in Muslim countries.

---

[108] Sax, 'The Public Trust Doctrine in Natural Resource Law', 474.

# 5

# Potential for Growth of Islamic Environmental Law

The teachings of the Sharī'ah and Prophetic instructions created an area around Makkah and Madinah where flora and fauna were to be protected and hunting was forbidden, an early model for today's national parks and other protected areas.[1]

Islamic law offers an array of environmental protection instruments that have proved their worth in the past and sometimes present themselves as cutting-edge tools. In fact, in Islamic law we can find principles and tools that resemble those that are at the core of modern environmental law (Section 5.1). These principles parallel those that form the basis of the Public Trust Doctrine. We can thus rely on them as foundations for the revival of Islamic environmental law in general and the "Atmospheric *Waqf* Doctrine or paradigm" more specifically. Most of these principles are used by environmental activists (Eco-Islam). This movement is in fact a reaction to the non-enforcement of statutory environmental law in Muslim countries (Section 5.2).

## 5.1 ISLAMIC ENVIRONMENTAL LAW PRINCIPLES: THE CORE OF THE ATMOSPHERIC *WAQF* PARADIGM

Atmospheric *Waqf* paradigm should be based on the environmental *Waqf* principle in the sense that it bears the idea of trusteeship over natural resources. The main legal argument of this suggested paradigm is grounded on the *Khilafa* principle, especially the environmental *Khilafa*.[2] Therefore, its main objective is to reinforce the fiduciary duty regarding natural resources and the climate system.

The Atmospheric *Waqf* Doctrine allows civil society to ask governments to fulfill their fiduciary duties: it considers the climate system similar to a *Waqf* asset that should be kept for the benefit of present and future generations. The Atmospheric

---

[1]  Nasr, 'God Is Absolute Reality and all Creation His Tajalli', 6.
[2]  On the idea of *Khilafa*, see Section 5.1.2.

86

*Waqf* paradigm does not mean that Muslim countries should not apply modern statutory law. It simply means that in these countries, citizens have an additional argument to advance in courts and in advocating strategies. It also means that the states can reframe their environmental laws according to the principle of the environmental *Khilafa*. The doctrine relies on the work of *Ulama* in collaboration with environmental scholars. It should be based on solid scientific arguments and also on legal and historical arguments.

The legal arguments on the Atmospheric *Waqf* Doctrine or paradigm have been advanced in previous chapters and will be discussed further in what follows. This doctrine is a simple way to bring authoritative legal instruments into the sphere of the climate. Because the planet's resources are depleting and mitigation and adaptation efforts are not taken seriously in many countries, a stronger doctrine should find its way into courts and parliaments and even into international organizations. In fact, the Atmospheric *Waqf* paradigm has its roots in the Muslim cultural soil, but its branches are universal. Comparative law can reveal the many similarities between the Trust, the PTD and the *Waqf*. It is time to exploit these multiple similarities and to revive the Atmospheric *Waqf*. Professor Peter Sand demonstrated many years ago that public trusteeship in international environmental law is rising.[3] The Atmospheric *Waqf* Doctrine or paradigm could fit perfectly within this international movement. The principles of international environmental law as described by Professor Sand are in fact already embedded within Islamic environmental law.

The Atmospheric *Waqf* Doctrine or paradigm should be integrated within a new branch of law: Islamic environmental law. This new branch finds its legitimacy in the principles existing within the scriptures and within the *Fiqh* and other complementary sources of *Sharia'*.[4] Seen from the angle of modern environmental law, these principles can be understood as follows: the sustainability principle, the adaptive management principle, the protected areas approach and animal rights. This section will delve into each principle and explain how it echoes modern environmental law principles and even anticipated them. The objective is to demonstrate that the foundations of Islamic environmental law and the Atmospheric *Waqf* Doctrine or paradigm exist and that it is possible to start from there in legal reforms and in environmental activism strategies in Muslim countries.

### 5.1.1 *Sustainability*

The principle of sustainable development encompasses the idea of protecting the environment for present and future generations, the idea of equity between

---

[3]    Peter H. Sand, 'The Rise of Public Trusteeship in International Environmental Law', at Third International Haub Prize Symposium, Murneau, 2013.

[4]    As explained in Chapter 2.

generations and the idea of integration of environmental considerations into economic policy.[5]

Sustainability is the current paradigm of environmental law. But it has always
existed under Islamic law and more particularly through the *Waqf*. In fact, the
common form of the private *Waqf*, for example, encompasses the intergenerational
principle.[6] The gift of income from the *Waqf* can thus last until the settlor's line dies
out. This same mechanism exists within the public *Waqf*. We have also seen earlier
that the idea of dedicating the public Trust to those who are yet to be born is at the
core of the PTD and more specifically of the Atmospheric Trust.[7]

Sustainability has particularly permeated international law and environmental
legislation in many countries following the Brundtland Report, *Our Common
Future*, in which reference is made to a global Trust.[8] In this sense, we can affirm
that sustainability is the essence of the Trust. It is also true for the *Waqf*.[9]

Indeed, in the *Waqf*, the interests of future generations are preserved by the rule
of perpetuity, which enjoins the *Mutawalli* to protect and manage it in a responsible
way for the benefit of the current beneficiaries but also for future generations. The
rule of perpetuity is also applicable for charitable Trusts and, as we have seen,
perpetuity is the very foundation of the Public Trust Doctrine.[10]

The rule of perpetuity in the *Waqf* has been interpreted as having disastrous
consequences for the economy in Islamic countries.[11] However, from an environmental standpoint, this rule has multiple benefits for the rights of future generations.
In fact, the rule of perpetuity "does not mean tying up the land, yet prohibiting its
use; it relates to tying up the asset in order to disallow the usage of the property and
to preserve it to constantly produce revenue"[12] for future generations, taking into
account that those revenues could also be ecosystem services.[13]

The Atmospheric *Waqf* paradigm therefore makes it possible to protect the object
of the *Waqf* (forest, water, biodiversity) for a very long period that goes far beyond
"political" time. It thus escapes all the political calculations that constitute major
impediments for environmental law. In fact, "this commitment to future
generations ... provides a strong moral foundation for [public Trust thinking]
PTT" in general.[14]

---

[5] World Commission on Environment and Development, *Our Common Future* (Oxford: Oxford
University Press, 1987). Available at: https://sustainabledevelopment.un.org/content/docu
ments/5987our-common-future.pdf
[6] Verbit, *The Origins of the Trust*, 129. See Section 4.1.4 'Similar Purposes'.
[7] See Section 4.1.4 'Similar Purposes'.
[8] World Commission on Environment and Development, *Our Common Future*.
[9] See for example the developments on the Trust for future generations (Section 4.1).
[10] See Section 3.2.
[11] Haitam Suleiman, 'The Islamic Trust *Waqf*: A Stagnant or Reviving Legal Institution?' (2016)
4, *Journal of Islamic and Middle Eastern Law*, 27–43.
[12] Ibid., at 34.
[13] See Sections 5.1.2 and 5.1.3.
[14] Hare and Blossey, 'Principles of Public Trust Thinking', 401.

According to Professor Mohamed Arafa, "[c]omparing [the notions linked to the principle of sustainable development] to the Islamic attitude on natural resources and environment, a great resemblance will be acknowledged. The core and purpose of maintainable growth exists in Islam as the term 'sustainable development' has been emphasized in light of the Sharia'a values".[15]

Scholars have also attempted to look at the many applications of Islamic law in the framework of the United Nations' Sustainable Development Goals (SDGs)[16] and found that the SDGs "reflect a universal set of values, much like Islam, intended to guide humanity along the right path. Both are grounded in a common objective: environmental practices that nurture, not harm, the environment for the betterment of generations to come".[17] The SDGs illustrate appropriately the idea of *Sharia'* as a way of life which covers both ethical and legal aspects.

The holistic nature of the SDGs encompasses the ethical obligations of humanity and can thus motivate the exploitation of Islamic law in order to protect the climate system. In fact, "[t]he fate of the planet Earth may well turn on how quickly human societies can improve the legal framework for sustainable development".[18] Professor Mohammad Abdullah finds that "most of the 17 developmental goals of the SDGs comfortably match with the long-term objectives of *Sharia'* and there is good scope for the stakeholders of Awqaf to develop *Waqf*-based development plan in line with the framework of SDGs".[19]

The congruence between the SDGs and the *Waqf* is not only theoretical. All *Awqaf* in Islamic countries have sufficient financial capacity to help those countries to "realize some of the most relevant and urgent Maqasid-oriented SDGs in a timely manner".[20]

More broadly, the implementation of the concept of *Khilafa* (stewardship)[21] is able to reframe environmental law into a more sustainable approach. This would translate into a profound paradigm shift in policy and environmental law. Here again the parallel with the Trust is appealing. Indeed, "nature's Trust would restructure permit systems to allocate only the interest portions of renewable resources to the present generations".[22] As for the *Waqf*, "[t]his concept does not hold any novelty: all of the so-called sustainability efforts aim towards this bottom

---

[15]  Mohamed A. Arafa, 'Islamic Policy of Environmental Conservation, 1,500 Years Old – Yet Thoroughly Modern' (2014) 16, 2, *European Journal of Law Reform*, 465–504 at 474.

[16]  For an analysis on the connection between Islamic law and the SDGs, see for example, Abdullah, 'Waqf, Sustainable Development Goals (SDGs) and Maqasidal-shariah'. See also Atih Rohaeti Dariah, Muhammad Syukri Salleh, and Hakimi M. Shafiai, 'A New Approach for Sustainable Development Goals in Islamic Perspective' (2016) 219, *Procedia – Social and Behavioral Sciences*, 159–66. See also Bin Hamad, 'Foundations for Sustainable Development'

[17]  Bin Hamad, *Foundations for Sustainable Development*, 1.

[18]  Ibid., 69.

[19]  Abdullah, 'Waqf, Sustainable Development Goals (SDGs) and Maqasidal-shariah', 158.

[20]  Ibid. See further Section 5.1.5. For more details on the notion of *Maqasid*, see Section 2.1.

[21]  See further Section 5.1.5.

[22]  Wood, *Nature's Trust*, 172.

line. However, such efforts lack the sound legal structure offered by the Trust that compels restraint".[23]

In parallel, the Atmospheric *Waqf* has the potential to convey a stronger and more sustainable approach which is more embedded within the spiritual principles of the existing *Sharia'* rules. According to Professor Mary Christina Wood, the sustainability of the Trust "means allowing present generations to use the 'yield' of the resource rather than depleting the natural 'capital' that sustains the yield. For non-renewable resources, it may mean rationing the resource between present and future classes of citizens".[24]

This idea resonates in the numerous lawsuits brought in the framework of Atmospheric Trust litigation where reference is made to the principle of sustainability, including *amicus curiae briefs* presented by religious groups.[25] In fact, the sustainability paradigm encompasses the idea of stewardship that is inherent to Islamic law.


### 5.1.2 *Green* Khilafa *or Stewardship*

The *Khilafa* (*Caliphate*) is a fundamental concept of Islamic public law. In fact, "for a vast majority of Muslims, a strong stewardship ethic (*Khilafa*) – in which humans are seen as divinely appointed 'managers' without whom nature cannot survive and has no meaning – remains the dominant paradigm".[26] The *Khilafa* principle has a scriptural basis in the verses: "I shall appoint a deputy on earth" (Qur'an 2.30); "It is He Who made you inheritors of the earth" (Qur'an 6.165); and "The earth has He spread out for all living beings, with fruit thereon, and palm trees with sheathed clusters [of dates], and grain growing tall on its stalks, and sweet-smelling plants".[27]

Another verse stipulates: "Do you not see that God has subjected to your use all things in the heavens and on earth and has made his bounties flow to you in exceeding measure, both seen and unseen?"[28] Each generation is only the Trustee: "[N]o one generation has the right to pollute the planet or to consume all its natural resources in a manner that leaves for posterity only a polluted planet or one seriously denuded of its resources".[29]

---

[23]  Ibid.

[24]  Ibid.

[25]  For example, in the *Amici Curia Briefs* presented by the Global Catholic Climate Movement and others in support of the plaintiffs in *Kesley Cascadia Rose Juliana et al. v. The United States of America; Barak Obama* (United States District Court, District of Oregon (Eugene Division), it is claimed that the Trust approach: 'provides tangible legal backing to the concept of intergenerational equity', 13. Available at: http://climatecasechart.com/case/juliana-v-united-states/

[26]  Richard Foltz, *Animals in Islamic Traditions and Muslim Cultures* (Oxford: Oneworld Publications, 2014), 85.

[27]  Özdemir, 'Toward an Understanding of Environmental Ethics from a Qur'anic Perspective', 23.

[28]  Qur'an, Surat Luq'mān, 31:20.

[29]  Weeramantry, *Islamic Jurisprudence: An International Perspective*, 61

On the idea of *Khilafa*, Professor Mohammad Hashim Kamali argues that it "implies holding a position of power, trust and responsibility that is exercised in harmony with the will of its principal party".[30]

The concept of *Khilafa* occurs in nine places in the Qur'an, and "in seven of these it is juxtaposed to the phrase fi'l-ard-in the earth – which signifies that its application is in relationship mainly to planet earth".[31] That is exactly how the *Waqf* functions.

Like the *Waqf*, the *Hima* is a perfect illustration of the idea of *Khilafa* (Trusteeship). It is "a good example of a human-centered development model where the human is viewed as a Trustee and a witness who is responsible for the 'construction of the world' (Emmarat Al-kawn)".[32] In the *Hima*, the fiduciary obligation is borne by the tribe, which is at the same time the beneficiary of the Trust. *Hima* illustrates the idea of Trusteeship. Therefore, it needs to be enforced in the framework of a comprehensive legal and institutional reform in order to insure its resurgence.[33]

The idea of *Khilafa* (Trusteeship) is common to both Islamic law and common law. In both legal systems it has been used for environmental purposes, even if it is not necessarily conveying the same idea. In Islamic law, the principle of *Khilafa* has a precise political meaning as it concerns the duty of the governor (*Hakim*), who embodies political authority. However, the principle is also used in broader terms in the ethical (including environmental context).[34]

It is the duty of the *Khalifa/Caliph*, as a political authority, to ensure strict observance of religious principles, to implement the legal provisions contained in the *Sharia'* and to administer the affairs of the community.[35]

The *Waqf* is one of the main illustrations of the principle of *Khilafa*. In the framework of the *Waqf*, the *Mutawalli* (or *Nazir*, the manager of the *Waqf* assets) is responsible for the "proper" management of the *Waqf*. According to Islamic law, the *Mutawalli* is also "responsible for any loss attained by the *Waqf* due to 'wilful neglect'".[36] Hence, "violating the stipulations of a '*Waqf*' is an 'enormity', basically a 'sin'. In case of complete mismanagement, the *Qadi* (judge) is to take

---

[30] Mohammmad Hashim Kamali, *Islam and the Environment: An Examination of the Source Evidence*, cited by Kaminski, 'The OIC and the Paris 2015 Climate Change Agreement', at 174 (note 6).

[31] Ibid.

[32] Odeh Rashed Al-Jayyousi, *Islam and Sustainable Development: New Worldviews* (Abingdon: Gower, Routledge, 2012), 89.

[33] Kakish, 'Facilitating a Hima Resurgence'.

[34] On the principle of *Khilafa* in a political perspective, see for example Gerhard Bowering, *Islamic Political Thought: An Introduction* (Princeton, NJ: Princeton University Press, 2015), 68.

[35] Ibid.

[36] Gaudiosi, 'The Influence of the Islamic Law of Waqf on the Development of the Trust in England', 135.

control of the *Waqf*, determine who are the beneficiaries, distribute the income and pay any debts".[37]

In modern *Waqf* laws in several Islamic countries, particular attention is given to the duties and responsibilities of the *Mutawalli*. In fact, due diligence on the *Mutawalli* does not always take place. Indeed, corruption and mismanagement were historically among major *Waqf* impediments.[38]

*Khilafa* concerns all areas of life (political, social, etc.) and can thus also be applied to the protection of the environment:

> [a]s a Khalifa, man is expected to interact with nature and its processes so as to transform the world ... God declared everything in creation subservient to humans, designed and/or redesignable to serve their happiness ... However, development or reconstruction of the earth is a pursuit that should be attained not in a greedy exploitative way, but through responsible and justly balanced means.[39]

The Qur'an declares that the natural world is not created just for humankind's use. Indeed, "[e]ven if humankind is the vicegerent of God on earth, it does not necessarily mean that the whole of nature and its resources are designed for humans' benefits only".[40] Muslim jurists have subsequently interpreted this idea. Al Biruni (one of the most learned Muslim scholars and compilers of the tenth century), for example, argues that "man does not have a right to exploit the other kingdoms for his own desires, which are insatiable, but may use them only in conformity with the law of God and in His way".[41]

In 1986, the Islamic Declaration on Nature stated that "[o]ur function as vice-regents, khalifa of God, is only to oversee the trust. The khalifa is answerable for his/her actions, for the way in which he/she uses or abuses the trust of God. Islam teaches us that we have been accountable for our deeds as well as our omissions. The khalifa will render an account of how he treated the trust of God on the Day of Reckoning".[42]

Therefore, as with the Public Trust Doctrine, the principle of *Khilafa* can constitute the overarching principle of Islamic environmental law, all the more so as Islam is recognized as a constitutional principle in all Muslim countries.

---

[37] Verbit, *The Origins of the Trust*, 135.
[38] See for example, Harasani, *Towards the Reform of Private Waqfs*.
[39] Safei El-Deen Hamed, 'Seeing the Environment Through Islamic Eyes: Application of Shariah to Natural Resources Planning and Management' (1993) 6, 2, *Journal of Agricultural and Environmental Ethics*, 145–64 at 149.
[40] Özdemir, 'Toward an Understanding of Environmental Ethics from a Qur'anic Perspective', 27.
[41] Ibid., 26.
[42] Islamic Declaration on Nature, The Assisi Declarations: Messages on Humanity and Nature from Buddhism, Christianity, Hinduism, Islam and Judaism. September 29, 1986. Available at: www.arcworld.org/

As a renewed branch of law, Islamic environmental law can use "a 'duty para-digm' in the sphere of the right to healthy environment, as a human being cannot destroy, deplete or unwisely use natural resources but has an obligation to develop and enhance them".[43]

Examples of the use of the principle of *Khilafa* in the framework of environ-mental conservation are illustrated in the aforementioned environmental *Fatwas* issued by the Majliss Ulama Indonesia (MUI). For example, in 2011 the MUI issued a *Fatwa* on "environmentally friendly mining"[44] which considers humanity as "stewards" on earth who "holds [sic] the 'Trust' (amanah) and have the responsibility to preserve the earth ... and its contents". The *Fatwa* stated that "the earth, water, and natural riches that are comprised in it including mined resources, represents a gift from God that may be 'explored and exploited' for the peace and prosperity of societies as 'maslahah amah'".[45] This *Fatwa* combines the principle of the Trust and *Maslaha* that represent the essence of the *Khilafa* paradigm. Therefore, it is possible to apply this paradigm whenever the natural order is threatened in order to reestab-lish the *Maslaha*.

Similarly the abovementioned *Fatwa* issued by the MUI in 2014 prohibiting hunting of endangered species, starts by considering that "human is created by God as a vicegerent on earth (*khalifa fi al-ard*) who carry [sic] out the mandate and is responsible for the prosperity of all creatures".[46]

The idea behind environmental (or green) *Khilafa* lies in the fact that it makes it possible to reframe the protection of the environment in the sense of a fiduciary duty. In this sense, the parallel with the Public Trust Doctrine is apparent. Such concerns become important particularly in the modern age, with its emphasis on environmental issues. The planet was inherited not by any one generation but by mankind in posterity, from generation to generation.

As for the Trust, the "Green" *Khilafa* could be custodial, managerial, proprietor-ial and of course spiritual and ethical. For example, the managerial stewardship relationship "marks a step up from the blanket duty of custodial stewardship. Stewards are required to

actively care for and manage the natural resources under their control. The managerial stewardship relationship goes further than the bare protection of the environment – stewards should not allow "damage to go untended". Good steward-ship means actively engaging with the mechanisms that seek to conserve and improve the state of the environment. Further, managerial stewardship does more

---

[43] Arafa, 'Islamic Policy of Environmental Conservation', at 470.
[44] Fatwa number 22 issued on May 22, 2011.
[45] Gade, 'Islamic Law and the Environment in Indonesia', 176.
[46] Fatwa number 04/2014 on Protection of endangered species to maintain the balanced ecosys-tems. The text of the fatwa is available at: https://assets.documentcloud.org/documents/1049328/indonesias-wildlife-traffickingfatwafull-text.pdf

than describe the type of duty: it ascribes the nature of that duty. By requiring stewards to be "careful" or "conservative", particular values of stewardship are injected into the general duty.[47]

The United States Supreme Court referred to the Trust over wildlife as an "attribute of government" and traced the Public Trust Doctrine back "through all vicissitudes of governmental authority".[48] This same idea is expressed by the Hawaii Supreme Court in *Re Water Use Permit Applications*. Professor Coplan commented on these decisions: "Public trust principles have been described as an essential attribute of sovereignty across cultures and across millennia".[49]

Therefore, similarly, the principle of *Khilafa* embedded within *Sharia'* and constitutions in several Muslim countries can serve as a basis for the nature's Trust principle. In parallel to or within the Atmospheric Trust litigation, it is possible to envisage Atmospheric *Khilafa* litigation. In common law countries, the fiduciary obligation of the state has been advanced as an argument in the framework of the Atmospheric Trust litigation which is, as mentioned earlier, an application of the PTD.[50] It is in fact the battleground of this litigation.

In *Juliana et al.* v. *the United States et al.*, for example, the plaintiffs evoke the government's "failure to prevent the present and looming climate crisis", which, according to them, "constitutes a breach in the government's basic duty of care to protect Plaintiffs' fundamental constitutional rights" (para. 98). They consider that "the United States has caused dangerous levels of $CO_2$ to build up in the atmosphere. That build-up seriously threatens the relatively stable climate system that enabled civilization to develop over the last 10,000 years. It impairs essential national public Trust resources required by Youth Plaintiffs and future generations" (para. 98). The plaintiffs also consider that "[a]s sovereign Trustees, the affirmative aggregate acts of Defendants [especially the approval by the Department of Energy of the export of liquefied natural gas ('LNG') from the Jordan Cove LNG terminal in Coos Bay, Oregon] are unconstitutional and in contravention of their duty to hold the atmosphere and other public Trust resources in Trust" (para. 310).[51]

In the same vein, in *Zoe and Stella Foster et al.* v. *Washington State et al.*, plaintiffs who sued the Washington Department of Ecology considered that this department failed to satisfy its duty under both the Public Trust Doctrine and chapter 70.235 (on Public health and safety – limiting greenhouse gas emissions) of the Revised Code of Washington, which requires it to report current science on

---

[47] Nathan J. Bennet, Tara S. Whitty, Elena Finkbeiner, Jeremy Pittman, Hannah Basset, Stefan Gelcich and Edward H. Allison, 'Environmental Stewardship: A Conceptual Review and Analytical Framework' (2018) 61, 4, *Environmental Management*, 597–614.

[48] *Geer v. Connecticut*, 161 US 519 (1896) cited by Wood and Galpern, 'Atmospheric Recovery Litigation', at 274.

[49] Coplan, 'Public Trust Limits on Greenhouse Gas Trading Schemes', at 311.

[50] Wood, *Nature's Trust*, 167. See further Chapter 4.

[51] Court orders and pleadings are available at: www.ourchildrenstrust.org

climate change to the legislature and make recommendations about greenhouse gas emission reductions.[52]

The idea of fiduciary duty can also be found in the previously cited *Urgenda* case and other similar cases filled in Pakistan and Colombia.[53] In the *Urgenda* case, for example, it is upheld that the duty of care

> principally means that a reduction of 25% to 40%, compared to 1990, should be realized in the Netherlands by 2020. A reduction of this extent is not only necessary to continue to have a prospect of a limitation of global warming of up to (less than) 2°C, but is furthermore the most cost effective. Alternatively, the Netherlands will need to have achieved a 40% reduction by 2030, compared to 1990. With its current climate policy, the State seriously fails to meet this duty of care and therefore acts unlawfully. (Para. 3.3)[54]

The claim of the state's fiduciary duty in the framework of the Atmospheric Trust litigation is a new and interesting phenomenon to analyze from the perspective of the Eco-Islam and Atmospheric *Waqf* paradigms. The Atmospheric Trust litigation is, in a way, an admission of failure of the statutory environmental law. Citizens rise to call for the implementation of the state's fiduciary duty because they consider that the sophisticated environmental law does not protect them enough. They rely on the basics: on Roman law (the notion of public Trust that belongs to all) and on the roots of the common law (the notion of Trust carrying the idea of the duty of care). The fact that the common law is a judge-made law is helpful. Indeed, it is the judges who have been able to extensively interpret the idea of the public Trust.

In Muslim countries, this idea of Trust is fundamental and foundational. The fact that it is imbued with religiosity, which is the very foundation of these countries, is likely to constitute an excellent legal argument in the hands of the civil society.

The implementation of these rules in the framework of natural resources management is a paradigm shift that is possible and necessary on the basis of the legal systems and constitutions in Islamic countries. This means that the burden of proof for the responsible management of natural resources will be borne by the agents responsible for this management, who can now be accountable. In fact, "[l]ike all trusts, public trusts require a strong legal foundation and must be enforceable by courts".[55]

---

[52] In fact, according to the Revised Code of Washington (RCW): (5)(a) 'The department shall adopt rules requiring persons to report emissions of greenhouse gases as defined in RCW 70.235.010 where those emissions from a single facility, source, or site, or from fossil fuels sold in Washington by a single supplier meet or exceed ten thousand metric tons of carbon dioxide equivalent annually'. https://app.leg.wa.gov/RCW/

[53] Peel and Osofsky, 'A Right Turn in Climate Change Litigation?'

[54] See *Urgenda Foundation v. The State of the Netherlands (District Court of the Hague)*, June 2015. Available at: https://elaw.org/nl.urgenda.15

[55] Sax, 'The Public Trust Doctrine in Natural Resource Law', at 557.

Of course, the implementation of the fiduciary obligation of the *Mutawalli* in the framework of environmental law will require great efforts towards raising awareness and legal reform. Indeed, even if the idea exists in the legal system, reorienting it to the management of natural resources is likely to lead to profound institutional changes. Besides, raising citizens' awareness of these rules is also paramount.

The corollary of the duty of care under the principle of *Khilafa* is to ensure an adaptive management of the *Waqf* or Trust assets.

### 5.1.3  *Adaptive Management*

Adaptive management is a concept of environmental sciences that represents "a vehicle for operationalizing a system-based understanding of social-ecological dynamics. It is based on recognition of non-equilibrium in social-ecological systems and the corresponding complexity, uncertainty and instability associated with both social and ecological systems and processes. Adaptive management is therefore seen as a key strategy for fostering the resilience of social-ecological systems".[56]

Like the Trust, the adaptive potential of the *Waqf* is broad. We have seen how the Public Trust Doctrine has evolved from the idea of the Trust and spread to natural resources since the nineteenth century.[57] As mentioned earlier, the PTD and the *Waqf* share several similarities.[58] As a matter of fact, "[t]he classic *Waqfiya* [the *Waqf* deed] contained a standard formulary, outlining operational alterations the *Mutawalli* was entitled to exercise. This point additionally supports the observation that the *Waqf* system offered operational flexibilities".[59]

Thus, when the environmental *Waqf* can no longer meet the initial objectives, the *Mutawalli* can improve its performance by modifying the management mode and even by disposing of the *Waqf* assets.[60] The manager of the *Waqf* can also dissolve the *Waqf* assets when they no longer fulfill their function of public utility or *Maslaha*. In this way, the *Waqf* is not an additional tool for putting nature "in a glass case" (*sous cloche*), but a flexible mechanism adapted to its rational management. This flexibility also characterizes *Waqf* assets.

The flexibility of the *Waqf* means that it can take several forms. It may "take the form of a land Trust dedicated in perpetuity to charitable purposes such as agricultural and range research, wildlife propagation and habitat development, a village woodlot, or a public cistern, well, or garden; or it may take the form of a fund or endowment for the financing of such projects"[61] (Figure 5.1).

---

[56] Melinda Harm Benson and Courtney Schultz, 'Adaptive Management and Law', in Craig R. Allen and Ahjond S. Garmestani (eds.), *Adaptive Management of Social-Ecological Systems* (Dordrecht: Springer, 2015), 40.

[57] See Chapter 4.

[58] Benson and Schultz, 'Adaptive Management and Law'.

[59] Suleiman, 'The Islamic Trust Waqf', 35.

[60] Which is an exception to the general principles of the *Waqf*.

[61] Bagader et al., 'Environmental Protection in Islam, 16.

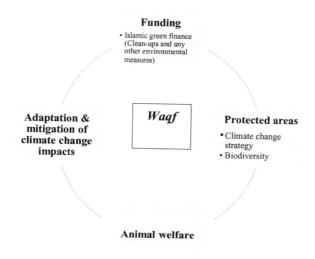

FIGURE 5.1 The multiple uses of the *Waqf*

In this regard, the combination of the environmental *Waqf* and Islamic finance offers numerous opportunities. For instance, the Islamic Green Funds (which resemble Socially Responsible Investment Funds (SRI)) and the Islamic Green Ṣukūk (which mimic the Green Bonds)[62] "can contribute significantly to the agenda of climate change".[63] The environmental *Waqf* can take several forms, such as a grant, an endowment or a donation. The environmental objectives of the *Waqf* could be broad or more specific (such as cleaning a bay or conducting environmental research) (Figure 5.1).

The *Waqf*, under the form of a grant, can have general environmental objectives. The *Mutawalli* "has the authority to determine which environmental needs should take precedence and be treated as a priority before advancing the next one". "However, in case of an environmental disaster, ... [he] can, with the judge's

---

[62] Green bonds are: any type of bond instrument where the proceeds will be exclusively applied to finance projects with environmental benefits. The Green Bond Principles (GBP), adopted in 2013 and updated in 2018, are 'voluntary process guidelines that recommend transparency and disclosure and promote integrity in the development of the Green Bond market by clarifying the approach for issuance of a Green Bond. The GBP are intended for broad use by the market: they provide issuers guidance on the key components involved in launching a credible Green Bond; they aid investors by ensuring availability of information necessary to evaluate the environmental impact of their Green Bond investments; and they assist underwriters by moving the market towards standard disclosures which will facilitate transactions'. International Capital Market Association (ICMA) Group, 'Green Bond Principles', 2018. Available at: www.icmagroup.org/

[63] Obaidullah, 'Managing Climate Change: Role of Islamic Finance', 33. See further Section 5.2.2.

permission, move the grant's resources, either wholly or partially, to address new and crucial environmental harms." Therefore, the Mutawalli may reallocate *Waqf* resources to other parts of the environment "as long as the new objective falls within the overall environmental purpose indicated by the donor".[64]

The flexibility of the *Waqf* enables it to play an important role in strengthening carbon sinks and reducing pollution and biodiversity loss.[65] The *Waqf* "may directly engage in the provision of goods and services related to mitigation and adaptation. Awqāf may also be dedicated to research and development and towards increasing consumer awareness and creating stronger support for action to mitigate climate change".[66] This may be facilitated by the creation of a global *Waqf* (Figure 5.2).[67]

Adaptive management is also at the core of the *Hima/Agdal*, which sometimes follows the system of the *Waqf*.[68] The *Hima* is a natural resource management system based on both the availability of these resources and the needs of the community. *Himas* were dedicated to prohibiting or limiting woodcutting, grazing, livestock or to providing welfare for communities suffering from drought or other natural catastrophes. Their "pragmatic flexibility ... has provided an important cultural precedent for protecting and managing public resources over which individuals enjoy usufructuary rights, including rights to grazing".[69] The adaptive management of *Hima* appears through the five types of *Hima*, where each one is dedicated to a different, specific purpose. In so doing, they best match the different nature protection needs.[70]

The same is true with regard to *Agdal*, which is the equivalent of *Hima* in North Africa. In fact, "[e]ach type of *agdal* has its own rules by which it operates, though always under the remote, watchful eye of the appropriate assembly and the *agdal* guard".[71] The *Agdal* (or *Hima*) "presents an astonishing capacity for adaptation and for resilience, in particular due to the ritual and symbolic system plasticity and to the hybridization and cross-breeding of norms observed on the ground".[72]

The *Agdal* or *Hima* has three processes that show its adaptive capacity: its flexibility as a "Knowledge–Practice–Institution–Belief complex",[73] its innovation in the face of ecological configurations and its accountability as a reengagement of the communities in the governance of natural resources.

---

[64] Arafa, 'Islamic Policy of Environmental Conservation', at 485.
[65] Jules Crétois, 'Islam: Comment les Habous peuvent sauvegarder l'environnement au Maroc', Tel Quel, June 6, 2016. Available at: https://telquel.ma/ See also Idllalène, 'Le *habous*, instrument de protection de la biodiversité?'
[66] Obaidullah, 'Managing Climate Change: Role of Islamic Finance', at 33.
[67] See further Section 5.2.
[68] Lutfallah, 'A History of the Hima Conservation System', at 218.
[69] Llewellyn, 'The Basis for a Discipline of Islamic Environmental Law', 214.
[70] See Section 2.2.
[71] Ilahiane, 'The Berber Agdal Institution', at 35.
[72] Auclair et al., 'Patrimony for Resilience', at 24.
[73] Ibid., at 24.

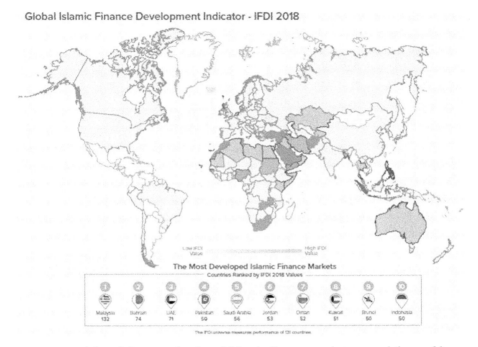

FIGURE 5.2 Map of the most developed Islamic finance markets around the world

Adaptive management appears, for example, through the system of opening and closing dates of the *Agdal* and *Hima*, which can vary according to climate variations. They "provide effective mechanisms for periodic biological rest essential to the regeneration of forage and wood species, enriching the areas biological diversity and slowing the effects of erosion so common in non-managed hills and slopes".[74]

Combining the adaptive capacity of the *Hima* (*Agdal*) and the *Waqf* can open multiple ecological opportunities today, especially taking into account that both can also represent an early answer to the tragedy of the commons.

### 5.1.4 *An Early Answer to the Tragedy of the Commons*

The "tragedy of the commons" is based on the idea that resources commonly used as public pastures will be overexploited because free riders will always benefit from these resources at the expense of others.[75] Therefore, it is important according to this theory to establish private property rights to avoid overexploitation of the resources. Islamic law offers a different alternative as an answer to the tragedy of the commons.

[74] Ilahiane, 'The Berber Agdal Institution', at 40.
[75] Garrett Hardin, 'The Tragedy of the Commons' (1968) 162, 3859, *Science*, 1243–48.

For instance, "the right to drinking water, free of charge, has a moral basis . . . and not a venal association with 'free-riders'".[76]

Islamic law answers the tragedy of the commons principally in two ways: the common and rational management of natural resources and the inalienability of these resources. As mentioned earlier, *Hima* (and *Agdal*) offers a concrete illustration of the traditional and common management modes of natural resources. Indeed, "*hima* became a symbol of redress and restoration of justice and gradually acquired a status close to that of haram . . . in that it denoted a sanctuary, with its flora and fauna receiving special protection".[77] Furthermore, the system of opening and closing the *Agdal* (or *Hima*) permits the community "to perpetuate the viability of common property among the users and to avoid any temptations of privatization that may arise from the cupidity of people or insistence upon customary utilization".[78]

The rule of inalienability used under Islamic law makes it possible, as mentioned in Section 4.1.3, to guarantee that the assets of the *Waqf* will not be sold and thus will be able to contribute to the protection of natural resources.[79] The classical *Waqf* was "developed in an economy in which land was scarce and represented the most valuable asset that could be owned. Since the particular *Waqf* tract of land had been dedicated in perpetuity to Allah, it could not be taken back and disposed of by mere mortals".[80]

Consequently, the application of *Waqf* to natural resources today could be justified by these same motives, namely the scarcity of natural resources. In many Islamic countries the protected areas instituted under statutory law are in general not effective. In Indonesia, for example, conservation policy "has largely been about excluding people and human activities from the country's 534 protected areas, including 50 national parks covering a total of 28.2 Mha".[81]

This phenomenon is not limited to those countries: a study estimated that since 1992 "around 50 percent of protected areas worldwide up to that time had been established on lands traditionally occupied and used by indigenous peoples".[82] It has been observed that, "in addition to the direct impacts of eviction, restrictions on access to and the use of vital resources, as well as restrictions on access to cultural and sacred sites, have led to the impoverishment of customary rights-holders and the erosion of traditional cultures".[83] The UNEP report on the environmental rule of

---

[76] James L. Wescoat, 'The "Right of Thirst" for Animals in Islamic Law: A Comparative Approach' (1995) 13, *Environment and Planning, Society and Space*, 637–54 at 643.

[77] Haq, 'Islam and Ecology', 166.

[78] Ilahiane, 'The Berber Agdal Institution', at 34.

[79] See further Section 4.1.3.

[80] Schoenblum, 'The Role of Legal Doctrine in the Decline of the Islamic Waqf', 1213.

[81] Jenny Springer and Fernanda Almeida, 'Protected Areas and the Land Rights of Indigenous Peoples and Local Communities, Current Issues and Future Agenda', Rights and Resources Initiative, May 2015.

[82] Ibid., 3.

[83] Ibid., 2.

law released in 2019 emphasized that one of the main factors of non-enforcement of environmental law is the failure to account for the interests of underrepresented groups such as indigenous communities.[84]

Stemming from the grassroots, the Islamic customary legal rules have a better chance to answer the tragedy of the commons than statutory environmental law. This is in line with anthropologist Eugene Anderson's observation on traditional societies. He states that all traditional societies that have succeeded in keeping their resources productive over time have done so in part through religious or ritual representation of resource management".[85]

Besides these applications of the *Agdals* and *Himas* as a response to the tragedy of the commons, Islamic law has also been ahead of the times in many other aspects. For example, some *Himas/Agdals* were dedicated to the protection of animals.

### 5.1.5 *Cutting-Edge Rules: The Recognition of Animal Rights*

All sources of Islamic law provide foundations for animal rights. The Qur'an contains many Surahs which bear the names of animals: Al-Baqara (The Cow), Al-Nahl (The Bee),[86] Al Anqabut (The Spider) and Al-Naml (The Ant). The Qur'an states that "There is no animal on the earth, or any bird that wings its flight, but is a community like you".[87] It is "especially noteworthy that this concept [community or *Umma*], which is [a] highly significant theme in Islamic tradition and literature, should also be used for animals".[88] Animals are thus considered in the Qur'an as part of the community, just like humans, which is paramount for animal protection under Islamic law.

In his commentary on those verses about animals in the Qur'an, Ibn Taymiyya, a famous legal scholar of the fourteenth century, underlined that "it must be remembered that God in his wisdom brought into being these creatures for reasons other than serving human beings".[89] The Hadith also echoes the Qur'an's previous Surah, as seen earlier, when it narrated a story about one of the prophet's companions, who asked: "are we also rewarded for kindness to animals?" The prophet answered: "There is a reward for kindness to every living being".[90]

---

[84] UNEP, 'Environmental Rule of Law: First Global Report'.

[85] Cited by Chandra Singh Negi, 'Religion and Biodiversity Conservation: Not a Mere Analogy' (2005) 1, 2, *The International Journal of Biodiversity Science and Management*, 85–96, at 86.

[86] One of its verses states, for example, 'We have also teaching from the cattle' (Qur'an 1909, 68). According to Professor Kula, an interpretation of this *Sourah* 'is that Man must learn from other species and from the natural order'. Kula, 'Islam and Environmental Conservation', 3.

[87] Qur'an 6: 38.

[88] Özdemir, 'Toward an Understanding of Environmental Ethics from a *Qur'anic* Perspective'.

[89] Cited by Haq, 'Islam and Ecology', 154.

[90] Sahih Al-Bukhari, 3:551. See Section 2.2. Another Hadith reported that the prophet said after he saw a camel suffering from mistreatment: 'do you not fear god regarding this animal, which God has put in your possession? It complains to me that you keep it hungry and overburden it, causing fatigue'. Sijistani Hadith: 2549.

A parallel can be drawn between this view and the modern concept of ecosystem in which humans, animals, plants, air, water and the soil form the same entity. The ecosystem approach is now enshrined in national and international environmental law.[91] Moreover, considering animals part of the same community as humans is a powerful idea that opens up new perspectives in the animal rights research agenda under Islamic law.

The *Fiqh* also offers numerous insights for animal protection through, for example, the writings of Izz Al-Din Ibn Abd Assalam, who in the thirteenth century wrote a book entitled *Rules for Judgment in the Cases of Living Beings*.[92] This book details the rules that must be followed by any owner of domestic animals, for example not to overburden them with loads, to provide them with shelter and food.[93] This book formulated, on the basis of *Sharia'*, "the bill of legal rights of animals in the thirteenth century".[94]

More philosophical, the writings of *Ikhwane Al Safa* (brothers of purity) indicate a developed sensitivity with regard to animal care. Their fable raises the question of "whether human beings are superior to animals, and if so in what respect". The answer they gave is that "human beings are superior to the animals – but not because they enjoy any higher moral or functional status, [but] because of their heavy burden, of being the custodians of the earth. As God's regent of the earth (khalifat Allah fi'l-Ard)".[95]

In Islamic law, "it is hardly possible to avoid discussion of the rights of animals in the context of conservation. The rights of animals, *huquq al-bahaim wa l-hayawan*, are enshrined as one of the categories of *huquq al-ibad*, the rights of God's servants, that is, human beings and animals".[96]

If modern law still has difficulty in finding a legal basis for animal rights, the *Sharia'*, based on religious principles that recognize charity towards animals, gave a

---

[91] See for example Vito De Lucia, 'Competing Narratives and Complex Genealogies: The Ecosystem Approach in International Environmental Law' (2015) 27, 1, *Journal of Environmental Law*, 91–117.

[92] 'Qawa'id al-ahkam fi masalih al-alanaam'. Al Shirazi Muhammad Al Hoseini also wrote a book on *Fiqh* and animal rights. Shirazi, *Fiqh, Huquq al-hayawan wa ahkamuh* (Bayrūt: Dār al-Maḥajjah al-Bayḍā' lil-Tibā'ah wa-al-Nashr wa-al-Tawzī', ed. 2011). Among the most famous books of Arabic literature and Islamic heritage on animals are the following: 'Camel books' from Abu Hatim al-Sijistani, 'Al-Khail' (The horses) from: Ibn Qutaiba, The 'sheep and will' from Abu Hassan Akhvash, 'The bird' from Ibn Shamil Sijtani, and the 'Animal' by Al Jahed.

[93] Richard Foltz, '"This She-Camel of God is a Sign to You", Dimensions of Animals in Islamic Tradition and Muslim Culture', in Paul Waldau and Kimberley Patton (eds.), *A Communion of Subjects: Animals in Religion, Science, and Ethics* (New York: Columbia University Press, 2006), 149–59.

[94] Islamic Declaration on Nature, The Assisi Declarations: Messages on Humanity and Nature from Buddhism, Christianity, Hinduism, Islam and Judaism. September 29, 1986. Available at: www.arcworld.org/

[95] Zayn Kassam, 'The Case of the Animals versus Man: Toward an Ecology of Being', in Paul Waldau and Kimberley Patton (eds.), *A Communion of Subjects: Animals in Religion, Science, and Ethics* (New York: Columbia University Press, 2006), 160–69.

[96] Llewellyn, 'The Basis for a Discipline of Islamic Environmental Law', at 233.

stimulating early answer to this question. For instance, it was totally normal to dedicate the *Waqf* to the protection of animals considered as the beneficiaries of the *Waqf*. This can be viewed as revolutionary today since this recognition took place long before the debate on this issue. There were *Awqaf* for the benefit of birds (birdhouses), cats and a *Waqf* for unwanted equestrian animals in Damascus (*al Sibai*) in the seventh century.[97] Besides, "[u]nder Islamic law, animals have a right to drinking water similar to that of human beings".[98]

Is this recognition of animal rights? Everything leads to the belief that it is, as can be deduced from the preceding. Careful study of the old *Waqfiats* (*Waqf* deeds) dedicated to animals could shed more light on this point. Unfortunately, the remaining *Waqf* archives are not always suitable for such research. In Turkey, for example, Professor Ismet Sungurbey reported that: "as only a few tens of thousands of *Waqfs* in our archives are read today, the *Waqfs* built for the benefit of animals cannot be fully identified".[99] Besides, research in the *Waqf* archives goes beyond the scope of environmental law and necessitates a strong knowledge both in history (including legal history) and in archive sciences.

Nevertheless, all scholars who raise this issue (animal rights in Islam and animal *Awqaf*), including in old *Fiqh* books, give the impression that this kind of *Waqf* was usual at that time. They report that animals had a great share in the Islamic social institutions and since the time of Ibn al-Bitar – the famous doctor of the seventh century[100] – Islamic civilization has known special *Awqaf* for the treatment of sick animals, and *Awqaf* to care for old animals. In Damascus, for example, the traces of animal *Awqaf* remain today. In the heart of the old city, in one of the oldest neighborhoods, is the Grand *Qaymariya* School, which in the middle of the twentieth century became a "palace" for Damascene cats.[101]

In the Mamluk period, many *Awqaf* establishments were devoted to animal welfare. There were complete architectural facilities dedicated to animals, such as the Green Basin, which was a *Waqf* created by Sultan Qaitbay in the Mamluk desert in order to provide water for animals but also a clinic attached to the basin.[102] This *Waqf* also stipulated that employers of veterinarians, trainers and those responsible for feeding and caring for animals would receive salaries

---

[97] Mohamed El Manouni, *Majallat Daawat Al Haq* (1983) 21 (in Arabic). Available at: http://www.habous.gov.ma/daouat-alhaq/
[98] Wescoat, 'The "Right of Thirst" for Animals in Islamic Law', at 637.
[99] Translation added. Ismet Sungurbey, 'Islam Hukukunda Hayvanlar Yararına Vakıflar ve Vakıf Mevzuatımızdaki Önemli Bir Eksiklik' (1990) 7, *Vakıf Haftası Dergisi*, 23–33. Available at: http://acikerisim.fsm.edu.tr. Professor Sungurbey gave the example of the General Directorate of Awqaf of the Department of Culture and Registration of 1959 in book numbers 488 and 360, registered in the city of Izmir in 1330 Hijri (1911).
[100] After Hijra (AH).
[101] Ragheb Al-Sarjani, *The Masterpieces of Endowments in Islamic Civilization* (Cairo: Nahdet Misr for Printing, Publishing and Distribution, 2010) (in Arabic).
[102] Ibid.

from the proceeds of agricultural land which were also instituted as *Awqaf* for this purpose.[103]

Architectural remains in Turkey also tell of a more favorable era for animals; fine stone carvings in the form of small castles served as birdhouses "called 'kuş köşkü' (bird pavilions) and 'serçe saray' (sparrow palace)". These "stunning birdhouses speak to the overall attitude that the Ottoman Turks had towards animals. Structures built during this time – between the 15th and 19th century – were designed with the care and protection of creatures in mind".[104]

This interest in animals through the *Waqf* is also translated into legal rules. In the Bayezid period (1481–1512), the criminal law (*Kanunname-i İhtisâb-i İstanbul al-Mahrûse*) prohibited the overburdening of horses, mules and donkeys (*Akgündüz* 295, Article 58). This legal provision "did not remain on paper and punishments were applied to those who harmed animals".[105] According to historians, this decree enacted by Sultan Ahmed III is probably the most comprehensive statute on animal care in Turkey.[106]

Moreover, evidence from *Waqf* for animals in the Islamic world also came from travelogues. According to Professor Priscilla Mary Işın, those writings reveal that "many foundations established during the Ottoman period contained substances for feeding and taking care of animals or birds, and there were even *Awqaf* established for this purpose alone".[107] For example, the observations of Lady Mary Wortley Montagu, the wife of the British ambassador who came to Istanbul during the reign of Sultan Ahmed III, are highly informative. In her memories of 1717–18, she wrote:

> Here are some little birds held in a sort of a religious reverence, and for that reason they multiply prodigiously: turtles, on the account of their innocence; and storks, because they are supposed to make every winter the pilgrimage to Mecca. To say truth, they are the happiest subjects under the Turkish government, and are so sensible of their privileges, that they walk the streets without fear, and generally build in the low parts of houses. Happy are those houses so distinguished, as the vulgar Turks are perfectly persuaded that they will not be that year attacked either by fire or pestilence. (Letter XXXVI)[108]

According to Professor Presilla Mary Işin, the following examples illustrate *Awqaf* dedicated to animals in Turkey:

---

[103] El Manouni, *Majallat Daawat Al Haq*.

[104] Sara Barnes, 'Elaborate Birdhouses Resembling Miniature Palaces Built in Ottoman-Era Turkey', *My Modern Met*, July 31, 2017. Available at: https://mymodernmet.com/ottoman-architecture-birdhouse-designs/

[105] Sungurbey, 'Islam Hukukunda Hayvanlar Yararına Vakıflar ve Vakıf Mevzuatımızdaki Önemli Bir Eksiklik'.

[106] Ibid.

[107] Translated from Priscilla Mary Işın, 'Yabancı Seyahatnamelere Göre Osmanlı Kültüründe Hayvan Hakları ve Hayvan Sevgisi', paper presented at the National Veterinary History and Professional Ethics Symposium in Konya (Turkey) (April 24–26, 2008).

[108] Lady Mary Wortley Montagu, *Letters* (Paris: Théophile Barrois Fils, 1816), 329.

- In the Beyazıt Mosque (1481–1512) an official was charged to feed birds living around the mosque. 30 gold pieces was allocated per year. This money continued to be paid until the end of the Ottoman period. Similarly, in the 1940s the mosque imam, Ali Hodja, treated injured birds, cats and dogs.
- In the *Waqf* deed of Mustafa Ağa of Keyfî Nâzın in İstanbul "Anadolu Hisarı": There was an article about giving 30 loaves of akçelik bread to dogs every day. Besides, the income of the two shops in Sivas was dedicated to "the birds who cannot migrate, in order not to starve in the snow in winter".
- Ödemişli Hacı İbrahim Ağa's *Waqf* dating from 1912 contained provision for feeding the storks living in Yeni Cami.

According to Professor Işın, other books contain information about these foundations in Turkey, Damascus, Jerusalem and Cairo.[109]

Moreover, one of the cities (Bursa) in the Ottoman Empire was provided with a stork hospital, "which was also known as the 'Gurabahâne-i Laklakan' (House for Injured Storks), [and] was established for storks whose wings were broken. The building, which is still standing, was also featured in many historical stories. When the storks were cared for and cured, they were then set free".[110] Interestingly, another hospital, also dedicated to the care of storks, was built in Morocco (Maristane Sidi Fredj in the city of Fès and Dar Bellardj in Marrakech).[111]

According to Professor Richard Foltz,

in better times, historically, non-human animals in Muslim societies benefited from protections and services that filled European visitors with astonishment. Already in the sixteenth century French essayist Michel de Montaigne noted that: "The Turks have alms and hospitals for animals". These institutions which were funded through religious endowments (*Awqaf*), would have appeared to most Europeans of the time as a frivolous waste of public resources.[112]

---

[109] The most stunning example of the care towards animals in the Islamic world is perhaps this story reported by Professor Thevenot, who visited Turkey in the middle of the seventeenth century. He wrote: 'There are those who leave a large amount of money to feed a certain number of dogs and cats a week when they die. They give money to the bakers or butchers for this job and they do this task faithfully. Every day the men who load the meat go and call the animal *Waqf*'s . . . I can give you a hundred more examples of the philanthropy of the Turks towards the animals'. Reported by Professor Sungurbey, 'Islam Hukukunda Hayvanlar Yararına Vakıflar ve Vakıf Mevzuatımızdaki Önemli Bir Eksiklik'.

[110] Ekrem Buğra Ekinci, 'The Ottomans' Exemplary Treatment of Street Animals', *Daily Sabah*, January 18, 2015. Available at: www.dailysabah.com

[111] Dar Bellardj was more a shelter than a hospital, but it is interesting to note the particular care addressed to this species of birds by Islamic *Waqf*. For further details see Idllalène, 'Le *habous*, instrument de protection de la biodiversité?'

[112] Foltz, *Animals in Islamic Traditions and Muslim Cultures*, 85.

In addition to these historical examples, analysis of the aforementioned "right of thirst" reveals that this right "divinely conferred upon humans and other animals . . . bears comparison with theological arguments for natural rights in the West".[113] In fact, the Arabic word *haq* is "more comparable to the Western notion of 'right' (Recht, droit) than [it is] to 'law' (Gesetz, loi)". Although shaped by pre-Islamic Arab, Jewish and Roman conceptions of rights, and the arid environment of Arabia, the right of thirst was reforged in terms of an Islamic understanding of the creation and of right conduct. It subsequently diffused across centuries and continents under the rubric of Islamic law.[114]

The United Arab Emirates (UAE) law on animal welfare enacted on September 4, 2007 (law number 16) and law number 5199 on animal protection in Turkey (June 24, 2004) are rare illustrations of how statutory law can encompass the Islamic conception of care towards animals. The UAE law includes a preamble on the scriptural basis while the Turkish law has provision on *Waqf* for animals.[115]

How, then, can we bring about a rediscovery and a revival of these principles in present-day Islamic societies? Animal rights activists in Egypt have exploited the scriptural basis in order to call for a dedicated animal rights law.[116] They finally succeeded in including an article on animal welfare in the new constitution.[117]

In the same way, in Indonesia, in Malaysia and in Yemen, environmental activists used the *Sharia'* rules on animal welfare in environmental *Fatwas*. However, they have not yet widely seized this opportunity to call for the institution of *Waqf* for animals.

In the aforementioned Indonesian environmental *Fatwa* on Wildlife Conservation for the Preservation of Ecosystem Balance, multiple references from the Qur'an, Hadith and Fiqh were cited as a basis for the protection of wildlife. The *Fatwa* summarized the Islamic foundations for animal welfare and duties of humans to protect them. It contains quotes from these three main sources of *Sharia'* and also from related Indonesian environmental statutory law. The *Fatwa* quotes, for example, the Surah: "There is not an animal [that lives] on the earth nor a being that flies on its wings, but [forms part of] communities like you. Nothing have we omitted from the Book, and they [all] shall be gathered to their Lord in the end".[118] It also quotes numerous Hadiths, among them the Hadith on charity towards animals.[119] Besides, the *Fatwa* includes principles of Islamic jurisprudence (or *Fiqh* principles) such as: "Avoiding a harm should come first before bringing in a

---

[113] Wescoat, 'The "Right of Thirst" for Animals in Islamic Law', at 645.
[114] Ibid.
[115] The Animal Protection Act in Turkey is available at: www.tbmm.gov.tr/kanunlar/k5199.html
    The UAE Animal Welfare law is available at: www.moccae.gov.ae/en/legislations.aspx
[116] For more details, see Stilt, 'Constitutional Innovation and Animal Protection in Egypt'.
[117] Ibid. See further Section 5.2.
[118] Qur'an, Al-An'am ([6]:38).
[119] See Chapter 1.

benefit". Furthermore, the *Fatwa* quotes *Ulamas'* writings, such as the book of Imam Ibn Hajar al-'Asqalani "Fath al-Bari", who stated that: "Ibn Battal said: 'The hadith [on God's order to love] encourages people to care for every creature, including believers and non-believers, and livestock owned and those owned by no one. It also specifies an instruction to feed and give water [to animals], to ease their loads and not overstep the boundary by beating [the animals]'". The *Fatwa* also cited Imam al-Sharbini in the book *Mughni al-Muhtaj*, who explained the obligation to protect rare animals and the prohibition on causing their extinction.

Finally, the *Fatwa* ruled that: "Killing, harming, assaulting, hunting and/or engaging in other activities which threaten endangered species with extinction are forbidden, except for cases allowed under shariah, such as self-defense" (para. 6).

In early 1992, the Grand Mufti in Yemen issued a Fatwa stating that

> Islam prohibits the killing of animals, except those slaughtered for their meat, or predatory animals for the protection of mankind. However, killing them to benefit from their horns, skin or other purposes, is prohibited and not allowed. Therefore, killing the rhinoceros for its horn must be prevented, and we must protect their existence and allow them their freedom until their natural death.[120]

In sum, the environmental *Fatwas* offer a rich compendium of Islamic foundations of animal welfare in a legal instrument aimed at the government, the legislator and the global community. This makes it an important legal basis for further reforms in the field of Islamic environmental law. These *Fatwas* could, for example, help to issue and revive the *Waqf* for animals.

In this regard, the sources and principles of Islamic law cited above (*Itihsan, Istislah, Qiyas, Khilafa*) should also be used for this reform.[121] Therefore, the *Waqf* deed formula could be interpreted in order to comprehend animal's rights. For example, in Kenya the *Waqf* formula is: "the ultimate benefit in the property the subject of the Wakf is expressly, or, in any case in which the personal law of the person making the Wakf so permits, impliedly, reserved for the poor or for any other purpose recognized by Muslim law as a religious, pious or charitable purpose of a permanent character".[122] The same could be said about other *Waqf* statutes in other countries. In fact, on the legal level, nothing prevents the *Waqf* being dedicated to the protection of animals or nature as a whole. In order to do that, it would suffice to interpret the notion of charity in a broad way. For example, in Turkey the law on *Waqf* announces that: "b) the purpose of the Foundation [Waqf]; It must be lawful, specific, understandable and continuous"[123] (Table 4.1).

---

[120] For more details on this *Fatwa* and on other environmental *Fatwas*, see: www.arcworld.org
[121] See further Section 2.1.
[122] The Republic of Kenya, Wakf Commissioners Act, Chapter 109, 4 (ii). Available at: www.kenyalaw.org. See also Table 4.1 for similar examples in other countries.
[123] Available at: www.vgm.gov.tr/

In sum, a wide interpretation of the definition of the *Waqf* and its purposes can support the dedication of the *Waqf* to animal welfare and nature conservation. The amendment of environmental laws and *Waqf* statutes might also become necessary.

In 1985, the biologist Michel Soulé published an article entitled: "What Is Conservation Biology?" in which he stated the belief that the anthropogenic extinction of species is a great moral wrong: "the diversity of organisms is good". Other species have value in themselves, "intrinsic value", which should motivate appreciation, respect and restraint in our dealings with them.[124]

Many centuries ago, Islamic law was already making practical developments related to this idea. However, even if Islamic tradition has much to say about the need to respect all parts of God's creation, even insects, "whatever teachings Islam may have to offer on the subject of human relations with non-human animal species, it is worth pointing out that people are usually only partially aware of what is taught by their own inherited tradition, and are often highly selective about those aspects that are known to them".[125]

Besides, if the *Waqf* of animals denotes a strong sensitivity towards these creatures, the law books are in fact rather devoted to the treatment of animals, their sale, and how to include them in the calculation of *Zakat*, their use for food and restrictions on hunting. In short, animals were widely discussed regarding their use by humans and not the obligations of humans towards them.[126]

Globally, according to the few recent books that deal with the place of animals in the law and culture of Islam, it appears that animals are only considered from the point of view of their interests and not their rights. Nevertheless, old books deal with animals in sections relating to "*Adats*" (customs).[127] In these sections, wild animals benefit from a certain degree of protection (especially in connection with the hunting season).[128]

The issue of animal rights in Islam is therefore not sufficiently analyzed neither in old books, because the concept of rights as we know it today did not exist, nor in modern books. Above all, the link between the *Waqf* of animals and the protection of these same animals is not analyzed by scholars. However, if we look at the very structure of the *Waqf*, we find that it consists of three main elements, namely the *Waqef*, the *Mawquf alayh* and the *Mutawalli*.[129] The *Mawquf alayh*, translated in the light of modern law, is equivalent to the beneficiary in the example of the Trust. It is noteworthy that in legal terms, the beneficiaries must be "entitled" to have rights. Yet history is full of examples of *Waqf* for animals that are placed as "beneficiaries" of *Waqf*.

---

[124] M. Soulé, 'What is Conservation Biology?' (1985) 35, *BioScience*, 727–34.
[125] Foltz, *Animals in Islamic Traditions and Muslim Cultures*, 4.
[126] Ibid., 31.
[127] Ibid.
[128] Ibid., 33.
[129] See further Section 2.2.

In the common law, the dedication to animal rights, made possible through the Trust, has not yet been translated by the Public Trust Doctrine.[130] Unlike in Islamic law, incorporating nature's rights is still a subject of debate under the common law.[131] Indeed, "[r]arely has a court acted to protect the resource itself from destruction or degradation (i.e., rarely has a court acted non-homocentrically)". However, there are already examples that could be interpreted as an attempt at incorporation. This is the case with the Florida Fish and Wildlife Conservation Commission.[132]

In another landmark case, the California Supreme Court stated:

> There is a growing public recognition that one of the most important public uses of the tidelands – a use encompassed within the trust – is the preservation of those lands in their natural state, so that they may serve as ecological units for scientific study, as open space, and as environments which provide food and habitat for birds and marine life and which favorably affect the scenery and climate of the area. (*Marks v. Whitney*)[133]

However, we can consider that it is somehow embedded in the idea of the fiduciary duty towards natural resources.

Charitable Trusts were the first to move towards recognition of the rights of nature. This was done first through the recognition of animal rights. Indeed, "[c]ases involving gifts promoting the prevention of cruelty to animals began to arise in the United Kingdom in the latter half of the 19th Century".[134] The Charities Act 2013 in England, for example, "shows an acknowledgement of the importance and relevance of environmental protection by the legislature".[135]

However, the PTD "has been used with some success as a right-based theory for relief in recent climate change cases outside the United States in nations such as Pakistan, the Philippines, and Ukraine".[136] Besides, "it is significant for purposes of Atmospheric Trust litigation momentum that the right based protection for the rivers in India were secured in courts".[137]

Nowadays, in the Muslim world, dedicating *Awqaf* to animals is a flexible way of injecting an animal rights dynamic into the law without necessarily resorting to broad legal reforms that would risk being rejected. If the religious concept of care towards animals is acknowledged in Muslim societies, it has a different connotation

---

[130] See further above, note 94.
[131] See Hare and Blossey, 'Principles of Public Trust Thinking'.
[132] See Gary D. Meyers, 'Variation on a Theme: Expanding the Public Trust Doctrine to Include Protection of Wildlife' (1989) 19, 3, *Environmental law*, 723–35.
[133] https://law.justia.com/cases/california/supreme-court/3d/6/251.html
[134] Rebecca Claire Byrnes, 'Filling the Gaps: Recognition of Environmental Protection as a Charitable Purpose', (2014), 31, *Environmental and Planning Law Journal*, 415–38, at 417.
[135] Ibid., at 421.
[136] Randall S. Abate, 'Atmospheric Trust Litigation: Foundation for a Constitutional Right to a Stable Climate System?' (2019) 10, 1, *George Washington Journal of Energy & Environmental Law*, 33–38, at 36.
[137] Ibid.

than animal rights. In Egypt, for example, it was possible to incorporate the idea of animal care into the constitution precisely because it was formulated according to its original conception in Islamic law.[138] The Atmospheric *Waqf* Doctrine should advance the argument of nature in the broad sense as an asset of the global Atmospheric *Waqf* in order to ask for its protection by government.[139]

In this overview, it appears that the seeds for the revival of Islamic environmental law and the institution of an Atmospheric *Waqf* Paradigm already exist implicitly either in the *Sharia'* or broadly within Islamic legal traditions.

History informs us about several applications of Islamic law to environmental protection. Comparative law sheds light on the similarities that exist between the Islamic environmental law and environmental common law, especially the law of trusts, and the historical divergence between those two legal systems.

The development of the environmental Trust in common law countries is also instructive. Indeed, it contrasts with the limited evolution of the environmental *Waqf* in the last few centuries. This contrast invites us to reflect once again on the environmental potential of Islamic law and the need to adapt this law to new ecological issues. It is paramount to strengthen *Waqf* and *Hima* in order to enable them to contribute to global climate protection. The legal and ethical grounds exist already within *Sharia'*. Having a striking contemporary aspect, ecological applications of *Waqf* and *Hima* gain from being reinvigorated in Muslim countries today.

The Atmospheric *Waqf* paradigm can allow the principles and approaches mentioned in Section 5.1 (sustainability, Green *Khilafa*, adaptive management, etc.) to be used in the contemporary legal system by reframing environmental law.

The following section will venture to present some avenues for legal reform in the framework of Islamic environmental law. These examples contribute to the conceptual foundations for the Atmospheric *Waqf* Doctrine.

## 5.2 CURRENT AND POTENTIAL APPLICATIONS OF ISLAMIC ENVIRONMENTAL LAW

Current initiatives regarding the application of Islamic law to the protection of natural resources are limited. Those initiatives are mostly undertaken by non-governmental groups (Eco-Islam). Besides, some Islamic countries have already adopted *Sharia'*-based measures in the area of environmental protection.

As mentioned in Chapter 1, "Eco-Islam" is a growing environmental grassroots movement. Interestingly, "Eco-Islam" is a reaction and an answer to the non-enforcement of statutory environmental law; this is provided by *Sharia'* and *Fatwas* (among other things), inasmuch as *Sharia'* encompasses ethics, religion and law.

---

[138] See further Section 5.2.1.4.
[139] See further Section 5.2.1.5.

In this regard, "Eco-Islam" is reminiscent, at least for the moment, of the movement which today accompanies the Atmospheric Trust litigation. Both movements reflect the recognition of the lack of environmental law, and both demonstrate the citizen's ability to change the law at the global level.

How then could "Eco-Islam" use Islamic environmental law as a tool in the Atmospheric Trust litigation or more broadly in the framework of environmental litigation?

Before answering this question, it is first important to conduct a brief overview of the evolution of this movement and how it intends to be both a solution to the non-enforcement of statutory environmental law and a promoter of Islamic environmental law.

### 5.2.1 *The Evolution of Eco-Islam: From Theory to Practice*

A lot has been said about the evolution of the grassroots environmental movement in Muslim countries: "Eco-Islam". In the past few years, scholars have become increasingly interested in Eco-Islam.[140] This movement carries enormous hopes for the implementation of environment law in the Muslim world. The United Nations now recognizes and welcomes this movement as part of its "Faith for Earth Initiative".[141] But the journey to achieving this recognition has been long and difficult (Figure 1.1). For many years, the ecological grassroots movement didn't attract civil society in Islamic countries. Authors attribute this inertia to historical reasons. According to some Muslim NGOs, environmental activism seems to be associated with colonialism. A few Muslims regarded the destruction of nature "as not their doing and believe that God will punish those who are destroying his creation".[142] Accordingly, some Muslim leaders think that secular/Western ideas on protecting nature are not acceptable.[143]

Yet some measures are being undertaken to encourage the revival of religious ethics for environmental protection in the Islamic world. Those measures are based on the work of scholars, especially philosophers, such as Professor Seyyed Hossein Nasr.[144] They have been undertaken mostly by civil society as a way to counter the non-enforcement of environmental statutory law. Further developments were possible through the work of Islamic legal scholars (*Fuqahas*).

---

[140] See Gade, 'Islamic Law and the Environment in Indonesia', at 176. See also: Khalid, 'Islam and the Environment'; Saidul Islam, 'Old Philosophy, New Movement'; Schwencke, 'Globalized Eco-Islam'; Vincenti, '"Green" Islam and Social Movements for Sustainability'. See Chapter 1.

[141] Available at: www.unenvironment.org/about-un-environment/faith-earth-initiative.

[142] Nawal Ammar, 'Islam and Deep Ecology', in David Landis Barnhill and Roger S. Gottlieb (eds.), *Deep Ecology and World Religions: New Essays on Sacred Ground* (Albany: State University of New York Press, 2001), 193–212, 206.

[143] Ibid.

[144] As mentioned, other philosophers and thinkers joined this movement. Amongst them Khalid Fazlun and Ibrahim Özdemir, etc. See further above in Chapter 1.

Those measures concern three spheres of action. First of all, during the past few decades, the Eco-Islam movement has been trying to revive Islamic environmental law by emphasizing the scriptural foundations of Islamic environmental ethics. Secondly, this movement stressed the role of Islam in the protection of the environment through field campaigns. In this regard, Islamic ethics was considered as a remedy to the ineffectiveness of statutory law. Thirdly, Eco-Islam groups started to use Islamic law more actively for environmental protection through *Fatwas*, constitutional reform and funding. However, those steps are not necessarily sequential.

### 5.2.1.1 The Use of Scriptural Sources as a Foundation for Environmental Protection in Islamic Countries:

The sources of Islamic law are the principal arguments of Eco-Islam.[145] In order to convince the government to reform the law or enact new legislation, or to change the behavior of polluting companies and raise awareness, the Eco-Islam movement relies on the sources of Islamic law – especially on the Qur'an as it is a non-controversial source of Islam, unlike other sources such as Hadith. But the Eco-Islam movement also relies on Hadith and the Fiqh because they are complementary sources and contain several arguments that can help serve their main objectives.

Other uses of scriptures by the Eco-Islam movement are illustrated by environmental *Fatwas*, which are supported by *Sharia'* sources (Qur'an, Hadith and Fiqh). Besides, constitutional reforms are opportunities for environmental groups to introduce environmental principles inspired by the *Sharia'* into the new constitutions. For example, in Egypt the inclusion of the Islamic conception of animal care into the new constitution was made possible because the concept of caring for animals was proposed in such a way that it appeared, to the commission that drafted the constitution in Egypt, as "locally authentic" rather than an imported concept.[146]

Even if "Eco-Islam" started by first focusing more on the "Why" (why from an Islamic point of view it is important to protect nature) rather than on the "How" (how this protection could be feasible), this movement has won legitimacy and is gaining momentum because it relies on *Sharia'* sources.[147] Therefore, as *Sharia'* is also the foundation of the legal system in Muslim countries, it is quite difficult for decision-makers to ignore this movement. Besides, the arguments put forward by

---

[145] On the sources of Islamic law, see Section 2.1 above.

[146] See above note 106. For more details, see Stilt, 'Constitutional Innovation and Animal Protection in Egypt'.

[147] Abdelzaher et al., 'Eco-Islam'.

this movement are quite similar to the grassroots legal actions in the framework of the Atmospheric Trust litigation.[148]

Moreover, Eco-Islam emerged as a means of pressure on the government in the sense that it embodies the *Khalifas* on earth and thus has a fiduciary duty towards natural resources. For example, in Iran, while "the Iranian government has not always matched its rhetoric in regard to environmental protection, NGOs still have the capacity – via the *Qur'ān* and other Islamic historical moral resources – to keep real pressure on the government to address environmental issues".[149] Being apolitical has helped the environmental groups to avoid government attacks and stay on the high moral ground.[150]

The Arab world has also expressed serious interest in the environment over the past few decades. Since 1983, a group of legal scholars in Jeddah formulated a short document that was published in multiple languages titled "Islamic Principles for the Conservation of the Natural Environment".[151] This document outlined the basis for environmental policy-making in Saudi Arabia and many other Muslim countries. The arguments in this document were drawn from Islam's most primary sources.[152] In this report, "ethical teachings are drawn almost exclusively from the *Qur'an* and *hadith*, and not from theological or philosophical studies or from commentaries on sacred texts".[153] The Islamic Principles for the Conservation of the Natural Environment concluded that: "Islam welcomes any regional or international endeavour in the field of conservation and invites all concerted, joint, and co-operative efforts in all fields to establish a balanced and planned international system for the protection and conservation of man and his environment and for the maintenance and perpetuation of a suitable, prosperous life for the present and future generations".[154]

Other major environmental conferences were held in Jeddah and Tehran following this initiative.[155] This movement brought about, as mentioned in Chapter 1, the "Islamic Declaration on Nature",[156] the "Islamic Declaration on Sustainable Development" adopted at the Conference of the ISESCO,[157] the

---

[148] Those arguments are based on *Shari'a* sources, especially the principle of *Khilafa*, but also the principles of sustainability, adaptive management and animal rights. The Atmospheric Trust litigation movement is also using as its main argument the principle of fiduciary duty and trusteeship. See further in Chapter 4.

[149] Kaminski, 'The OIC and the Paris 2015 Climate Change Agreement', 178.

[150] Eco Islam encompasses also entities that have close attaches to the government as is the case for Majliss Ulama Indonesia.

[151] Bakader et al., *Islamic Principles for the Conservation of the Natural Environment*.

[152] Vincenti, '"Green" Islam and Social Movements for Sustainability', 220 and following.

[153] Wescoat, 'Islam and Environmental Ethics', 868.

[154] Bakader et al., *Islamic Principles for the Conservation of the Natural Environment*, 24.

[155] See Schwencke, 'Globalized Eco-Islam'. See also Vincenti, '"Green" Islam and Social Movements for Sustainability'.

[156] Available at: www.arcworld.org

[157] Available at: www.isesco.org.ma/fr/wp-content/uploads/sites/2/2015/05/Developmt-durable1.pdf

"Islamic Declaration on Global Climate Change" and, more recently, the Rabat Declaration on the "Role of Cultural and Religious Factors in the Protection of the Environment and Sustainable Development" in Rabat (Morocco) in October 2019 at the eighth Islamic Conference of Environment Ministers.[158]

The "Islamic Declaration on Global Climate Change" was adopted at the Islamic Climate Change Symposium held in Istanbul in August 2015.[159] This symposium gathered the most distinguished international Islamic scholars and religious leaders from twenty countries.[160] It was organized by four NGOs (Islamic Relief Worldwide, Islamic Foundation for Ecology and Environmental Sciences (IFEES), GreenFaith and the Climate Action Network) in collaboration with three Islamic organizations: the Organization of Islamic Cooperation (OIC), the International Islamic Fiqh Academy (IIFA) and the Islamic Educational, Scientific and Cultural Organization (ISESCO).

As "an 'eco-Islamic Manifesto', the Islamic Declaration on Global Climate Change marks the new global ambitions of the current 'eco-Islamic' movement".[161] The Declaration is addressed to Muslims and the world population, including Islamic endowments (*Awqaf or Waqfs*) without any specification. That means that its recommendations are aimed at the *Awqaf* administrations in Muslim countries (Ministries of *Awqaf*) and also the private *Awqaf* held by NGOs or the private sector. The Declaration is more specifically addressed to the Conference of the Parties (COP) to the United Nations Framework Convention on Climate Change (UNFCCC) and the Meeting of the Parties (MOP) to the Kyoto Protocol taking place in Paris in December 2015 in order "to bring their discussions to an equitable and binding conclusion". It is also addressed to wealthy nations and oil-producing states and to corporations, finance and business. In this regard, it calls for divestment from fossil fuel and scaling up of renewable energy and calls to "Recognize the moral obligation to reduce consumption so that the poor may benefit from what is left of the earth's non-renewable resources" (para. 3.2).

The Declaration states that the

> current rate of climate change cannot be sustained, and the earth's fine equilibrium (*mīzān*) may soon be lost. As we humans are woven into the fabric of the natural world, its gifts are for us to savour. But the same fossil fuels that helped us achieve

---

[158] Rabat Declaration draws from previous conferences of Environment Ministers, held in the framework of the ISESCO Islamic Programme for Sustainable Development of Jeddah, Kingdom of Saudi Arabia in 2002 and its updated versions of 2006, 2010, 2012 and 2015. Even if it does not contain any reference to the scriptural basis, it automatically draws from those sources as it is based on the previous declarations.

[159] Available at: www.ifees.org.uk/wp-content/uploads/2016/10/climate_declarationmMWB.pdf. See also for an overview of the global framework of this Declaration: Hancock, 'Faith and Creation', and Damian, 'An Islamic Declaration on Climate Change'.

[160] For example, the Grand Muftis of Lebanon and Uganda and the chair of the Indonesian Council of *Ulamas*.

[161] Vincente, '"Green" Islam and Social Movements for Sustainability', 67.

most of the prosperity we see today are the main cause of climate change. Excessive pollution from fossil fuels threatens to destroy the gifts bestowed on us by God, whom we know as Allah – gifts such as a functioning climate, healthy air to breathe, regular seasons, and living oceans. But our attitude to these gifts has been short-sighted, and we have abused them.[162]

The Declaration called for people to reclaim their viceregency and to "tackle habits, mindsets, and the root causes of climate change, environmental degradation, and the loss of biodiversity in their particular spheres of influence". It then gives a supplementary argument that could be possibly used in the framework of the Atmospheric *Waqf/Khilafa* litigation. The Declaration adds that the citizens should reclaim their viceregency according to the prophet Muhammad in order to "bring about a resolution to the challenges that now face us".[163]

The Declaration is invoking the *Sharia'* for the protection of the environment not only by quoting from the Qur'an and Hadith, but also by bringing scientific evidence and by emphasizing the *Sharia'* principles that should be applied, that is, *Khilafa* and *Mizan* (balance).[164]

The "Eco-Islam" movement has gained momentum in the last few years mainly through fieldwork.

### 5.2.1.2 Eco-Islam as a Cure for Non-enforcement of Statutory Environmental Law: The Fieldwork

The Islamic Foundation for Ecology and Environmental Sciences (IFEES) plays an important role in forming a bridge between scriptures (Why) and the enforcement of Islamic principles in field conservation projects (How). With the help of the Alliance of Religions and Conservation (ARC) and other international NGOs, the project on the island of Misali in Tanzania and other field projects were successfully realized. Those projects, especially the Misali Island Project, are now well known in the "Eco-Islam" literature. They are an illustration of how Islamic ethics is applied in order to tackle the non-enforcement of statutory environmental law.

The island of Misali in the Indian Ocean "is a wonderful example of the remarkable role that religious values can play in confronting the environmental

---

[162] Islamic Declaration on Global Climate Change (2015). Preamble, 1.3. See also Kaminski, 'The OIC and the Paris 2015 Climate Change Agreement', at 180.

[163] Islamic Declaration on Global Climate Change (2015) (para. 3.6).

[164] For example, paragraph 1.4 states: "We note that the Millennium Ecosystem Assessment (UNEP, 2005), backed by over 1,300 scientists from 95 countries, found that overall, people have made greater changes to ecosystems in the last half of the 20th century than at any time in human history ... these changes have enhanced human well-being, but have been accompanied by ever increasing degradation (of our environment)". In paragraph 1.5: 'A study by the Intergovernmental Panel on Climate Change (IPCC) comprising representatives from over 100 nations, published in March 2014, gave five reasons for concern'.

crisis in the Islamic world".[165] The coral reef that surrounds this island is home to a rich variety of fish and turtles that were endangered by overfishing. The island is more than 95 percent Muslim, and local religious leaders were able to restore sustainable fishing and rich marine life by highlighting Islamic teachings on conservation. Government bans had virtually no impact on changing the attitudes of fishermen, who depleted the fish stocks by using dynamite. A local fisherman summed up the reason for the success of the religious message while the government decrees had failed. "It's easy to ignore the government", he said, "but no one can break the law of God".[166]

The Misali Island Project also led to the world's first Islamic conservation guide, launched by an NGO (IFEES) and government representatives (Directorate of Fisheries).[167] The guide on protecting marine life "used lessons from the Islamic Ecological Paradigm (IEP) to teach fishers how vital marine resources should be used, and protected and prohibited them from using unsustainable practices".[168]

Professor El-Ansary also cited the case of the government's annual tree-planting campaign in Nigeria, which was unsuccessful until the plantation project was established by an NGO that used religious precepts. The annual tree-planting campaigns were mostly organized by the government with no results until the project was carried out by environmental activists. Indeed, "Environmentalists have carried out tree planting projects using the Islamic notion of tenderness towards the natural environment and the induction encouraging planting of trees".[169]

The impact of Islamic environmental success stories has led more environmentalists in the region to become interested in exploring the Islamic input into solving specific ecological problems. The cases of Misali in Tanzania, tree planting in Nigeria and other Eco-Islam field projects illustrate how it is possible to respond to the non-enforcement of statutory environmental law by exploiting the potential of religion through collaboration, on the ground, between international NGOs, local religious groups and the government.[170]

This collaboration is now encouraged by the UN "Faith for Earth Initiative" and by the recent Rabat Declaration which states that:

[165] Waleed El-Ansary, 'Islamic Environmental Economics and the Three Dimensions of Islam: "A Common Word" on the Environment as Neighbor', in Waleed El-Ansary and David Linnan (eds.), *Muslim and Christian Understanding: Theory and Application of 'A Common Word'* (New York: Palgrave Macmillan, 2010), 143–57.

[166] Ibid.

[167] Abdelzaher and Abdelzaher, 'Beyond Environmental Regulations'. See also further examples of Eco-Islam practices in this article.

[168] Ibid.

[169] El-Ansary, 'Islamic Environmental Economics and the Three Dimensions of Islam', 143.

[170] Ibid. For an overview, see for example Abdelzaher and Abdelzaher, 'Beyond Environmental Regulations'.

we shall seek to promote the understanding and capacity of environmental communication between Muftis, Ulemas, imams, preachers, and promoters of the Islamic faith and activists in relevant associations through forums, short workshops and other information media in order to vulgarize the hallmarks of the crisis and the issue of sustainable development from a scientific, religious and cultural perspective, show their social and economic implications on the future of communities and encourage academic research in the field. (Para. 9)[171]

It could be argued that this potential can also be more systematically highlighted by the exploitation of Islamic environmental law, especially the *Waqf*, either by civil society or by the government itself. This is what a few NGOs have already undertaken in the field of funding.[172] They have also used the ecological potential of Islamic law through environmental *Fatwas*.

### 5.2.1.3  Environmental Fatwas: The Legal Weapon of Eco-Islam

The mobilization of Islamic law by environmental activists in Muslim countries is done through the environmental *Fatwas* adopted by *Ulamas* in countries such as Indonesia, Malaysia and Egypt.[173]

The environmental *Fatwas* allow the rules of *Sharia'* to be applied in the sphere of the environment. They can also help in reviving the idea of the environmental *Waqf* and more broadly in conveying the principle of the Atmospheric *Waqf* and encouraging its adoption and spread in the Islamic world (Table 2.1)

Environmental *Fatwas* are usually prepared in collaboration between *Ulamas* and environmentalists (activists and scholars) generally in the framework of international nature conservation programs supported by international NGOs such as the Alliance of Religions and Conservation (ARC).[174] This resulted in the *Fatwas* encompassing both religious and scientific principles. For example, the *Fatwa* on "Wildlife Conservation for the Preservation of Ecosystem Balance" issued by the MUI Indonesia in 2014 offers an illustration of this rich content.[175] This *Fatwa* of twenty-eight pages contains numerous *Sharia'* references, including *Sharia'* sources, *Fiqh* principles and quotes from authoritative *Fiqh* books. To these sources are added citations of Indonesian environmental regulations and scientific recommendations on how to monitor the wild animal species. The *Fatwa* is addressed to a vast array of interlocutors: the government, legislators, regional administrations, businesses, religious leaders and the global community.

---

[171] UNEP, UNEA, 4, Faith for Earth Dialogue, 7.
[172] See further Section 5.2.2.2.
[173] See above in Chapter 2 and Section 5.2.1.4.
[174] Mangunjaya and Gudah, 'Fatwas on Boosting Environmental Conservation in Indonesia'.
[175] Ibid., 6. The text of this *Fatwa* is available in English at: www.arcworld.org/downloads/Fatwa-MUI-English-Jun-2014.pdf

Arguably the environmental *Fatwas* are a kind of *soft law* because, theoretically, they are not legally binding. *Fatwas* are opinions given by the committee of *Ulamas* on demand (by individuals or group of individuals, a court or the state). Therefore, "environmental *Fatwas* are not enforceable by the state and can only be regarded as non-state, ground-up responses to the imperfections of existing environmental policies and laws".[176]

For instance, in Indonesia, like many other Islamic countries, the *Sharia'* does not cover environmental matters and is restricted mostly to family law. Nevertheless, this did not prevent the environmental NGOs from resorting to one of the *Sharia'* tools, the *Fatwa*, and expanding it to cover environmental issues.

Religious institutions in Indonesia have also established close cooperation with the ministerial departments responsible for nature conservation, with universities and with international NGOs. For example, the aforementioned Majliss Ulama Indonesia (MUI) has adopted a Memorandum of Understanding with the Ministry of Oceans and Fisheries (*Kementerian Kelautan dan Perikanan*), the Ministry of Forestry (*Kementerian Kehutanan*) and the Ministry of Environment (*Kementerian Lingkungan Hidup*) in order to press for the enforcement of *Sharia'*-based rules in the framework of environmental policy.[177] According to a statement by an Indonesian minister, the Majliss Ulama Indonesia (MUI) *Fatwa* on environmentally friendly mining "reinforces positive law and serves as a normative reference for the government and mining firms in the management of the environment".[178]

From Asia, to the Middle East, to America, environmental *Fatwas* have gained momentum as a tool for environmental protection. A recent example is the statement on "climate change and fossil fuel divestment" issued on September 1, 2019 by the *Fiqh* Council of North America, which is the Council of Islamic Religious Scholars. This is the first *Fatwa*-like statement in the world issued by a *Fiqh* Council that is addressed to the fossil fuel industry. It calls upon Islamic investment houses and other investment fund administrators and managers "to immediately develop fossil fuel-free investment vehicles and portfolios that include investments in renewable and clean energy companies".[179]

This statement should be followed by upcoming environmental *Fatwas*. In this way it forms a junction between the past and the present, between the Islamic Declaration on Global Climate Change, Eco-Islam movements and the

---

[176] Ramlan, 'Religious Law for the Environment'.

[177] In this context, the Ministry of Environment also encourages traditional Quranic schools disseminated throughout the country, to spread the teachings of Islam on the environment (*Ekopesantren*). See Mangunjaya et al., 'Faiths from the Archipelago', 111.

[178] MUI Fatwa on Environment Normative Reference. Available at: https://en.antaranews.com/news/74166/mui-fatwa-on-environment-normative-reference

[179] Available at: https://financingthefuture.global/statement-of-fiqh-council-of-north-america-on-fossil-fuel-divestment/.

international legal climate system. As such it represents an important milestone in the Atmospheric *Waqf* paradigm.

In sum, the evolution of the Eco-Islam movement towards increasing use of the law was possible thanks to *Ijtihad*. *Ijtihad* systematizes many concepts from the Qur'an and the Hadith.[180] For example, as we have seen, the *Waqf* is a creation of *Ijtihad* by interpreting general rules of the Qur'an and Hadith related to charity and by using *Istihsan* in order to bring customary law into the *Sharia'*.[181] The use of *Ijtihad* is thus what reinvigorates Islamic environmental law through environmental *Fatwas*. Even if they lack a legally binding effect, these *Fatwas* are paving the way for a new understanding of *Sharia'*-based environmental law.

Besides, the environmental *Fatwas*, as general non-binding legal tools, are using as a basis the main sources of the *Sharia'* (Qur'an, Hadith and Fiqh). Their strength comes from the fact that they use those sources in the field of the environment. They therefore have a strong symbolic effect.

Environmental *Fatwas* use a bottom-up approach. They are "regarded as non-state, ground-up responses to the imperfections of existing environmental policies and laws. However, this does not mean that they are not 'enforced' in the broad sense".[182] The MUI's Board in collaboration with NGOs such as Conservation International, Alliance for Religions and Conservation, CARE international and the Islamic Foundation for Ecology and Environmental Sciences "initiated the 'socialization' (*sosialisasi*) or implementation of three of their environmental fatwas".[183] At least two guidebooks have been published, on how the *Fatwas* can be used as a legal basis in the religious schools (*pesantren*) to teach eco-friendly practices, and on the training and capacity building of preachers (*da'i*) and local volunteers in advocacy and practical implementation.[184]

*Fatwas* can thus serve as a first step to promote the legal tools (such as the environmental *Waqf* and the *Hima*) to be used for the protection of the environment. Environmental *Fatwas* can prompt the government to adopt those tools. This could lead to a change in other countries, as has been witnessed in the case of Malaysia and Singapore.[185] The re-greening of the *Sharia'* could be contagious, especially with the support of international environmental organizations, such as the UN "Faith for Earth Initiative".[186] This initiative can promote the implementation of Islamic environmental law through the "Eco-Islam" movement. It can also impacts on government programs.

---

[180] See further details on *Ijtihad* above in Section 2.1 ('The Sources of Islamic Environmental Law').

[181] See Section 2.2.

[182] Ramlan, 'Religious Law for the Environment', at 16.

[183] Ibid.

[184] Ibid.

[185] Those countries have in fact been influenced by the experience of environmental *Fatwas* in Indonesia. Ibid.

[186] See the introduction.

It is noteworthy that, according to the *Fiqh*, *Fatwas* can be binding if they are endorsed by judges (*qadi*) in court.[187] *Ulamas* who are able to issue the *Fatwa* (the *muftis*) have served in the past as experts in court. This possibility is conceivable today. Indeed, *Fatwas* can be used in "Atmospheric *Khilafa* litigation" as a legal argument to strengthen a plaintiff's arguments, as seen in public Trust litigation.[188]

In this case, one of the main arguments of the Atmospheric Trust litigation is that the government has failed in its obligations as a Trustee. By transposing this argument into the context of Islamic law, nothing would prevent a *mufti* from declaring, for example, that authorizing a large polluting company to open or continue its activity is contrary to the government's fiduciary duty and *Khilafa* principle. All the environmental *Fatwas* released so far invoke the principle of *Khilafa* in their arguments. When advanced before a court, this argument will be hard to dismiss as it is based on both religion and the constitution (Islamic Supremacy clause). This has already occurred in other countries where environmental litigation was also based on religious principles, such as those included in the *Laudato Si'*. A parallel could be drawn between the *amicus curiae briefs* presented by religious groups in the Atmospheric Trust litigation, for example, and the environmental *Fatwas* that could be used in courts (including *Sharia'* courts) in the framework of the Atmospheric *Khilafa* litigation. It is very important for the litigation to be based on this grounded principle because it would give more strength to this movement and reinforce its anchorage. As Pope John Paul II declared: "We need to recognize that, while atmospheric trust litigation may provide a cataclysm for urgent climate action, legal movements need backing from a moral culture that inspires support and respect from the people".[189]

Environmental *Fatwas* can thus be used as technical tools to encourage governments, individuals and the business sector to use the environmental *Waqf* or *Hima* in order to protect natural resources and to contribute to climate change mitigation efforts. Environmental *Fatwas* can also strengthen the idea of a green *Khilafa*, which is the essence of the environmental *Waqf* and the Atmospheric *Waqf* paradigm. For example, a *Fatwa* can recommend using the *Waqf* as a tool for protecting the climate system. This recommendation could be generalized to further environmental *Fatwas* around the world, as we have seen with the example of the statement of the Fiqh Council of North America on fossil fuel divestment.

---

[187] According to Al-Qarāfī (thirteenth-century jurist). See Ramlan, 'Religious Law for the Environment: Comparative Islamic Environmental Law in Singapore, Malaysia, and Indonesia', at 10.

[188] See Chapter 1.

[189] Mary Christina Wood, 'Nature's Trust: A Legal and Sacred Covenant to Protect Earth's Climate System for Future Generation', in Gerald Magill and Kiarash Aramesh (eds.), *The Urgency of Climate Change: Pivotal Perspectives* (Newcastle upon Tyne: Cambridge Scholars Publishing, 2017), 362–87, 375.

The UN Faith for Earth Initiative, for instance, can support such environmental *Fatwas* through the empowerment of the *Ulamas* and *muftis*.

One of the environmental *Fatwas* released in 2014 by the Majlis Ulamas Indonesia recommends the use of *Waqf* and *Zakat* for the Construction of Clean Water and Sanitation Facilities for Communities (Table 2.1). It is a good example of the revival of *Waqf* for water; which through history has been one of the main types of *Waqfs* in the Islamic world.[190] This *Fatwa* could be a first step towards the recommendation of other kinds of environmental *Waqfs* in environmental *Fatwas*.

Again, a parallel is possible through the example of the *amicus curiae briefs*, which advocate for the use of the Public Trust Doctrine in the Atmospheric Trust litigation. In the *amicus curiae briefs* brought by religious groups it was stated, for example, that: "[i]n the papal encyclical, *Laudato Si'*, Pope Francis issued a clarion call for 'the establishment of a legal framework which can set clear boundaries and ensure the protection of ecosystems'. The ancient yet enduring public Trust principle, which safeguards crucial natural resources as common property of all citizens, offers just such a legal framework".[191]

Paraphrasing this statement in the framework of Islamic environmental law is tempting: "the ancient yet enduring [*Waqf* institution/principle], which safeguards crucial natural resources offers just such a legal framework", "which can set clear boundaries and ensure the protection of ecosystems". The analysis of the impacts of environmental *Fatwas* in a country like Indonesia, for example, shows that they create stimulus for the legislator and the society.[192] They can also help to convey in court the idea of the "Trust in the higher sense".[193] The Atmospheric *Waqf* can be used as a higher principle and not necessarily as a formal institution.

Nevertheless, because *muftis* cannot answer beyond the parameters of the question that has been put to them (by individuals, group of individuals, courts or the state), it is important that the question is asked properly.[194] This reverses the burden

---

[190] See for example, Valentine Denizeau, 'Conduire l'eau dans le Caire mamluk: installations hydrauliques et polititıqes d'aménagement dans la capital égyptienne (1250–1517)' (PhD thesis, University Aix Marseille, 2010).

[191] United States District Court, District of Oregon, Eugene Divison, *Kelsey Cascadia Rose Juliana, M. Xiuhtezcatl Tonatiuh, plaintiffs v. The United States of America*; Barak Obama, federal defendants, Amici Curiae Brief in Support of Plaintiffs, Case 6:15-cv-01517, p. 4. Available at https://ord.uscourts.gov/index.php

[192] See for example Mangunjaya and Gudah, 'Fatwas on Boosting Environmental Conservation in Indonesia'.

[193] See further developments above on this idea in Section 4.2.3 ('An Overarching Principle').

[194] According to Professor Shazny Ramlan 'Muftis, at the end of the day, only provide their legal opinion based on the abstraction or the limited facts provided by the petitioner in her question. Thus, unlike judicial decisions resulting from court proceedings where clearer facts and supporting evidence are presented, the *fatwa* only addresses questions of law (ie, "In case of X, or situations similar to X, the law is Y. Otherwise, the law is Z."). Keeping in mind that *fatwas* "present the law of Islam, and should therefore have an objective form", it is imperative that *muftis* clearly state the position of Islamic law on a given issue, and conclude with the invocation ('And Allah *wallahu a'lam*) as a mark that "the *muftī* gives ... only the best that Man

of action on environmental groups, faith-based groups and also on individuals who should reframe their request for an advisory opinion in terms that would allow the evolution of Islamic environmental law.'[195]

For instance, an environmental NGO may ask if the extraction of sand by a company in the vicinity of a village is contrary to *Sharia'* by attaching to the question scientific evidence of the impacts of the extractions on the groundwater, on biodiversity and on the landscape. Or the question could be more broadly asked on what *Sharia'* provides for climate change impacts by using, as an argument, the Islamic Declaration on Global Climate Change and the Statement on Climate Change and Fossil Fuel Divestment issued by the *Fiqh* Council of North America, among other arguments. The *Fatwa* could then seize this opportunity to recommend environmental *Waqfs* or even the Atmospheric *Waqf*.

One of the main shortfalls of Eco-Islam, as demonstrated in the example of the constitutional reform in Egypt, is the limited knowledge by environmental activists of *Fiqh* and Islamic law. However, Egyptian environmental activists, who were secular, preferred to "Islamize" their advocating strategy in order to improve their chances of success in incorporating the protection of animals article into the draft Egyptian constitution.[196] This may result in a growing use of environmental *Fatwas* by environmental groups in Muslim countries, even by secular groups.

The lack of scientific knowledge could represent one of the main impediments to the Eco-Islam movement. Yet it appears from the analysis of the Atmospheric Trust litigation that scientific evidence in such litigation is powerful. Therefore, the *Ulamas* have to strengthen their role by opening up to science. The *Mufti* should be able to understand the IPCC reports, for example, in order to play an effective role in the Atmospheric *Waqf/Khilafa* litigation. They should be able to link science

---

can determine for what God's will really is'". Ramlan, 'Religious Law for the Environment', at 10–11. See also Muhammad Khalid Masud, Brinkley Messick and David S. Powers, 'Muftis, Fatwas, and Islamic Legal Interpretation', in Muhammad Khalid Masud, BrinkleyMessick and David S Powers (eds.), *Islamic Legal Interpretation: Muftis and Their Fatwas* (New York: Harvard University Press, 1996), 20–26.

[195] An official document entitled 'Procedures for Determining and Applying Fatwas about the Environment and Management of Natural Resources' explains this procedure. It lays out four kinds of 'tasks and functions' involved in deriving a *Fatwa*: (1) the *mustafti* (the party seeking the *fatwa*); (2) the *mufti* (the author of the *fatwa*); (3) the issue to be determined; and (4) the users (*pengguna*) of the *fatwa* or 'related parties'. The 'framework' for developing and applying the *fatwa* includes a 'workshop' to be attended by the *mufti*, the *mustafti*, as well as 'experts in the area and personages from the society who will utilize the *fatwa*'. The goal at this stage of the process is to achieve a 'comprehensive and holistic' formulation of the issue with an eye to an implementable solution, through 'various sources of Islamic law' as well as 'comparative study and/or field research'. See Gade, 'Islamic Law and the Environment in Indonesia', at 176.

[196] Stilt, 'Constitutional Innovation and Animal Protection in Egypt'.

with the enjoinments of *Sharia'* in order to reinforce their arguments.[197] The parallel with legal arguments presented by religious groups, as reflected in *amicus curiae briefs* filed with the Supreme Court in the United States is also enlightening here. In the November 2002 statement (reiterated in twenty-one state-level statements in 2003, 2004 and 2005), *Amici* and senior religious leaders from a diverse array of Christian and Jewish denominations and groups stated: "We are deeply distressed by evidence that ... [g]lobal greenhouse gas emissions are projected to increase average temperatures by 2.5–10.4 degrees Fahrenheit into the next century – bringing rising seas, weather and agricultural disruptions, floods, refugees, migrating diseases and other dis-locations which most harm the planet's poor and vulnerable".[198] Therefore, "based on the Christian tenets of stewardship for the natural world and solicitude for the most vulnerable members of the human community, Amici have joined a growing number of people of faith to support concerted action to control emissions of greenhouse gases such as carbon dioxide".[199]

The power of bringing science into the religious discourse in courts lies in the fact that it could reinforce the religious arguments of environmental *Fatwas* or any other means used for bringing a lawsuit. This is a way to bring ethics into environmental sciences and vice versa.[200]

One of the first uses of climate science in an environmental *Fatwa*-like document occurred recently, in September 2019. The abovementioned Statement on Fossil Fuel Divestment adopted by the *Fiqh* Council of North America declares:

> We affirm that it is the overwhelming consensus of climate scientists that this clear and present danger is caused by the continued burning of fossil fuels. To go beyond the 1.5-degree limit will endanger all human civilization and planetary life. Scientists are already projecting that 1 in four species, 1,000,000 species, are in danger of extinction by the end of this century. According to current scientific information, the burning of the proven reserves, presently identified by the fossil fuel industry, will create at least 3,000 gigatons of greenhouse gas emissions which is six times this threshold level.[201]

This demonstrates that there is a continuum and evolution in the environmental *Fatwas* and an acknowledgment of the importance of using this tool to protect the

---

[197] Here also the example of *Ekopesantren* (traditional religious schools dedicated to spread the teachings of Islam on the environment) could be helpful in extending the environmental teaching to *Ulamas*.

[198] Supreme Court of the United States, *Commonwealth of Massachussetts, et al., Petitioners v. Environmental Protection Agency, et al., Respondents*, On Writ of Certiorari to the United States Court of Appeals for the District of Columbia Circuit, Brief of the National Council of the Churches of Christ in the USA, Church World Service, and National Catholic Rural Life Conference as Amici Curiae in Support of Petitioners. Available at: www.supremecourt.gov/

[199] Ibid.

[200] See Section 5.1.5 (and specifically the statement by the biologist Michel Soulé).

[201] This statement is available at: https://financingthefuture.global/statement-of-fiqh-council-of-north-america-on-fossil-fuel-divestment/

climate system. It also demonstrates how the *Ulamas* are willing to use climate science in Islamic legal instruments.

At the same time, the *Ulamas* have to use more *Ijtihad* in order to answer to the questions put to them by referring not only to the Qur'an and Hadith, but also to Qiyas, Istihsan and Istislah.[202] Consequently this will open to a much more possibilities of evolution for Islamic environmental law.

Considering the form of the environmental *Fatwas*, they can either follow a classical formula or use new technologies and the internet, as is the case in some countries such as Indonesia, Malaysia, Singapore, Egypt and Yemen.[203] This will offer more practical solutions for environmental NGOs that seek prompt legal advice on the issues they are dealing with. The same environmental *Fatwas* could afterwards be used as an argument in the courts or constitute a conceptual basis for statutory reforms and government programs. This will also facilitate its use by other countries (the oil-stain effect).

If resorting to environmental *Fatwas* by faith-based groups to seek more effective environmental protection is now turning into a movement in itself in some Muslim countries, that does not mean that environmental *Fatwas* are the only legal tool to promote Islamic environmental law. Islamic environmental law principles can also be included through constitutions.

### 5.2.1.4 Islamic Environmental Law as Part of the Constitution

Constitutions in Islamic countries encompass the Islamic supremacy clause. This principle is generally formulated as follows: "the principles of Islamic Sharia are the main source of legislation".[204] This means that the entire legal system is submitted to Islamic law. Consequently, the Islamic supremacy clause renders Islamic law as a body of supra-constitutional standards like an "Islamic *Grundnorm*", according to which "the common source of validity for all legal rules belonging to the same (legal) order".[205] This kind of *Grundnorm* is nevertheless not harmoniously interpreted by the judges.[206]

---

[202] See further Section 2.1.

[203] Available for Singapore at: www.muis.gov.sg/officeofthemufti/Fatwa and for Malaysia at: http://e-smaf.islam.gov.my/e-smaf/index.php/main/mainv1/fatwa/3 and for Indonesia at: https://mui.or.id/ and for Egypt at: www.dar-alifta.org. For an analysis of the first three *Fatwas*' councils, see Ramlan, 'Religious Law for the Environment'. See Table 2.1.

[204] Article 2 of the Constitution of the Arab Republic of Egypt. For more examples, see Table 1.1 and also https://constituteproject.org/

[205] It is the definition of 'Grundnorm' according to Professor Hans Kelsen. See further Nathalie Bernard-Maugiron and Baudouin Dupret, 'Les principes de la sharia sont la source principale de la législation', *Égypte/Monde arabe* (1999) 2. Available at: https://journals.openedition.org/ema/992

[206] A detailed study of all the jurisprudence of the High Constitutional Court relating to Article 2 (on Islamic supremacy clause) of the Egyptian constitution concluded that the constitutional judge did recognize the symbolic value of the *Sharia*' in the Egyptian legal order, but he went

According to this norm or clause, any legal provision can be enforced within the *Grundnorm* perspective, though this possibility is not exploited in the framework of environmental protection. Yet many Islamic constitutions also encompass environmental principles, especially the right to a safe environment (Table 1.1). Therefore, the combination of those two principles can constitute the foundations of Islamic environmental law. It could also strengthen the legal arguments in the Atmospheric Trust litigation cases. Examples of this litigation around the world show that they are based on the constitution, especially on the duty of care principle and on the right to a safe and healthy environment.[207] Adding the Islamic Supremacy clause argument to this legal strategy could lead to significant results in Muslim countries. Only a few constitutions include the *Waqf*, yet the majority of Islamic countries have a legal basis for this institution in statutory law (Table 4.1).

Constitutional reform in Egypt offers an interesting example of the combination of the Islamic Supremacy clause and the Environmental clause. As mentioned in Section 5.1.4, activists have pushed the drafters to include an Islamic conception of the principle of care towards animals in the new constitution. "*Al-Rifq-Bi-Al Hayawan*" (care towards animals) was included in the constitution following its Islamic formula. This triggered the incorporation of another provision related to environmental resources conservation into the Egyptian Constitution.[208] Article 45 of the Egyptian Constitution reads as follow:

The state commits to protecting its seas, beaches, lakes, waterways, groundwater, natural reserves. It is prohibited to encroach upon, pollute, or use them in a manner that contradicts their nature. Every citizen has the right to enjoy them as regulated by law. The state also commits to the protection and development of green space in urban areas; the protection of plants, livestock and fisheries; the protection of endangered species; and the prevention of cruelty to animals. All the foregoing takes place as regulated by law.

The Islamic formulation of the principle appears more clearly in the Arabic version of Article 45, which includes the same formula adopted by Imam al Bukhari in his compilation of Hadiths (nineteenth century), that is "al rifq-bil-hayawan." Instead of a generic formula following the Western statutes model, environmental activists in Egypt conveyed an Islamic principle which was integrated as such into the constitution.[209]

little further than this simple recognition. As for statutory law, it has appropriated the religious normative corpus. Ibid. See also Michiel, *Sharia and National Law in Muslim Countries*, 8; Dawood and Ginsburg, 'Constitutional Islamization and Human Rights'.

[207] UNEP, 'The Statute of Climate Change Litigation: A Global Review', 2017, 15 and 32. See also Peel and Osofsky, 'A Right Turn in Climate Change Litigation?'

[208] Stilt, 'Constitutional Innovation and Animal Protection in Egypt'.

[209] Ibid.

Apart from Egypt, not many countries have adopted the principle of protection of animals and natural resources in its religious formula.[210] However, several Muslim countries' constitutions incorporate the principle of environmental protection. Combined with the Islamic Supremacy clause, it can be said that environmental protection can very well be seen and interpreted from an Islamic legal perspective, especially by courts.

### 5.2.1.5 Islamic Law: A Basis for Environmental Litigation

Islamic law is used as a basis in environmental litigation in a few Islamic countries. Environmental activists play an important role in this litigation. It is noteworthy that this movement is comparable to the environmental justice movement that "served as a platform for climate justice litigation, which in turn laid a common-law foundation for atmospheric trust litigation".[211]

In Pakistan and in Egypt "the inclusion of Islamic law as a part of the state's democratic constitutional framework allows for the invocation of Islamic values before national courts in public interest claims".[212] The Islamic Supremacy clause in the constitution has been "used as a basis for activists to challenge the 'un-Islamic' character of laws and government actions in the courts".[213] For example, in Pakistan, Article 2A of the constitution (Islamic Supremacy clause) played a vital role to expand the horizon of Article 184A (on social justice), facilitating access to justice. The courts utilized Article 2A, successfully strengthening the existing legal principles of the common law.[214]

It is interesting to note that among the cases dealt with by the judges, one of them concerned the legitimacy (according to *Sharia'*) of the decision taken by an environmental agency which had not carried out an Environment Impact Assessment (EIA) before the construction of a cement factory. The judge in this case retained the *Fiqh* principle "*amr [bil] ma'rūf wa nahi [ani]munkar* (prohibiting good and preventing evil) to allege that the agency failed to protect "the health of citizens when it continued to allow local cement plant to emit harmful air pollutants".[215]

In Pakistan, the Supreme Court acted according to the Islamic Supremacy clause, combining Islamic and secular principles of justice. The court asserted that "right to social justice was like a fundamental right under the Islamic principles, although it was not enshrined in any way in the Constitutional scheme".[216]

---

[210] Except the United Arab Emirates. See further Section 5.1.5.
[211] Abate, 'Atmospheric Trust Litigation', at 33.
[212] Ramlan, 'Religious Law for the Environment', at 7.
[213] Ibid.
[214] Aman Ullah, 'Public Interest Litigation: A Constitutional Regime to Access to Justice in Pakistan' (2018) 19, 2, *Pakistan Vision*, 167–81, at 177.
[215] Ramlan, 'Religious Law for the Environment', 7.
[216] Ullah, 'Public Interest Litigation', 177.

Similarly, this court embraced the public interest litigation principles. It held, for example, that Article 184(3) should be interpreted in the light of Article 2A.[217] In sum, "the incorporation of the Objectives Resolution enhanced the power of judicial review of the Higher Courts, along with the doctrine of Public Interest" in this country.[218]

A parallel with the Public Trust Doctrine is thus possible. The public interest is at the core of the *Waqf* as it is for the PTD. Thanks to its emphasis on the public interest, "[the PTD and the *Waqf*] expansion is expected to be associated with moralistic rather than individualistic or traditionalistic politic structure".[219] Besides, the history of the Atmospheric Trust litigation in the United States, for example, shows that "environmental justice is rooted in several social movements within the US, including the Civil Rights movements of the 50s, 60s, 70s".[220] Similarly, environmental issues in the Muslim world are the product of social injustice.[221]

Moreover, the principles of Islamic environmental law, especially those entrenched in the *Waqf* (fiduciary duty, Khilafa, Trusteeship), could also be cited as a basis of *amicus curiae briefs* presented by religious groups in environmental and climate change litigation. For instance, in the *amicus curiae brief* in support of the plaintiffs presented by the Global Catholic Climate Movement and Leadership Council of Women Religious in the case of *Kelsley Cascadia Rose Juliana et al.* v. *the United States of America et al.*, it is stated that the public Trust principles represent: "(1) an ethic toward future generations; (2) an affirmation of public rights to natural assets; and (3) a condemnation of waste". These are moral precepts "not only to the foundations of human experience, but are mirrored in the religious teachings of many faiths [such as encompassed by the Islamic Declaration on Global Climate Change]".[222]

---

[217] This article states: 'Without prejudice to the provisions of Article 199, the Supreme Court shall, if it considers that a question of public importance with reference to the enforcement of any of the Fundamental Rights conferred by Chapter I of Part II is involved have the power to make an order of the nature mentioned in the said Article'.

[218] Ullah, 'Public Interest Litigation'.

[219] According to Professor Daniel Elazar, the typology of state political cultures, the *moralistic* political culture emphasizes 'the commonwealth conception as the basis for democratic government', the *individualistic* political culture emphasizes 'the conception of the democratic order as a market-place' and the traditionalistic culture emphasizes the role of government as a preserver of the status quo. Cited by Lawler and Parle, 'Expansion of the Public Trust Doctrine in Environmental Law', at 139.

[220] Abate, 'Atmospheric Trust Litigation', 34.

[221] Khalid, 'Islam, Ecology, and Modernity'.

[222] In *The United States Courts of Appeals for the Ninth Circuit, The United States of America, et al., v. United States District for the District of Oregon and Kelsey Cascadia Rose Juliana, et al.*, On Petition for Writ of Mandamus in Case No. 6:15-cv-01517-TC-AA (D. Or.), Motion for Leave to File Brief of Amici Curiae Global Catholic Climate Movement, et al., in Opposition to Petition for Writ of Mandamus, Case: 17-71692, 09/05/2017, ID: 10569948, DktEntry: 24, p. 23 of 31. Available at: www.ourchildrenstrust.org

It is, in fact, the first time that the Islamic ethics principles have been used in the framework of the Atmospheric Trust litigation. This was possible because the same ethical foundations, as conveyed through the Islamic Declaration on Global Climate Change for example, are commonly shared by all religions.

We can therefore foresee the application of the principles of *Waqf*, and more broadly of Islamic law principles in *amicus curiae briefs*, presented by religious groups in the Atmospheric Trust litigation, especially as it is supposed that climate change litigation "will appear with increasing frequency in the Global South", including in Muslim countries.[223]

The common ground between all religions could be fruitfully promoted in order to call for effective protection of the climate system. The Islamic Declaration on Global Climate Change encourages adopting such an approach. It states: "we welcome the significant contributions taken by other faiths, as we can all be winners in this race – If we each offer the best of our respective traditions, we may yet see a way through our difficulties" (para. 3.5). This call could be considered as the ethical ground for a global Atmospheric Trust movement based on the principle of Trust/ *Waqf* thinking.

The call was reiterated in the Rabat Declaration on the "Role of Cultural and Religious Factors in the Protection of the Environment and Sustainable Development" at the eighth Islamic Conference of Environment Ministers. The declaration emphasizes that: "environmental challenges, despite being a new topic in man's understanding and scientific interests, are consistent with the fundamental relevant answers relating to the challenges of protecting the environment given in religious texts and the principles of social education and upbringing in all beliefs and cultures regardless of their differences" (para. 9). The declaration represents, in fact, a bridge between the previous environmental declarations issued by Muslim international organizations and the UN Faith for Earth Initiative. In this sense, it makes it easier to spread Islamic environmental law at the global level.

Another interesting example of the use of Islamic law, especially the *Waqf*, in a court decision in a manner that could be extended to Atmospheric *Khilafa* litigation, is the suit filed by a *Waqf* administrator against the Saudi Electricity Company. In this case, the company had installed a high-voltage electricity cable over a *Waqf* farm. This impacted on the value and productivity of the *Waqf*. The court held that the company had to compensate the *Waqf* farm or remove its cables from the location.[224]

In sum, "the type of new interpretive insights generated through legal challenges tell us something about how prevailing institutional readings of justice standards never fully exhaust the broader range of possibilities". A "component of established

---

[223] UNEP, 'The Statute of Climate Change Litigation: A Global Review', 25.
[224] Ibid.

standards is prized open to newer developments in society. Law is tested against the burden of proof of deepening ecological problems, the rightness claims of competing actors, the value orientations of contemporary publics, as well as technical-pragmatic claims as to how best to attain common goals".[225]

Therefore, environmental activists in Muslim countries could provide a platform for the Atmospheric *Khilafa* litigation and push towards legal reform. They could participate not only within the political boundaries of those countries, but could also add their voices to the ongoing global environmental justice movement.

This universalist reach is already happening through Islamic finance, including green finance. Islamic green finance is more the prerogative of the governments and the private sector. But NGOs (including faith-based groups) also participate in the global trend through funding of environmental initiatives. For example, in the United Kingdom, the NGO Islamic Relief Worldwide has been successfully managing *Waqf* funds collected through cash *Waqf*. It has assisted various projects in many countries around the world, such as the Kharan Water Project in Pakistan and Tsunami Response in Indonesia.[226]

These achievements are also supported by governments. A few of the achievements are related to environmental *Waqf*.

### 5.2.2 *Environmental* Waqf *Initiatives and Islamic Green Finance*

A few states have already started to use the *Waqf* for environmental purposes. The explosion of Islamic finance helped to create new *Awqaf*-based financial products through the private sector.

#### 5.2.2.1 Examples of Environmental *Waqf* in Muslim Countries

The *Waqf* is also used as a funding mechanism for environmental projects such as clean-ups and trees plantings. The emergence of Sustainable Development Goals and Corporate Social Responsibility "has made people think of waqf as a potential instrument to address these goals, which has led to more and more non-Muslims becoming aware of the concept".[227]

In general, Islamic countries have dedicated state departments for managing the *Awqaf* (generally called Ministry of *Awqaf* and Islamic Affairs). Their duties can be extended to the protection of the environment, but for now they mostly focus on managing mosques and religious schools. However, in the last decade these

---

[225] Tracey Skillington, 'Changing Perspectives on Natural Resource Heritage, Human Rights, and Intergenerational Justice' (2019) 23, 4, *International Journal of Human Rights*, 615–17 at 624.

[226] See for example the Kharan Water Project in Indonesia. More information is available at: www .islamic-relief.org/wp-content/uploads/2014/06/2010-Annual-Report.pdf

[227] Available at: www.worldbank.org/en/country/malaysia; www.inceif.org; www.isra.my

ministries have started to embrace the ecological movement through specific actions such as the Green Mosques.[228]

Environmental *Awqaf* are present in a few countries today, including Kuwait, Indonesia, Malaysia, Saudi Arabia[229] and even in the United Kingdom, France, Australia and New Zealand.[230]

Environmental *Awqaf* in Kuwait seem to present one of the best models, "which aimed at participating in the efforts of revival and the consolidation of the values and principles of waqf".[231] The Kuwait Awkaf Public Foundation (KAPF) has "played a major role in pulling the public attention to the importance of environmental waqf".[232] KAPF created a dedicated *Waqf* company (Kuwaiti Company for the Environmental Services), which is providing cleaning services and an environmental fund. This fund, called the Kuwait Regional Organization (KRU), was instituted by the Kuwait Regional Convention of the Protection of the Marine Environment in the Gulf. KRU is "one of the beneficiaries that received considerable financial aid from the Health Fund to support its environmental task, especially that most member states in the organization do not pay their financial dues".[233] Again, Islamic law is replacing and supplementing the failing statutory environmental law.[234]

In Indonesia, environmental *Awqaf* are scattered programs used for tree planting or cultivating, building wells and clean water installations.[235] However, these types of *Awqaf* "are continuously running and getting increasing support from the people".[236] The Indonesian *Waqf* fund (TWI) is focused on animal husbandry,

[228] Ahmad Hafiz Bin Abdul Aziz, Wei Zhang, Baharom Abdul Hamid, Mahomed Ziyaad, Said Bouheraoua, Noor Suhaida Kasri and Mohamed Al-Amine Sano, *Maximizing Social Impact Through Waqf Solutions* (Washington, DC: World Bank Group, 2019). Available at: http://documents.worldbank.org/curated/en/930461562218730622/Maximizing-Social-Impact-Through-Waqf-Solutions

[229] Norma Md Saad, Salina Kassim and Zarinah Hamid, 'Best Practices of Waqf: Experiences of Malaysia and Saudi Arabia' (2016) 2, 2, *Journal of Islamic Economics Lariba*, 57–74.

[230] 'Awaqf New Zealand' for example was established by an NGO.

[231] Ibrahim Ahmed Khalil, Yunus Ali and Mohammad Shaiban, 'Waqf Fund Management in Kuwait and Egypt: Can Malaysia Learn from Their Experiences?', Proceeding of the International Conference on Masjid, Zakat and Waqf (IMAF 2014), December 1–2, 2014, Kuala Lumpur, Malaysia.

[232] Budiman Mochammad Arif, 'The Role of Waqf for Environmental Protection in Indonesia', Aceh Development International Conference (ADIC), Kuala Lumpur, March 26–28, 2011.

[233] Nada Al-Duaij and Eisa Al-Anezy, 'The Environmental Laws and Regulations in Islamic Waqf: Application to the Situation in Kuwait', paper, September 2009, www.google.com/url?sa=t&rct=j&q=&esrc=s&source=web&cd=&ved=2ahUKEwjnoa7yltLsAhXyDmMBHbTSDB8QFjAFegQICxAC&url=https%3A%2F%2Fworks.bepress.com%2Feisa_al_enizy%2F2%2F2%2Fdownload%2F&usg=AOvVaw1xSQCD7sckCcvBNp7JnnVi

[234] For further details see Section 5.2.1.2.

[235] Arif, 'The Role of Waqf for Environmental Protection in Indonesia'.

[236] Ibid. For example, in 2007 Tabung Wakaf Indonesia (TWI) launched a program named 'Tree waqf'. The endowment consists of rubber seeds. The community provided land and takes care of the rubber trees until they can be harvested.

agriculture, farming, trade ventures and business facility.[237] The Green *Waqf* Program was launched by the local *Zakat* Agency Board. It combines social and ecological objectives. By "choosing rubber trees for the program, [the agency] expected to push down the poverty level of the community and reduce severe environmental degradation as well".[238]

Indonesia has *Waqfs* for supply and purification of water. For example, Badan Wakaf Al-Quran (BWA) builds clean water wells in several regions of Indonesia under the program Water Action for People.[239] Indonesian *Waqfs* also have an international scope. *Waqf* Dhompet Dhuafa (DD) provides funds for building artesian wells and clean water installations for the people of Gaza in Palestine.[240]

Australia,[241] France,[242] the United Kingdom[243] and New Zealand have their own *Awqaf*. These are dedicated to a variety of charitable objectives, including conservation of natural resources, clean-ups, tree planting and animal welfare services.

*Himas* (e.g., wildlife reserves, public gardens or wells) can also be "secured and protected in a more permanent and sustainable setting because a *Waqf* may take, for example, the form of a fund or endowment for the financing of nature conservation projects".[244] The international NGO BirdLife International led a project launched in 2011 to finance the enforcement and revival of *Himas* in four sites in the Middle East region.[245] In fact, one of the main areas of *Waqf* is funding.

### 5.2.2.2 Islamic Green Finance as a Framework for Environmental *Waqf*

Islamic finance is constantly evolving in both Muslim and non-Muslim countries. It is based on three main principles, namely the prohibition of interest, the prohibition of contract ambiguity and the prohibition of speculation. It also encompasses the obligation of profit and risk sharing.[246]

Islamic finance is now estimated to amount to US$3.4 trillion.[247] Islamic banking accounted for 71 percent of the industry's total assets in 2017 and "there is a

---

[237] Asmak Ab Rahman, *New Developments in Islamic Economics: Examples from Southeast Asia* (Bingley: Emerald Group Publishing, 2018), 70.

[238] Al-Duaij and Al-Anezy, 'The Environmental Laws and Regulations in Islamic Waqf'.

[239] The BWA disburses *Waqf* funds of 45 million rupiahs for this program. Ibid.

[240] Ibid.

[241] Awqaf in Australia are recognized in the Charity Act. Available at: www.acnc.gov.au

[242] Available at: http://waqfrance.fr/qui-est-waqf.html

[243] *Awqaf* in United Kingdom are for example led by the NGO Muslim Hands. See further at: https://muslimhands.org.uk/donate/waqf

[244] Vincenti, '"Green" Islam and Social Movements for Sustainability', 198.

[245] Ibid.

[246] Abbas Mirakhor and Iqbal Zaidi, 'Profit-and-Loss Sharing Contracts in Islamic Finance', in M. Kabir Hassan and Mervyn K. Lewis (eds.), *Handbook of Islamic Banking* (Cheltenham: Edward Elgar, 2007), 49.

[247] Ahmed Sekreter, 'Green Finance and Islamic Finance' (2017) 4, 3. *International Journal of Social Sciences & Educational Studies*, 115–21, at 116.

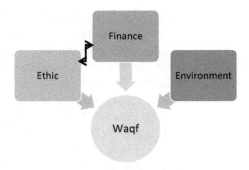

FIGURE 5.3 The potential of Islamic finance to foster environmental *Waqf*

continuing trend of consolidation within the Islamic banking industry, with some large mergers and acquisitions taking place in the biggest markets such as Malaysia and the GCC [Gulf Cooperation Council countries]".[248]

Islamic financial assets in the Organization of Islamic Cooperation countries, for example, were estimated to be around 98 percent of global *Sharia'* assets in 2011 with an average annual compound growth of 27.7 percent.[249]

Muslim countries which are intensively using Islamic finance are also among the main producers of greenhouse gases in the world (Gulf Region and MENA Region).[250] Therefore, it is critical that these countries implement the growing Islamic green finance. Islamic finance could be mobilized in ecological projects by using instruments that fit within *Sharia'* rules such as the *Mudaraba* and the Green *Sukuk*.[251]

*Mudaraba* is a type of Islamic financing based on a profit and loss sharing system. It permits a partnership between a bank (the investor or *Rab Al Mal*) and a contractor (*Mudarib*) in which the bank pledges to fully finance the project while the contractor has to manage it. The remuneration is based on a distribution key fixed beforehand in the form of the entrepreneur's profit percentage.[252]

Green *Sukuk* (plural of *Sak*, bond) are green Islamic bonds representing "ownership interest in defined assets, usufruct or services, as well as equity in a project or investment activity".[253] Many Islamic and non-Islamic countries are already using Islamic green finance: among Islamic countries, Indonesia, Malaysia and United Arab Emirates.

[248] See further at: www.isdb.org
[249] Organization of Islamic Cooperation (SESRIC), Islamic Finance in OIC Member Countries, OIC Outlook Series, May 2012, p. 1. Available at: www.sesric.org/files/article/450.pdf
[250] Ibid., at 119.
[251] Sekreter, 'Green Finance and Islamic Finance'.
[252] More information on Islamic finance is available at: www.financialislam.com/
[253] Umar F. Moghul and Samir H. K. Safar-Aly, 'Green Sukuk: The Introduction of Islam's Environmental Ethics to Contemporary Islamic Finance' (2014) 27, 1, *Georgetown International Environmental Law Review*, at 34.

Malaysia is one of the largest *Sukuk* markets in the world. Its financial regulator (*Suruhan Sekuriti* – Securities Commission Malaysia) issued guidelines for a "Socially Responsible Investment (SRI) *Sukuk*" that cover a comprehensive range of eligible projects, including those that: "(1) preserve and protect the environment and natural resources; (2) conserve the use of energy; (3) promote the use of renewable energy; (4) reduce greenhouse gas emission; or (5) improve the quality of life for the society".[254]

Among the eligible projects for *Sukuk*, the guidelines include investments within *Waqf*.[255] The SRI guidelines cite examples of *Waqf* that would cover the following areas:

(1) sustainable land use; (2) sustainable forestry and agriculture; (3) biodiversity conservation; (4) remediation and redevelopment of polluted or contaminated sites; (5) water infrastructure, treatment and recycling; (6) sustainable waste management projects; (7) new or existing renewable energy (solar, wind, hydro, biomass, geo-thermal and tidal); (8) efficient power generation and transmission systems; and (9) energy efficient which results in the reduction of greenhouse gas emissions or energy consumption per unit output.[256]

One of the examples of implementation of Green *Sukuk* is the financing of a 50-megawatt photovoltaic project in Indonesia in 2012 by Australian solar companies ($100 million).[257]

According to Professors Moghul and Safar-Aly, "contemporary Islamic finance has three tools to bring green principles into its legal sphere: (A) standards and structures for transactions and products; (B) criteria for a fatwa; (C) enhanced compliance auditing".[258] Islamic finance can set new standards or model its standards after those of the International Finance Corporation (IFC) on Environmental and Social Sustainability (Performance Standards) and World Bank Environmental, Health, and Safety (EHS) guidelines.[259]

Interestingly, *Fatwa* can also be used here as an approval (or disapproval) instrument in order to provide comfort to potential investors and customers. They can tap into the *Fiqh* principles in order to create a set of rules for Islamic finance. These kinds of *Fatwas* are not exactly the same as the environmental *Fatwas* used by the Eco-Islam movement. Yet they can be considered as a kind of environmental or green *Fatwas* as well.

Compliance auditing should be used, according to Professors Moghul and Safar-Aly, by *Sharia'* supervisory boards' audit institutions in order to "summarize efforts

---

[254] Ibid.
[255] Ibid., at 48.
[256] Ibid.
[257] Ibid., at 50.
[258] Ibid., at 54.
[259] Ibid., at 55.

undertaken to avoid and ameliorate negative environmental impacts that is known *ex ante*, and any that may have arisen ex post. It should also set forth any positive impact the institution has affected".[260]

The Islamic Development Bank (IDB), through its stated *Waqf*-based agenda, is taking measures to "emphasize on the potential role of *Awqaf* for the accomplishment of maqasid-based SDGs-like developmental goals, particularly among IDB member countries".[261]

The IDB also adopted the *Awqaf* sector development program, which is focused on advice, training, research and knowledge sharing. The ongoing *Waqf* programs led by the IDB research institute (Islamic Research Institute) are divided into the following areas:

a. Creating enabling environment – developing model *Waqf* law
b. Strengthening information flow
d. Capacity building – preparing awqaf training package (manual and courses)
d. Knowledge creation – conducting awqaf research studies and events
e. Knowledge and information sharing – developing awqaf database and publications.[262]

These programs can help in the promotion of environmental *Waqf* and their expansion to new areas. Research projects can, for example, focus on studying the multiple different uses of *Waqf* in the area of climate change, combating pollution or instituting *Waqf* for animals.

In Morocco, for example, the Islamic Development Bank recently showed its interest in *Waqf* assets managed by the *Awqaf* Ministry (Ministry of *Habous*) and proposed to finance their development through its Awqaf Property Investment Fund (APIF).[263] In several Muslim countries *Waqf* lands are dormant assets not exploited for economic welfare even if they represent a rich potential. These lands can thus serve for environmental purposes such as green finance projects. This will provide more financial stability through the perpetuity rule. The institution of *Waqf* "can transform social capital into social and public infrastructure. It provides a permanent social safety net in the case of perpetual *Waqf* to the beneficiaries".[264] Cash *Waqf*[265]

---

[260] Ibid., at 57.
[261] Abdullah, 'Waqf, Sustainable Development Goals (SDGs) and Maqasidal-shariah', at 160.
[262] Saad Kassim Hamid, 'Best Practices of Waqf: Experiences of Malaysia and Saudi Arabia' (2016) 2, 2, *Journal of Islamic Economics Lariba*, 57–74 at 72.
[263] Noureddine El Aissi, 'La BID convoite les biens Waqf au Maroc', *L'Economiste*, August 30, 2018. Available at: www.leconomiste.com/article/1032875-la-bid-convoite-les-biens-waqf-au-maroc
[264] Salman Ahmed Shaikh, Abdul Ghafar Ismail and Muhammad Hakimi Mohd Shafiai, 'Application of Waqf for Social and Development Finance' (2017) 9, 1, *ISRA International Journal of Islamic Finance*, 5–14 at 9.
[265] Cash *Waqf* derives from *Waqf* on movables (for example jewelry). See above in Chapter 2, note 95.

(which is the form of most contemporary *Awqaf*) can pool resources to be used for any ecological purposes.

The *Waqf* can be established "by dedicating movable or immovable asset(s) in order to enable people to contribute in creating a *Waqf* even if they do not personally own any real estate".[266] In order to do so, it is suggested to "keep a distinction between the perpetuity of the object [of the *Waqf*] itself and its 'dedication' of benefits".[267]

Among the wide spectrum of welfare services a *Waqf* can provide are services for other living beings.[268] For example, "animal protection programs and environmental preservation expenditures can be provided more flexibly through Waqf".[269]

Environmental *Waqf* can also play a role in coping with the humanitarian crises resulting from climate change.[270] The *Waqf* "may directly engage in provision of goods and services related to mitigation and adaptation".[271] This can be done both by governments and by NGOs. The *Waqf* can also be devoted to research and development "that includes a movement along the learning curve resulting in a fall in clean technology prices". It can be dedicated to increasing consumer awareness and support for action to mitigate climate change impacts.[272]

*Waqf* could also serve as a mechanism for funding environmental litigation, including the Atmospheric *Khilafa* litigation. Similarly, Clean Development Mechanisms can take the form of the *Waqf*, including Green *Sukuk*.

As mentioned in Section 5.1.2, for example, Islamic financial growth is considerably higher in countries with a mixed common law/*Sharia'* legal system.[273] Those countries are in fact the pioneers in Islamic finance. Accordingly, the chances for environmental *Waqf*-based tools are better in these countries as there are synergies between *Waqf* and Trusts. In this regard, faith-based groups can help in securing sustainable financing mechanisms and in fundraising.[274]

---

[266] Shaikh et al., 'Application of Waqf for Social and Development Finance', 10.

[267] Ibid.

[268] See examples of environmental Awqaf in the previous section.

[269] Shaikh et al., 'Application of Waqf for Social and Development Finance'.

[270] Obaidullah, 'Managing Climate Change', 33. See also, for a brief overview, Crétois, 'Islam'.

[271] Obaidullah, 'Managing Climate Change', 48.

[272] Ibid.

[273] See above, in Chapter 1 and in Chapters 4 and 5. In Chapter 1, I advanced the hypothesis according to which environmental *Waqf* is mainly used in Islamic countries that have mixed legal systems (*Sharia'* and common law). I brought a parallel argument from Islamic finance which grows most readily in those countries considered as pioneers. Consequently, I defended the idea that similarities between the common law and Islamic law have favored environmental *Waqf* and could therefore also be explored in the framework of Public Trust Doctrine, including through litigation and especially the Atmospheric Trust litigation. See Grassa and Gazdar, 'Financial Development and Economic Growth in GCC Countries', 165.

[274] Professor Elizabeth Mcleod and Martin Palmer talk about the advantages of faith-based organizations in the Christian world that 'have been fundraising for centuries, if not millennia, and have established methods. [Thus] [l]ooking together at such long established funding

It is important to build partnership between conservation organisms and religious groups "to achieve both social and ecological benefits while also accessing large public funding opportunities that support the priorities of both groups".[275] There is "great potential for religious and conservation grounds to work together to achieve joint environmental objectives according to their core teachings, beliefs, and practices".[276] This collaboration is encouraged, as mentioned, by the UN "Faith for Earth Initiative", whose mission is: "[t]o Encourage, Empower and Engage with Faith-Based Organizations as partners, at all levels, toward achieving the Sustainable Development Goals and fulfilling Agenda 2030".[277] It is also encouraged by the Rabat Declaration on the "Role of Cultural and Religious Factors in the Protection of the Environment and Sustainable Development".

The "Faith for Earth Initiative" acknowledges that "[r]eligious investments may be governed by beliefs and religious laws. Islamic financial institutions, for example, ban interest on investment and use the Sharia law of finance including Mudaraba (Profit and loss sharing), Wadiah (safekeeping), Musharaka (joint venture), Murabaha (cost plus), and Ijar (leasing)".[278] Those instruments are gaining momentum in many countries. Their success is due to the fact that they place equal emphasis on the ethical, moral, social and religious dimensions, to enhance equality and fairness for the good of society as a whole.[279]

In this regard, the "Faith for Earth Initiative" relies on the UN Environment Finance Initiative (UNEP-FI), which could provide a partnership platform with the global financial sector in order to "facilitate the most needed coupling of remodeling investment and the impact of financial reforms needed to achieve the SDGs involving faith-based investments".[280]

The UN Faith for Earth Initiative is also associated with the Economics of Ecosystems and Biodiversity (TEEB), whose mission is to mainstream the values of biodiversity and ecosystem services into decision making at all levels, and with the green economy, "where faith-based organizations could be natural partners where greening of own establishments, or investments could lead to mutual benefits".[281] This has resulted in an ambitious strategy concerning Islamic green finance: "innovative green and sustainable investments such as promoting investments in large scale renewable energy, sustainable transport, and sustainable cities projects".[282] The environmental *Waqf* and the *Hima*

---

sources – church tax; special appeal days; religious family Trusts – can open new doors'.
Mcleod and Palmer, 'Why Conservation Needs Religion', at 249.
[275] Ibid.
[276] Ibid., at 244.
[277] UNEP, UNEA, 4, Faith for Earth Dialogue.
[278] UNEP, 'Engaging with Faith Based Organizations', 12.
[279] Ibid.
[280] Ibid.
[281] Ibid.
[282] Ibid.

could thus be creatively inserted into the faith-based investments included in this strategy.

Another possible convergence between Islamic green finance and environmental *Waqf* are Islamic taxes or *Zakat*. *Zakat* could reach $500 billion annually.[283] A few financial initiatives are trying to make the *Zakat* more impactful on the daily lives of Muslims around the world by using digitalization. These initiatives can also help in encouraging the environmental *Awqaf*.[284] One of the outcomes of this program is the world's first *Waqf* platform (waqfworld), announced at the twelfth World Islamic Economic Foundation Forum (WIEF) held in Jakarta in November 2016.[285]

Environmental *Waqf* and Islamic finance have convergent roles. The *Waqf* can serve as a tool for green finance. This can occur in small villages, bigger cities and even at the global level. A global "Atmospheric *Waqf*" can be dedicated to the protection of the climate system as a whole. This could be achieved within the United Nations or any other international organization and could be used as a fund for adaptation and mitigation or any other form of support for the enforcement of the Paris Climate Agreement. The Atmospheric *Waqf* can serve as a platform where all initiatives related to the protection of the climate system can converge and create a dynamic at both global and local levels.

The Atmospheric *Waqf* can be supervised by both environmental specialists and Islamic law scholars (*Ulamas*). It should not only collect funds (from individuals, organizations and governments), but also help to issue environmental *Fatwas*, to institute local environmental *Waqfs* and to re-create or reinforce *Himas/Agdals*.

As a charitable institution, the global Atmospheric *Waqf* can join the work of other faiths (in the framework of the Alliance of Religions and Conservations, for example) and work closely with local and international faith-based groups. The Atmospheric *Waqf* paradigm should also take into account the specificity of Islamic law, which is pragmatic, ethical and ecological.

The potential for the growth of *Sharia'*-based environmental law in Muslim countries is enormous and promising. Environmental principles that are both

---

[283] UNDP, 'UNDP and World Zakat Forum Launch New Partnership to Unlock Zakat for the SDGs', November 5, 2019. Available at: http://www.id.undp.org/content/indonesia/en/home/presscenter/pressreleases/2019/UNDP-World-Zakat-Forum-SDGs.html

[284] For example, the global *Sadaqah* is a crowdfunding platform run by a leading global company focused on the Islamic economy. The platform facilitates charitable donations Sadaqah, *Zaka* and *Waqf* by bringing together corporate donors, the public, charity partners and community leaders to crowdfund campaigns online. Available at: www.globalsadaqah.com/

[285] According to the founder of this new platform: 'Waqf is an institution that can unite and bring socio-economic development to the Muslim World. Ummah development is the focus of WaqfWorld.org. We use technology to improve Cash Waqf flows to Partner Mutawali (authorised or recognised Waqf Trustees or managers) and Charities for their campaigns including Islamic microfinance, education or human capital development, humanitarian relief, social enterprise or religious activities/assets'. Maziah Ghuraba, 'World First Islamic Endowment Crowdfunding Plateform Launched', *Eprantis*, November 18, 2016. Available at: www.eperantis.com/worlds-first-islamic-endowment-crowdfunding-platform-launched

modern and ancient are embedded in legal and financial instruments such as Islamic finance, environmental *Waqfs*, atmospheric litigation and environmental *Fatwas*. For example, the principle of sustainability is entrenched within the *Sharia'*. *Waqf* is a landmark *Sharia'* tool that encompasses dedication to future generations. *Khilafa* is an overarching principle in Islamic law and carries the idea of fiduciary obligation which, comparatively, permits the expansion of the Public Trust Doctrine in common law countries. Adaptive management is illustrated through the flexibility of the *Waqf* and could thus be used for a wide range of environmental purposes. Moreover, *Himas*, which can also be created through *Waqf*, represent an early answer to the tragedy of the commons because they provide ecological services for the tribe according to ancestral, negotiated rules. Nothing prevents both *Hima* and *Waqf* being dedicated to nature conservation in general. The concept of charity is broad under both the *Sharia'* and *Waqf* legal texts in Islamic countries (Table 4.1).

These principles and instruments are essential ingredients for the Atmospheric *Waqf* paradigm or Doctrine. They pave the way for further developments in Islamic environmental law. Some of these tools are already more or less successful (Islamic finance and environmental *Fatwas*), while others are still limited in their scope of action (litigation, environmental *Waqf*).

*Waqf*-based environmental litigation, for example, lacks the appropriate environmental legal principles. Many Islamic countries do not have the preconditions for *Sharia'*-based environmental litigation. This kind of litigation is favored by the social justice movement, which is still largely limited in those countries.[286] However, since the Arab Spring, social and environmental movements are gaining momentum and this could be reflected in the litigation. For instance, in Egypt it was possible for environmental activists to add a new article (on animal protection) to the draft constitution, even in the midst of the citizens' revolution (Arab Spring), because they found a way to link animal protection with the issue of human rights. Indeed, in a context where human rights are flouted, the issue of environmental conservation may look frivolous and devoid of interest, even if it is wrapped in religious discourse. The environmental *Waqf* can introduce (or rather reintroduce) this idea by contributing to the transformation of society.

Concerning Asian countries where the majority of Muslims live, some of them have already started the Atmospheric Trust litigation based on the common law because they are also common law countries (for example, Pakistan). In parallel, Indonesia looks like a pioneer in environmental *Fatwas*.

Certainly, the use of Islamic law and ethics may seem controversial in many countries given the international geopolitical context where the rise of terrorism is

---

[286] On the Arab Spring movement and its legal impacts, see, for example, Antoni Abat i Ninet and Mark Tushnet (eds.), *The Arab Spring: An Essay on Revolution and Constitutionalism* (Cheltenham: Edward Elgar, 2015).

associated with the Islamic State project. The attempts at the revival of Islamic environmental law could be interpreted as an "Islamization strategy" at a time when secular human rights movements are struggling to impose their ideas. Governments and political authorities may be cautious regarding Eco-Islam movements as it is difficult to embrace environmental Islamic ethics without considering other controversial/debated aspects of Islamic law.[287] This might partly explain why Atmospheric Trust litigation led by activists in countries like Pakistan or India did not sufficiently tap into the legal and ethical arguments brought by *Sharia'*, even if those arguments are available in their legal systems. Instead, they have used the common law and more specifically their own constitutions.

This possibility cannot be found, or at least is more difficult to find in civil law Muslim countries as they do not have the equivalent of the Public Trust Doctrine within the civil law system. As an alternative, these countries might use the *Sharia'*-based environmental law and, more specifically, the Atmospheric *Waqf* Doctrine.

Thirty years ago Professor Donald L. Horowitz underlined the apprehension regarding the revival of *Sharia'* ideas and admitted that: "[t]he Islamic revival ... is frequently pictured as backward-looking, destructive, obscurantist, and xenophobic". There is however, "an institution-building side to Islamic revival that is modernizing, ... and by no means hostile to Western ideas".[288]

In fact, using the *Sharia'* in environmental litigation offers an argument as strong as the one provided by the common law. Similarities between the Trust and the *Waqf* facilitate bringing *Sharia'* arguments into environmental litigation and more especially in Atmospheric Trust litigation in Muslim countries.

Islamic environmental law has already been used by Eco-Islam, both at the technical level (the *Fatwas*) and conceptually (interpretations of Islamic environmental principles and sources). Admittedly, environmental *Fatwas* are not binding legal rules and their impact has not yet been proven, but the combination of other legal and financial tools to protect the environment within the framework of the Atmospheric Waqf paradigm is promising.

The environmental *Waqf* is already being used in several countries and all the technical aspects (financing, water, clean-ups) could be extended to many other applications. But this expansion will require that governments support the reform. This is happening, for example, at the level of organizations such as ISESCO, which brings together annually the environment ministers of Muslim countries. As mentioned earlier, ISESCO recently adopted the Rabat Declaration on the "Role of Cultural and Religious Factors in the Protection of the Environment and

---

[287] For example, in some Muslim countries, the reform of inheritance law is currently an object of debate. See for example Claudia Mende, 'Islamic Inheritance Law in Morocco and Tunisia, Feminist Asma Lamrabet Under Pressure', October 2018. Available at: https://en.qantara.de/content/islamic-inheritance-law-in-morocco-and-tunisia-feminist-asma-lamrabet-under-pressure

[288] Donald L. Horowitz, 'The Qur'an and the Common Law: Islamic Law Reform and the Theory of Legal Change' (1994) 42, 2, *American Journal of Comparative Law*, 233–93.

Sustainable Development" at the eighth Islamic Conference of Environment Ministers in Rabat, Morocco. This declaration could represent, along with the Islamic Declaration on Global Climate Change, a further argument in the framework of the Atmospheric *Khilafa* litigation. Besides, these declarations influence environmental law in Muslim countries. Many other Islamic organizations, such as the Organization for Islamic Cooperation, can also serve the purpose of "regreening" the *Sharia'* and setting the legal foundations for a healthy and safe climate system.

Eco-Islam can represent a real springboard for revitalizing environmental Islamic law. Its actions extend to advocating, as well as to fieldwork. It engages with Islamic scholars (*Ulamas*); with the state (Indonesia and Malaysia), with scientific institutions, international NGOs and has even contributed to constitutional reform in some countries (Iran and Egypt).

Eco-Islam is an original environmental grassroots movement.[289] However, the movement is still largely limited concerning its arguments, its legal strategy and its geographical scope. Its actions, in particular via the internet, will nevertheless allow it to expand its experience to other Muslim countries.

The use of the Islamic Declaration on Global Climate Change in the Atmospheric Trust litigation in a non-Muslim country, the United States, is a good sign, predicting the evolution and expansion of the Eco-Islam movement and Islamic environmental law in general.

---

[289] See further Section 5.2.1.

# Conclusion

*Religious leaders can instigate the "massive mobilisation of public opinion" needed to stem the destruction of ecosystems around the world in a way that governments and scientists cannot.*

Partha Dasgupta[1]

Islamic environmental law has the potential to reframe the environmental legal system and thus could contribute further gravity to international efforts for climate action. In fact, Islamic environmental law could benefit from the opportunity offered at the global level. On one hand, it could benefit from the global ecological movements based on religion and spirituality (Eco-Islam). On the other hand, it could connect to the civil society movement related to environmental justice and protecting the climate system, especially the Atmospheric Trust litigation. Moreover, Islamic environmental law could benefit from the revival of the *Waqf* as part of the SDGs agenda.[2]

This book has addressed the legal foundations for the resurgence of Islamic environmental law from the *Sharia'* and its sources, and from a comparative law approach. It permits us to confront the main environmental legal instruments in both the *Sharia'* and common law, namely the *Waqf* and the Trust.

Faced with the non-enforcement of statutory environmental law, the use of traditional institutions could be the answer. The *Waqf* as a charitable trust is likely to apply to several aspects of environmental protection. The *Hima or Agdal* (traditional protected areas) can replay their ecological role if they are reshaped in a more integrated way.

The revival of these legal tools will nevertheless require efforts on the part of governments and civil society. This revival could benefit from the experience of

---

[1]    Cited by Chaplin, 'The Global Greening of Religion', p. 3.
[2]    The World Bank Group, INCEIF and ISRA, 'Maximizing Social Impacts through Waqf Solutions', May 2019. Available at: http://documents.worldbank.org/curated/en/930461562218730622/text/Maximizing-Social-Impact-Through-Waqf-Solutions.txt

Trusts in the common law as both institutions have similar functioning modes. In fact, "flexible doctrines are especially important so that the law can 'leapfrog' societal norms".[3]

In the case of *Waqf* and *Hima*, social norms are already imbued with these concepts, which constitute the very backbone of the legal and social system, and can be receptive to their revival in the field of the environment. *Sharia'* in Islamic countries could constitute the core of environmental protection as it has the potential of sustainability, adaptability and resilience. Based on scriptures claimed by governments as the very foundation of their authority, *Sharia'*-based environmental law could have a better chance of enforcement and effectiveness.

In the fourteenth century, Imam Al Shatibi stated that any independent interpretation of the principles of jurisprudence must be based on the *Maslaha* (public benefit), which is to achieve benefit and prevent harm. According to him "it is a matter of bearing human interest or benefit in mind when seeking to understand any relevant text or when drawing an analogy between two rulings".[4]

This objective should also be triggered today in the field of environmental law. It is the only way to establish the environmental *Waqf* "in the higher sense", that is, the "Atmospheric" *Waqf*.

Similar to the classical *Waqf*, the Atmospheric or global *Waqf* will have three components: the settlor, which would be the global community, the trustee, which would encompass the government and decision-makers at all levels; and the beneficiary, which would be the global community itself, including non-human beings, natural resources and the climate system at large.

The global *Waqf* is similar to the global trust as conceived by Gro Harlem Brundtland in her report "Our Common Future". What distinguished it from the global Trust is the *Sharia'* aspect that would particularly attract Muslim countries.

It has been stated that, in general, the use of charity law for environmental protection has two main shortfalls – namely anthropocentrism and the "ad-hoc law" aspect.[5] Charitable Trusts, for example, "do not necessarily target the greatest need, but rather target the issues in which the individual donors or members of an organisation have particular interests".[6]

Therefore, while charity law might lack a systematic approach, it can "fill the gaps" in the sense of encouraging environmental protection in areas of public interest that might not receive adequate protection or adequate funding under

---

[3]   Sagarin and Turnipseed, 'The Public Trust Doctrine', at 484.
[4]   Raysuni, 'Theory of the Higher Objectives', 7.
[5]   According to Professor Rebecca Claire Byrnes, charity law has at least two main shortfalls: 'First, the requirement of "public benefit" meant, at least historically, that the charity or trust could not be intended to protect the environment only for the environment's sake, without also an element of human benefit. Second, charity law is ad hoc and lacks systematic approach to environmental protection'. Byrnes, 'Filling the Gaps', at 417.
[6]   Ibid.

statutory environmental law regimes.[7] However, this limit is not necessarily applicable to Islamic law in which charity is the main component.

The challenges that arise in Muslim countries are precisely to recreate incentives that will push people to donate for the protection of the environment. The first step would be to remind the citizens and the potential donors of the examples of the ancient environmental *Waqfs* and how Muslims of the sixth century considered that charity was also valid for non-human beings, for example. If the consultant has experience with environmental issues and is able to persuade and encourage the *Waqif* (*Al Waqef*) that environmental safety is vital for a clean and healthy environment, the donor may well be inspired to aim for that purpose.[8]

The success of Islamic finance offers a great opportunity for the revival of Islamic environmental law inasmuch as it is increasingly using green finance tools. As the *Waqf* benefits from support at the local and national levels, "the sector need not operate at the periphery of socio-economic activity, but should rather be mainstreamed within the state's legal, social and economic systems".[9] In this regard, it may become a social obligation to endow properties as *Waqf*.[10]

In addition to raising awareness and integrating the *Waqf* into environmental law, reinvigorating Islamic environmental law through the *Waqf* or *Hima* requires collaboration between environmental legal scholars and *Ulamas* in coordination with environmental sciences scholars. *Ijtihad* is an essential tool for imagining new applications of environmental *Waqfs*, for example. According to Faqih Al-Zarqa (1907–99), "everything in waqf is subject to *ijtihad* and there is no single ruling in it that gained unanimity except that the *waqf* purpose must be benevolent (*birr*)".[11]

From there, and considering that charity (*birr* or *sadaqa*) is also valid for non-human beings, and could thus be expanded to nature in general, it is conceivable to use *Ijtihad* to extend to infinity the different applications of *Waqf* (Figure 5.1). Similarly, it is possible to consider ecosystem services provided by a *Waqf*-based protected area as a charity for current and future generations, including nature itself, just as the *Waqf* for birds, for example, existed many centuries ago.

The founding principles of the Trust, similar to the *Waqf*, are used in trials around the world to ask governments to fulfill their fiduciary responsibilities and protect the climate system. Using sources of Islamic law and *Ijtihad* will certainly favor the exploitation of these principles as a higher sense *Waqf* or *Khilafa*.

The environmental *Waqf* can indeed be a tool through which *Khilafa* ethics is introduced effectively into Islamic countries' legal and institutional systems.

---

[7] Ibid.

[8] Al-Duaij and Al-Anzi, 'The Environmental Laws and Regulations in Islamic Waqf, 19.

[9] M. H. Dafterdar, 'Toward Effective Legal Regulations and an Enabling Environment for Inalienable Muslim Endowments Awqaf' (2011) *Islam and Civilisational Renewal*, 654–68, at 665.

[10] Abdullah, 'Waqf, Sustainable Development Goals (SDGs) and Maqasid al-Shariah', at 168.

[11] Cited by Dafterdar, 'Toward Effective Legal Regulations', 656.

The review of the history of the *Waqf* shows that this institution has been more of a statement of what ought to be the law than an accurate reflection of how the law actually operates. *Ijtihad* and *Qiyas* played a major role in expanding the *Waqf*.

Current criticisms of the *Waqf* and Islamic environmental law in general (as dormant, rigid or unrealistic) lose sight of its potential for future use.[12] To paraphrase Professor Mary Christina Wood, the new Atmospheric *Waqf* paradigm "must push beyond the current boundaries [of the *Waqf*]" in order to be successful.[13]

The ecological movement in Muslim countries, Eco-Islam, has already started to use Islamic legal principles for the protection of natural resources. This movement has exploited the environmental *Fatwas* based on scriptural sources and the *Fiqh* principles in order to create a compendium of contemporary environmental Islamic legal rulings. This compendium can be used in courts, as well as in banking systems and regulations.

Eco-Islam has contributed to constitutional reform in some countries. It has undertaken many actions in the field that has shown their effectiveness compared to statutory law. Similarly, Atmospheric Trust litigation has succeeded in transforming a traditional idea (the Public Trust Doctrine) into a revolutionary legal tool, thanks to grassroots environmental movements, as well as judges, lawyers and legal scholars.[14]

Similarly, the role of Eco-Islam can be crucial in the context of Muslim countries. In fact, Eco-Islam can foster the Atmospheric *Waqf* Doctrine/paradigm. The essential elements of this doctrine already exist. Islamic law has a huge ecological potential which is still untapped today. More research is needed to explore and systematize this potential. In particular, a new legal research agenda should be oriented towards a new interpretation of this potential in the light of comparative law and ecological sciences. More importantly, this potential should be implemented and experienced through the law and through NGOs and governmental programs.

According to Judge Ann Aiken, "federal courts too often have been cautious and overly deferential in the arena of environmental law, and the world has suffered for it".[15] This same statement can be made for Islamic environmental law. In fact, not only judges have ignored it, but governments and civil society did not pay much attention to its expansion either.

---

[12] I am paraphrasing the very inspiring article written by Professor Timothy Patrick Brady in 1990, predicting the fabulous evolution of the Public Trust Doctrine, in which he wrote: 'The public trust doctrine can be a tool through which the stewardship ethic can be introduced effectively into American law and society. A review of the history of the public trust doctrine shows that the doctrine has been more of a statement of what ought to be the law than an accurate reflection of how the law actually operates. Current criticisms of the public trust doctrine, by focusing on the past and present uses of the doctrine, lose sight of its potential for future use'. Brady, 'But Most of It Belongs to Those Yet to Be Born', at 646.

[13] Wood, *Nature's Trust*, 16.

[14] See further developments in Chapter 4. This evolution by scholars has two main milestones. Sax, 'The Public Trust Doctrine in Natural Resource Law'. See also Wood, Nature's Trust.

[15] *Juliana v. United States*, D. Oregon, Eugene Division, 217 F. Supp. 3d at 1262. Available at: https://www.leagle.com/decision/infdco20161114p76

Off course there are several gaps in applying Islamic environmental law in Muslim countries. This use can be turned against them. Indeed, the use of public trust principles or Atmospheric *Waqf* Doctrine necessitates preliminary conditions of democracy and human rights. As Professor Joseph Sax, the founder of the environmental Public Trust Doctrine, put it fifty years ago, the idea of fiduciary duty on natural resources appeals to citizens and not to serfs.[16] This means that "certain interests are so intrinsically important to every citizen that their free availability" is a duty of the Trustee or *Khalifa*. Among these duties the protection of natural resources should be a main component, especially as the *Khalifa* principle is at the core of Islamic law applicable to natural resources. It is also claimed to legitimate the political authority of the *Khalifa* or public authority in several Muslim countries.

"[I]t will in any case be a significant struggle for Muslim campaigners to raise the profile of ecological issues within Muslim communities while issues of integration, discrimination, security and extremism continue to dominate their agenda."[17] Nevertheless, the consensus through, for example, the Islamic Declaration on Global Climate Change, the Rabat Declaration on the "Role of Cultural and Religious Factors in the Protection of the Environment and Sustainable Development" and the UNEP "Faith for Earth" Initiative shows that it is possible for such consensus to lead to effective local responses. In fact, since the historic open letter on Muslim–Christian relations "endorsed by an impressively wide range of prominent Islamic scholars", it has been clear that "broadly based consensus at least among representative elites on key global issues is in principle attainable".[18]

Besides, the Atmospheric *Khalifa* litigation will necessitate a shift in the Eco-Islam movement as the legal system must be taken into account. Comparatively, the success of the Atmospheric Trust litigation in common law countries is due, in particular, to the fact that it took place in countries where the principal source of the law is case law. Moreover, in common law countries, "the judiciary is potentially a crucial player in forcing carbon reduction, because it tends to be a less politicized branch of government ... with power to order swift and decisive relief".[19] From this perspective, applying Atmospheric *Khalifa* litigation will not be an easy task in many Muslim countries where those conditions are not found.

Nevertheless, at least two opportunities are available for environmental activists in Muslim countries: first, they can benefit from the current prevalence of Atmospheric Trust litigation around the world, including in non-common law

---

[16] Sax, 'The Public Trust Doctrine in Natural Resource Law', at 521.

[17] Chaplin, 'The Global Greening of Religion', 4.

[18] Ibid. This letter is available at: www.acommonword.com/the-acw-document/

[19] Mary Christina Wood, 'Atmospheric Trust Litigation across the World', in Ken Coghil, Charles Sampford and Tim Smith (eds.), *Fiduciary Duty and the Atmospheric Trust* (New York: Routledge, 2016), 99–164, at 105.

countries; second, they can tap into the potential of Islamic environmental law and Atmospheric *Waqf* Doctrine as a means for social justice.

Even in civil law countries, legal scholars are "pushing the limits of the law" in order to emphasize the state's "climate inaction" through lawsuits.[20] The prevalence of this litigation all over the world is an indicator of a new phenomenon: environmental law appears increasingly as a tool for democracy and human rights.[21] This is exactly what the Atmospheric *Waqf* Doctrine/paradigm ought to be.

This book has attempted to claim a "green *Khilafa* principle" guaranteed by the legal system, in the framework of the Atmospheric *Waqf* paradigm.

---

[20] Martin Aude, "'L'Affaire du Siècle" veut repousser les limites du droit', *Alternatives Economiques*, May 28, 2019. Available at: www.alternatives-economiques.fr
[21] Michael C. Blumm and Mary Christina Wood, "'No Ordinary Lawsuit": Climate Change, Due Process, and the Public Trust Doctrine' (2017) 67, 1, *American University Law Review*, 1–87.

# Select Bibliography

Aassouli, Dalal, Asutay, Mehmet, Mohieldin, Mahmoud and Chiara Nwokike, Tochukwu, 'Green Sukuk, Energy Poverty, and Climate Change: A Roadmap for Sub-Saharan Africa', Policy Research Working Paper 8680, 2018.

Abat i Ninet, Antoni and Tushnet, Mark (eds.), *The Arab Spring: An Essay on Revolution and Constitutionalism* (Cheltenham: Edward Elgar, 2015).

Abate, Randal, S., 'Atmospheric Trust Litigation: Foundation for a Constitutional Right to a Stable Climate System?' (2019) 10, 1, *George Washington Journal of Energy & Environmental Law*, 33–38.

Abbasi, Muhammad Zubair, 'The Classical Islamic Law of Waqf: A Concise Introduction' (2012) 26, 2, *Arab Law Quarterly*, 121–53.

'Sharī'a under the English Legal System in British India: Awqāf (Endowments) in the Making of Anglo-Muhammadan Law', (PhD thesis, Oxford University Abbasi School of Law, 2013).

Abdelzaher, Dina M. and Abdelzaher, Amir, 'Beyond Environmental Regulations: Exploring the Potential of "Eco-Islam" in Boosting Environmental Ethics Within SMEs in Arab Markets' (2015) 145, 2, *Journal of Business Ethics*, 357–71.

Abdelzaher, Dina M., Amr, Kotb and Akrum Nasr, Helfaya, 'Eco-Islam: Beyond the Principles of Why and What, and Into the Principles of How' (2019) 155, 3, *Journal of Business Ethics*, 623–43.

Abdul Aziz, Ahmad Hafiz Bin, Zhang, Wei, Hamid, Baharom Abdul, Mahomed, Ziyaad, Bouheraoua, Said, Kasri, Noor Suhaida and Sano, Mohamed Al-Amine, *Maximizing Social Impact through Waqf Solutions (English)* (Washington, DC: World Bank Group, 2019), http://documents.worldbank.org/curated/en/930461562218730622/Maximizing-Social-Impact-Through-Waqf-Solutions

Abdullah, Mohammad, 'Waqf, Sustainable Development Goals (SDGs) and Maqasidal-shariah' (2018) 45, 1, *International Journal of Social Economics*, 158–72.

Al-Bukhari, Muhanimed Ibn Ismaiel, *Sahih Al-Bukhari* (Darus Salam: Publishers & Distributors, 1997).

Al-Duaij, Nada and Al-Anezy, Eisa, 'The Environmental Law and Regulations in Islamic Waqf: Application to the Situation in Kuwait', paper, September 2009, www.google.com/url?sa=t&rct=j&q=&esrc=s&source=web&cd=&ved=2ahUKEwjnoa7yltLsAhXyDmMBHbTSDB8QFjAFegQICxAC&url=https%3A%2F%2Fworks.bepress.com%2Feisa_al_enizy%2F2%2Fdownload%2F&usg=AOvVaw1xSQCD7sckCcvBNp7JnnVi

Al-Jayyousi Odeh, Rashed, *Islam and Sustainable Development: New Worldviews* (Abingdon: Gower, Routledge, 2012).

Al Sarihi, Aicha, 'Implications of Climate Policies for Gulf States Economic Diversification Strategies', The Arab Gulf States Institute in Washington, July 9, 2018.

Al-Sarjani, Ragheb, *The Masterpieces of Endowments in Islamic Civilization* (Cairo: Nahdet Misr for Printing, Publishing and Distribution, 2010) (in Arabic).

Al Suwaidi, Ahmed, 'Developments of the Legal Systems of the Gulf Arab States', (1993) 8, 4, *Arab Law Quarterly*, 289–301.

Ammar, Nawal, 'Islam and Deep Ecology', in David Landis Barnhill and Roger S. Gottlieb (eds.), *Deep Ecology and World Religions: New Essays on Sacred Ground* (Albany, NY: State University of New York Press, 2001), 193–212.

Arafa Mohamed, A., 'Islamic Policy of Environmental Conservation, 1,500 Years Old – Yet Thoroughly Modern' (2014) 16, 2, *European Journal of Law Reform*, 465–504.

Asmak Abd, Rahman, *New Development in Islamic Economics: Examples from Southeast Asia* (Bingley: Emerald Group Publishing, 2018).

Auclair, Laurent, Baudot, Patrick, Genin, Didier, Romangy, Bruno and Simenel, Romain, 'Patrimony for Resilience: Evidence from the Forest Agdal in the Moroccan High Atlas Mountains' (2011) 16, 4, *Ecology and Society*, 24–35.

Aude, Martin, '"L'Affaire du Siècle" veut repousser les limites du droit', *Alternatives Economiques*, May 28, 2019, www.alternatives-economiques.fr

Austin, Bodetti, Islam and eco-theology : The future of environmentalism, *The New Arab*, 5 August 2020, https://english.alaraby.co.uk/english/society/2020/8/5/islam-and-eco-the ology-the-future-of-environmentalism

Azziman, Omar, 'La tradition juridique islamique dans l'évolution du droit privé marocain', in Jean Claude Santussi (ed.), *Le Maroc actuel, une modernisation au miroire de la tradition* (Aix-en-Provence: Institut de recherches et d'études sur les mondes arabes et musulmans, Éditions du CNRS, 2013), 251–72.

Bagader, Abubakr Ahmed, El-Sabbagh, Abdullatif Tawfik El-Chirazi, Al-Glayand, Mohamad As-Sayyid, Samarrai, Mawil Tousuf Izzi-Deen and Llewellyn, Othman Abd-ar-Rahman, 'Environmental Protection in Islam' (Gland: Environmental Policy and Law Paper No. 20, 2d ed., IUCN, 1994).

Bakader, Abou Bakr Ahmed, Al Sabagh, Abdul Latif Tawfik El Shirazy, Al Glenid, MohamedAl Sayyed and Samarrai, Mawil Y. Izzi Deen, *Islamic Principles for the Conservation of the Natural Environment* (Gland, Switzerland: International Union for Conservation of Nature and Natural Resources, 1983).

Barnes, Sara, 'Elaborate Birdhouses Resembling Miniature Palaces Built in Ottoman-Era Turkey', *My Modern Met*, July 31, 2017.

Bennet, Nathan J., Whitty, Tara S., Finkbeiner, Elena, Pittman, Jeremy, Basset, Hannah, Gelcich, Stefan and Allison, Edward H., 'Environmental Stewardship: A Conceptual Review and Analytical Framework' (2018) 61, 4, *Environmental Management*, 597–614.

Benson, Melinda Harm and Schultz, Courtney, 'Adaptive Management and Law', in Craig R. Allen and Ahjond S. Garmestani (eds.), *Adaptive Management of Social-Ecological Systems* (Dordrecht: Springer, 2015), 9–16.

Bernard-Maugiron, Nathalie and Dupret, Baudouin, 'Les principes de la sharia sont la source principale de la législation' (1999) 2, *Égypte/Monde arabe*, http://journals.openedition .org/ema/992

Bhala, Raj. *Understanding Islamic Law* (New York: LexisNexis, 2011).

Bin Hamad, Norah, 'Foundations for Sustainable Development: Harmonizing Islam, Nature and Law' (SJD dissertation, Pace University, New York, 2017).

Bin Muhammad, Ghazi , Aftab, Ahmed and Shah-Kazemi, Reza, *'The Holy Qur'an and the Environment'* (Amman: Royal Aal al-Bayt Institute for Islamic Thought, 2010).

Bint, Maidin Ainul Jaria, 'Challenges in Implementing and Enforcing Environmental Protection Measures in Malaysia', *The Malaysian Bar*, November 17, 2005.

Black, Ann, Esmaeili, Hossein and Hosen, Nadirsyah, *Modern Perspectives on Islamic Law* (Cheltenham: Edward Edgar, 2013).

Blumm, Michael C. and Wood, Mary Christina, *The Public Trust Doctrine in Environmental and Natural Resources Law* (Durham, NC: Carolina Academic Press, 2d ed., 2015).

Bogert, George Gleason, *Handbook of the Law of Trusts* (Eagan, MN: West Publishing, 1921).

Bowering, Gerhard, *Islamic Political Thought: An Introduction* (Princeton, NJ: Princeton University Press, 2015).

Brady, Timothy Patrick, '"But Most of It Belongs to Those Yet to Be Born": The Public Trust: Common Law Doctrine. NEPA and the Stewardship Ethic' (1990) 17 *Boston College Environmental Affairs Law Review*, 621.

Brennan, Paul, 'Perpetual and Inalienable Islamic Endowments, A Practical Introduction', 2017, www.academia.edu/32035700/WAQF_perpetual_and_inalienable_Islamic_endowments

Brown, Nathan J. and Revkin, Mara, 'Islamic Law and the Constitution', in Emon M. Anver and Ahmed Rumee (eds.), *The Oxford Handbook of Islamic Law* (Oxford: Oxford University Press, 2018).

Bruch, Carl, Coker, Wole and VanArsdale, Chris, *Constitutional Environmental Law: Giving Force to Fundamental Principles in Africa* (Washington, DC: Environmental Law Institute, UNEP, 2d ed., 2001).

Budiman, Mochammad Arif, 'The Role of Waqf for Environmental Protection in Indonesia'. Aceh Development International Conference (ADIC), Kuala Lumpur, March 26–28, 2011.

Byrnes, Rebecca Claire, 'Filling the Gaps: Recognition of Environmental Protection as a Charitable Purpose' (2014) 31, *Environmental and Planning Law Journal*, 415–38.

Cahen, Claude, 'Réflexions sur le waqf ancien' (1961) 14, *Studia Islamica*, 37–56.

Carlarne, Cinnamon P., 'Reassessing the Role of Religion in Western Climate Change Decision-Making', in Waleed El-Ansary and David K. Linnan (eds.), *Muslim and Christian Understanding: Theory and Application of 'A Common Word'* (New York : Palgrave MacMillan, 2010).

Chaplin, Jonathan, 'The Global Greening of Religion' (2016) 2, *Palgrave Communications*, 16–47, www.nature.com/articles/palcomms201647

Cizakca, Murat, 'Awqaf in History and Its Implications for Modern Islamic Economics' (1998) 6, 1, *Islamic Economic Studies*, 43–70.

 *A History of Philanthropic Foundations: The Islamic World from the Seventh Century to the Present* (Istanbul: Bogazici University Press, 2000).

Clarry, Daniel, 'Fiduciary Ownership and Trusts in a Comparative Perspective' (2014) 63, 4, *International and Comparative Law Quarterly*, 901–33.

Coplan, Karl S., 'Public Trust Limits on Greenhouse Gas Trading Schemes: A Sustainable Middle Ground?' (2010) 35, 2, *Columbia Journal of Environmental Law*, 287–336.

Crétois, Jules, 'Islam: Comment les Habous peuvent sauvegarder l'environnement au Maroc', *Tel Quel*, June 6, 2016.

Crone, Patricia, *Roman, Provincial and Islamic Law: The Origins of the Islamic Patronate* (London: Cambridge University Press, 1987).

Dafterdar, M. H., 'Toward Effective Legal Regulations and an Enabling Environment for Inalienable Muslim Endowments Awqaf' (2011) 2, 4, *Islam and Civilisational Renewal*, 654–68.

Damian, Howard S. J., 'An Islamic Declaration on Climate Change', *Thinking Faith*, October 25, 2015, www.thinkingfaith.org

Darby, Megan, 'Muslim Leaders Tell Petropowers to Lead on Climate Change', *Climate Change News*, August 18, 2015.

Dawood, Ahmed and Ginsburg, Tom, 'Constitutional Islamization and Human Rights: The Surprising Origin and Spread of Islamic Supremacy in Constitutions', University of Chicago Public Law & Legal Theory Working Paper, No. 477 (2014).

De Lucia, Vito, 'Competing Narratives and Complex Genealogies: The Ecosystem Approach in International Environmental Law' (2015) 27, 1, *Journal of Environmental Law*, 91–117.

Ekinci, Ekrem Bugra, 'The Ottomans' Exemplary Treatment of Street Animals', *Daily Sabah*, January 18, 2015, www.dailysabah.com/

El Aissi, Noureddine, 'La BID convoite les biens Waqf au Maroc', *L'Economiste*, No. 5340 of August 30, 2018, www.leconomiste.com

El-Ansary, Waleed, 'Islamic Environmental Economics and the Three Dimensions of Islam: "A Common Word" on the Environment as Neighbor', in Waleed El-Ansary and David Linnan (eds.), *Muslim and Christian Understanding: Theory and Application of "A Common Word"* (New York: Palgrave MacMillan US, 2010), 143–57.

El-Ansary, Waleed and Linnan, David K. (eds.), *Muslim and Christian Understanding: Theory and Application of "A Common Word"* (New York: Palgrave MacMillan, 2010).

El Khatir, Aboulkacem, 'Droit coutumier amazigh face aux processus d'institution et d'imposition de la législation nationale au Maroc', International Labour Organization (undated), www.ilo.org

El Manouni, Mohamed, *Majallat Daawat Al Haq* (1983) 21 (in Arabic), www.habous.gov.ma

Emon, Anver M., 'Shari'a and the Modern State', in Anver M. Emon, Mark Ellis and Benjamin Glahn (eds.), *Islamic Law and International Human Rights Law: Searching for Common Ground* (London: Oxford University Press, 2012), 52–81.

Fletcher, Madelein, 'How Can We Understand Islamic Law Today?' (2006) 17, 2, *Islam and Christian–Muslim Relations*, 159–72.

Foltz, Richard C., 'Islamic Environmentalism in Theory and Practice', in Richard C. Foltz (ed.), *Worldviews, Religion, and the Environment: A Global Anthology* (Belmont, CA: Wadsworth, 2003), 358–67.

Denny, Frederick and Baharuddin, Azizan (eds.), *Islam and Ecology: A Bestowed Trust* (Cambridge, MA: Harvard University Press, 2003).

'Islamic Environmentalism: A Matter of Interpretation', in Richard C. Foltz, Frederick Denny and Azizan Baharuddin (eds.), *Islam and Ecology: A Bestowed Trust* (Cambridge, MA: Harvard University Press, 2003), 249–79.

'This She-Camel of God Is a Sign to You: Dimensions of Animals in Islamic Tradition and Muslim Culture', in Paul Waldau and Kimberley Patton (eds.), *A Communion of Subjects: Animals in Religion, Science, and Ethics* (New York: Columbia University Press, 2006), 149–59.

*Animals in Islamic Traditions and Muslim Cultures* (New York: Simon and Schuster, 2014).

Freedman, Bradley and Shirley, Emily, 'England and the Public Trust Doctrine' (2014) 8, *Journal of Planning and Environmental Law*, 839–48.

Gade, Anna M., 'Islamic Law and the Environment in Indonesia: *Fatwa* and *Da'wa*' (2015) 19, *Worldviews*, 161–83.

Gary, Suzan N, 'History and Policy: Who Should Control Charitable Gifts?', in *Social Welfare Organisations: Better Alternatives to Charity?* (New York: National Center on Philanthropy and the Law, Conference Proceedings, 2016), 1–30.

Gaudiosi, Monica M., 'The Influence of the Islamic Law of Waqf on the Development of the Trust in England: The Case of Merton College' (1988) 136, 4, *University of Pennsylvania Law Review*, 1231–61.

Geertz Clifford, 'Local Knowledge: Fact and Law in Comparative Perspective', in *Local Knowledge: Further Essays in Interpretive Anthropology* (New York: Basic Books, 2008), 167–234.

Gottlieb, Roger S. (ed.), *Oxford Handbook on Religion and Ecology* (Oxford: Blackwell, 2006). 'Introduction: Religion and Ecology – What Is the Connection and Why Does It Matter?', in Roger S. Gottlieb (ed.), *Oxford Handbook on Religion and Ecology* (Oxford: Blackwell, 2006), 1–21.

Grais, Wafik and Pellegrini, Matteo, 'Corporate Governance and Shariah Compliance in Institutions Offering Islamic Financial Services', World Bank Policy Research Working Paper 4054 (2006).

Grassa, Rihab and Gazdar, Kaouthar, 'Financial Development and Economic Growth in GCC Countries: A Comparative Study between Islamic and Conventional Finance' (2014) 41, 6, *International Journal of Social Economics*, 493–514.

Habib, Ahmed, 'Role of Zakat and Awqaf in Poverty Alleviation' (Jeddah: Islamic Research and Training Institute, Occasional Paper 8, 2004).

Haghamed, Naser, 'The Muslim World Has to Take Climate Action', *Al Jazeera*, November 4, 2016, www.aljazeera.com

Hallaq, Wael B., 'Was the Gate of Ijtihad Closed?' (1984) 16, 1, *International Journal of Middle East Studies*, 3–41.

*An Introduction to Islamic Law* (New York: Cambridge University Press, 2009).

Hamed, Safei El-Deen, 'Seeing the Environment through Islamic Eyes: Application of Shariah to Natural Resources Planning and Management' (1993) 6, 2, *Journal of Agricultural and Environmental Ethics*, 145–64.

Hancock, Rosemary, 'Faith and Creation: Possibilities of an "Islamic" Environmental Ethic', *ABC Religion & Ethics*, September 11, 2018.

Haq, S. Nomanul, 'Islam and Ecology: Toward Retrieval and Reconstruction', in Richard C. Foltz, Frederick Denny and Azizan Baharuddin (eds.), *Islam and Ecology: A Bestowed Trust* (Cambridge, MA: Harvard University Press, 2003), 121–54.

Harasani, Hamid, *Towards the Reforms of Private Waqfs: A Comparative Study of Islamic Waqf and English Trusts* (Leiden: Brill-Nijhoff, 2015).

Hardin, Garrett, 'The Tragedy of the Commons' (1968) 162, 3859, *Science*, 1243–48.

Hare, Darragh and Blossey, Bernd, 'Principles of Public Trust Thinking' (2014) 19, 5, *Human Dimensions of Wildlife*, 397–406.

Haskell, Paul G., *Preface to the Law of Trusts* (Mineola, NY: Foundation Press, 1975).

Hennigan, Peter C., *The Birth of a Legal Institution: The Formation of the Waqf in Third-Century A. H. Hanafi Legal Discourse* (Leiden: Brill, 2004).

Holdsworth, William Searle, Goodhart, Arthur L., Hanbury, Greville Harold, and Burke, John McDonald, A *History of English Law* (London: Methuen, 1903).

Horowitz, Donald L., 'The Qur'an and the Common Law: Islamic Law Reform and the Theory of Legal Change' (1994) 42, 2, *American Journal of Comparative Law*, 233–93.

Hudson, Alastair, *Equity and Trusts* (London: Cavendish Publishing, 4th ed., 2005).

Huffman, James L., 'Why Liberating the Public Trust Doctrine Is Bad for the Public' (2015) 45, 2, *Environmental Law*, 337–77.

Hugues, Aaron W., 'Why Is Islam So Different in Different Countries?', *The Conversation*, February 18, 2016.

Hulley, N. J., 'New Zealand's Public Trust Doctrine', LLM Research Paper, Victoria University of Wellington (2018).

Idllalène, Samira, 'Le *habous*, instrument de protection de la biodiversité? Le cas du Maroc dans une approche de droit comparé' (2013) 4, 1, *Développement durable et territoires*, https://journals.openedition.org/developpementdurable/9732

Ilahiane, Hsain, 'The Berber Agdal Institution: Indigenous Range Management in the Atlas Mountains' (1999) 38, 1, *Ethnology*, 21–45.

Işın, Priscilla Mary, 'Yabancı Seyahatnamelere Göre Osmanlı Kültüründe Hayvan Hakları ve Hayvan Sevgisi', National Veterinary History and Professional Ethics Symposium, Konya (Turkey), 2008.

James, Philip S., *Introduction to English Law* (London: Butterworths, 1979).

Jenkins, Willis, 'Islamic Law and Environmental Ethics: How Jurisprudence (*Usul Al Fiqh*) Mobilizes Practical Reform' (2005) 9, 3, *Worldviews*, 338–64.

Jenkins, Willis and Key, Chapple Christopher, 'Annual Review, Religion and Environment' (2011) 36, *Annual Review of Environment and Resources*, 441–63.

Jihadi, H., 'Agdal, ressemblance et divergence de deux législations, l'Agdal Amazigh et le Habous arabe' (in Arabic), in E. Ouaazzi and L. Aït Bahcine (eds.), *Droit et société au Maroc* (Rabat: Institut Royal de la Culture Amazigh, Série colloque et séminaires, no. 7, 2005), 259–65.

Jung, Dietrich, Petersen, Marie Juul and Sparre, Sara Lei, *Politics of Modern Muslim Subjectivities: Islam, Youth, and Social Activism in the Middle East* (New York: Palgrave MacMillan, 2014).

Kakish, Kamal, 'Facilitating a Hima Resurgence: Understanding the Links between Land Governance and Tenure Security', West Asia–North Africa Institute: WANA, 2016, http://wanainstitute.org/

Kamali, Mohammad Hashim, *Principles of Islamic Jurisprudence* (Cambridge: Islamic Texts Society, 2004).

Kaminski, Joseph J., 'The OIC and the Paris 2015 Climate Change Agreement: Islam and the Environment', in Leslie A. Pal and M. Evren Tok (eds.), *Global Governance and Muslim Organizations*. International Political Economy Series (Cham: Springer International Publishing, 2019), 171–95.

Kassam, Zayn, The Case of the Animals Versus Man: Toward an Ecology of Being', in Paul Waldau and Kimberley Patton (eds.), *A Communion of Subjects: Animals in Religion, Science, and Ethics* (New York: Columbia University Press, 2006), 160–69.

Kempin Jr., Frederick G., *Historical Introduction to Anglo-American Law in a Nutshell* (St. Paul, MN: West Publishing, 3d ed., 1990).

Khalfoune, Tahar, 'Le Habous, le domaine public et le trust' (2005) 57, 2, *Revue internationale de droit compare*, 441–70.

Khalid, Fazlun, 'Islam and the Environment – Ethics and Practice, an Assessment' (2010) 4, 11, *Religion Compass*, 707–16.

'Exploring Environmental Ethics in Islam: Insights from the Qur'an and the Practice of Prophet Muhammad', in John Hart (ed.), *The Wiley Blackwell Companion to Religion and Ecology* (Oxford: Wiley Blackwell, 2017), 130–45.

Khalil, Ibrahim Ahmed, Yunus, Ali and Shaiban, Mohammad, 'Waqf Fund Management in Kuwait and Egypt: Can Malaysia Learn from Their Experiences?', Proceedings of the International Conference on Masjid, Zakat and Waqf (IMAF 2014), December 1–2, 2014, Kuala Lumpur, Malaysia.

Kilani, Hala, Serhal, Assaad and Llewellyn, Othman, 'Al-Hima: A Way of Life' (Amman: IUCN West Asia Regional Office, 2007).

Kozlowski, Gregory C., *Muslim Endowments and Society in British India* (Cambridge: Cambridge University Press, 1985).

Kula, E., 'Islam and Environmental Conservation' (2001) 28, 1, *Environmental Conservation*, 1–9.

Kundis Graig, Robin, 'Adapting to Climate Change: The Potential of State Common Law Public Trust Doctrines' (2010) 34, *Vermont Law Review*, 781–853.

Lau, Martin, 'The Introduction to the Pakistani Legal System, with Special Reference to the Law of Contract' (1994) 3, *Yearbook of Islamic & Middle East Law*, 21–28.

Lawler, James J. and Parle, William M., 'Expansion of the Public Trust Doctrine in Environmental Law: An Examination of Judicial Policy Making by State Courts' (1989) 70, 1, *Social Science Quarterly*, 134–48.

Legrand, Pierre, *Le droit comparé* (Paris: Presse Universitaire de France, 3d ed., 2011).

Llewellyn, Abd-Ar-Rahman Othman, 'The Basis for a Discipline of Islamic Environmental Law', in Richard C. Foltz, Frederick Mathewson Denny and Azizan Haji Baharuddin (eds.), *Islam and Ecology: A Bestowed Trust* (Cambridge, MA: Harvard University Press, 2003), 185–248.

Lutfallah, Gari, 'A History of the Hima Conservation System' (2006) 12, 2, *Environment and History*, 213–28.

Magill, Gerald and Aramesh, Kiarash (eds.), *The Urgency of Climate Change, Pivotal Perspectives* (Newcastle upon Tyne: Cambridge Scholars Publishing, 2017), 362–87.

Mahadi, Ahmad, 'Cash Waqf: Historical Evolution, Nature and Role as an Alternative to Riba-Based Financing for the Grass Root' (2015) 4, 1, *Journal of Islamic Finance*, 63–74.

Makdisi, John, 'Legal Logic and Equity in Islamic Law' (1985) 33, 1, *American Journal of Comparative Law*, 63–92.

'The Islamic Origins of the Common Law' (1999) 77, 2, *North Carolina Law Review*, 1635–739.

Mangunjaya, Fachruddin Majeri and McKay, Jeanne Elizabeth, 'Reviving an Islamic Approach for Environmental Conservation in Indonesia' (2012) 16, *Worldviews*, 286–305.

Mangunjaya, Fachruddin Majeri and Praharawati, Gudah, 'Fatwas on Boosting Environmental Conservation in Indonesia' (2019) 10, 570, *Religions*, 1–14.

Mangunjaya, Fachruddin Majeri, Tobing, Imran S. L., Binawan, Andang, Pua, Evangeline and Nurbawa, Made, 'Faiths from the Archipelago: Action on the Environment and Climate Change' (2015) 19, 2, *Worldviews: Global Religions, Culture, and Ecology*, 103–22.

Mansoor, Khan M. and Bhatti, Ishaq M., 'Islamic Banking and Finance: On Its Way to Globalization' (2008) 34, 10, *Management Finance*, 708–25.

Martinez, Ignacio Arroyo, 'Trust and the Civil Law' (1982) 42, 5, *Louisiana Law Review*, 1709–20.

Massoud, Mark Fathi, 'How an Islamic State Rejected Islamic Law' (2018) 66, 3, *American Journal of Comparative Law*, 579–602.

Masud, Muhammad Khalid, Messick, Brinkley and Powers, David S., 'Muftis, Fatwas, and Islamic Legal Interpretation', in Muhammad Khalid Masud, Brinkley Messick and David S. Powers (eds.), *Islamic Legal Interpretation: Muftis and Their Fatwas* (New York: Harvard University Press, 1996), 20–26.

Mawil, Izz-Deen, 'Islamic Environmental Ethics, Law and Society', in J. Ronald Engel and Joan Gibb Engle (eds.), *Ethics of Environment and Development* (London: Belhaven Press, 1990).

Mcleod, Elizabeth and Palmer, Martin, 'Why Conservation Needs Religion' (2015) 43, 3, *Coastal Management*, 239–40.

Mekouar, Mohamed Ali, *Etudes en droit de l'environnement* (Rabat: Okad, 1988).

Mende, Claudia, 'Islamic Inheritance Law in Morocco and Tunisia, Feminist Asma Lamrabet Under Pressure', *Qantara*, October 2018.

Messaoudi, L., 'Grandeurs et limites du droit musulman au Maroc' (1995) 47, 1, *Revue internationale de droit comparé*, 146–54.

Meyers, Gary D., 'Variation on a Theme: Expanding the Public Trust Doctrine to Include Protection of Wildlife' (1989) 19, 3, *Environmental law*, 723–35.

Michiel, Jan Otto, *Sharia and National Law in Muslim Countries: Tensions and Opportunities for Dutch and EU Foreign Policy* (Leiden: Leiden University Press, 2008).

Mikhail, Alan, *Nature and Empire in Ottoman Egypt: An Environmental History* (Cambridge: Cambridge University Press, 2011).

Miller, Howard S., *The Legal Foundations of American Philanthropy 1176–1844* (Madison: State Historical Society of Wisconsin, 1961).

Milsom, S. F. C. F. B. A., *Historical Foundations of the Common Law* (London: Butterworths, 1969).

Moghul, Umar F. and Safar-Aly, Samir H. K., 'Green Sukuk: The Introduction of Islam's Environmental Ethics to Contemporary Islamic Finance' (2014) 27, 1, *Georgetown International Environmental Law Review*, 1–60.

Mohsin, M. I. A., Dafterdar, H., Cizakca, M., Alhabshi, S. O., Razak, S. H. A., Sadr, S. K., Anwar, T. and Obaidullah, M., *Financing the Development of Old Waqf Properties: Classical Principles and Innovative Practices around the World* (New York: Palgrave MacMillan, 2016).

Nasr, Seyyed Hossein, *Man and Nature: The Spiritual Crisis of Modern Man* (London: George Allen & Unwin, 1968).

'Islam, the Contemporary Islamic World, and the Environmental Crisis', in Richard C. Foltz, Frederick Denny and Azizan Baharuddin, *Islam and Ecology: A Bestowed Trust* (Cambridge, MA: Harvard University Press, 2003), 85–105.

'God Is Absolute Reality and All Creation His Tajalli', in John Hart (ed.), *The Wiley Blackwell Companion to Religion and Ecology* (Oxford: John Wiley, 2017), 1–11.

Negi, Chandra Singh, 'Religion and Biodiversity Conservation: Not a Mere Analogy' (2005) 1, 2, *International Journal of Biodiversity Science and Management*, 85–96.

Noor, Mohammad, 'Environmental Law and Policy Practices in Malaysia: An Empirical Study' (2011) 5, 9, *Australian Journal of Basics and Applied Sciences*, 1248–60.

Obaidullah, Mohammed, 'Managing Climate Change: Role of Islamic Finance' (2018) 26, 1, *Islamic Economic Studies*, 31–62.

Olawuyi, Damilola, 'Can MENA Extractive Industries Support the Global Energy Transition? Current Opportunities and Future Directions' (2020) *The Extractive Industries and Society*, 10.1016/j.exis.2020.02.003.

Opwis, Felicitas, 'Maṣlaḥa in Contemporary Islamic Legal Theory' (2005) 12, 2, *Islamic Law and Society*, 182–223.

Özdemir, Ibrahim, 'Toward an Understanding of Environmental Ethics from a Qur'anic Perspective', in Richard C. Foltz, Frederick Denny and Azizan Baharuddin (eds.), *Islam and Ecology: A Bestowed Trust* (Cambridge, MA: Harvard University Press, 2003), 3–37.

*The Ethical Dimension of Human Attitude towards Nature: A Muslim Perspective* (Merter: Insan Publications, 2d ed., 2008).

Pal, Leslie A. and Evren, Tok M. (eds.), *Global Governance and Muslim Organizations*. International Political Economy Series (Cham: Springer International Publishing, 2019).

Peel, Jacqueline and Osofsky, Hari M., 'A Right Turn in Climate Change Litigation?' (2018) 7, 1, *Transnational Environmental Law*, 37–67.

Pope Francis, *Laudato Si'* [Encyclical Letter on Care for Our Common Home] (May 24, 2015), http://w2.vatican.va

Powers, David S., 'Orientalism, Colonialism, and Legal History: The Attack on Muslim Family Endowments in Algeria and India' (1989) 31, 3, *Comparative Studies in Society and History*, 535–71.

Raissouni, Ahmed, *Islamic Waqf Endowment: Scope and Implication* (Rabat: ISESCO, 2001).

Ramazotti, Marco, 'Customary Water Rights and Contemporary Water Legislation, Mapping Out the Interface', FAO *Legal Papers*, 76, December 2008.

Ramlan, Shazny, 'Religious Law for the Environment: Comparative Islamic Environmental Law in Singapore, Malaysia, and Indonesia', NUS Centre for Asian Legal Studies Working Paper 19/03, Centre for Asian Legal Studies. Faculty of Law, National University of Singapore, 2019, http://law.nus.edu.sg/wps/

Rauf, Feisal Abdul, *Islam: A Sacred Law* (Brattleboro: Qiblah Books, 2000).

Raysuni, Ahmad, *'Theory of the Higher Objectives and Intends of Islamic Law'*, (Translated by Nancy Roberts). International Institute of Islamic Thought, 2005.

Rehman, Schehrazade S. and Askari, Hossein, 'How Islamic Are Islamic Countries?' (2010), 10, 2, *Global Economy Journal*, www.en.islamic-sources.com

Rohaeti Atih, Dariah, Salleh, Muhammad Syukri and Shafiai, Hakimi M., 'A New Approach for Sustainable Development Goals in Islamic Perspective' (2016) 219, *Procedia – Social and Behavioral Sciences*, 159–66.

Saad, Norma Md, Kassim, Salina and Hamid, Zarinah, 'Best Practices of Waqf: Experiences of Malaysia and Saudi Arabia' (2016) 2, 2, *Journal of Islamic Economics*, 57–74.

Sachs, Wolfgang, 'The Sustainable Development Goals and Laudato Si': Varieties of Post-Development?' (2017) 38, 12, *Third World Quarterly*, 2573–87.

Sagarin, Raphael D. and Turnipseed, Mary, 'The Public Trust Doctrine: Where Ecology Meets Natural Resources Management' (2012) 37, *Annual Review of Environmental Resources*, 473–97.

Saidul Islam, Muhammad, 'Old Philosophy, New Movement: The Rise of the Islamic Ecological Paradigm in the Discourse of Environmentalism' (2012) 7, 1, *Nature and Culture*, 72–94.

Saniotis, Arthur, 'Muslim and Ecology: Fostering Islamic Environmental Ethics', (2012) 6, 2, *Contemporary Islam*, 155–71.

Saritoprak, Zeki, 'Qur'an', in Bron R. Taylor and Jefferey Kaplan (eds.), *Encyclopedia of Religion and Nature* (New York: Thoemmes Continuum, 2008), 1321–24.

Sax, Joseph L., 'The Public Trust Doctrine in Natural Resource Law: Effective Judicial Intervention' (1970) 68, 3, *Michigan Law Review*, 471–566.

Schacht, Joseph, *An Introduction to Islamic Law* (Oxford: Clarendon Press, 1964). *Introduction au droit musulman* (Paris: Maisonneuve & Larose, 1983).

Schoenblum, Jeffrey A., 'The Role of Legal Doctrine in the Decline of the Islamic Waqf: A Comparison with the Trust' (1999) 32, *Vanderbilt Journal of Transnational Law*, 1191–203.

Schwencke, A. M., 'Globalized Eco-Islam: A Survey of Global Islamic Environmentalism' (Leiden Institute for Religious Studies (LIRS), Leiden University, 2012).

Sekreter, Ahmed, 'Green Finance and Islamic Finance' (2017) 4, 3, *International Journal of Social Sciences & Educational Studies*, 115–21.

Sellers, Mortimer, 'An Introduction to the Rule of Law in Comparative Perspective', in M. Sellers and T. Tomaszewski (eds.), *The Rule of Law in Comparative Perspective. Ius Gentium: Comparative Perspectives on Law and Justice*, vol. 3 (Dordrecht: Springer, 2010).

Shaikh Salman, Ahmed, Ghafar, Ismail Abdul and Mohd, Muhammad Shafiai Hakimi, 'Application of Waqf for Social and Development Finance' (2017) 9, 1, *ISRA International Journal of Islamic Finance*, 5–14.

Shatzmiller, Maya, 'Islamic Institutions and Property Rights: The Case of the "Public Good" Waqf' (2001) 44, 1, *Journal of the Economic and Social History of the Orient*, 44–74.

Silecchia, Anne Lucia, '"Social Love" as a Vision for Environmental Law: Laudato Si' and the Rule of Law' (2016) 10, 3, *Liberty University Law Review*, 371–98.

Skillington, Tracey, 'Changing Perspectives on Natural Resources: Heritage, Human Rights, and Intergenerational Justice' (2019) 23, 4, *International Journal of Human Rights*, 615–37.

Slade, David C., *Putting the Public Trust Doctrine to Work* (Washington, DC: Coastal States Organization, 2d ed., 1997).

Smith, Lionel (ed.), *The Worlds of the Trust* (New York: Cambridge University Press, 2013).

Soulé, Michel, 'What Is Conservation Biology?' (1985) 35, *BioScience*, 727–34.

Sponsel, Leslie E., 'Spiritual Ecology as an International Environmental Movement' (2014) 15, *Advances in Sustainability and Environmental Justice*, 275–93.

Stibbard, Paul, Russel, David, QC and Bromeley, Blake, 'Understanding the Waqf in the World of the Trust' (2012) 18, 8, *Trust and Trustees*, 785–810.

Stilt, Kristen A., 'Constitutional Innovation and Animal Protection in Egypt' (2017) 43, 4, *Law and Social Enquiry*, 1364–90.

Suleiman, Haitam, 'The Islamic Trust Waqf: A Stagnant or Reviving Legal Institution?' (2016) 4, *Journal of Islamic and Middle Eastern Law*, 27–43.

Sungurbey, Ismet, 'Islam Hukukunda Hayvanlar Yararına Vakıflar ve Vakıf Mevzuatımızdaki Önemli Bir Eksiklik' (1990) 7, *Vakıf Haftası Dergisi*, 23–33.

Taylor, Bron R. and Kaplan, Jeffrey (eds.), *The Encyclopedia of Religion and Nature* (London: Thoemmes Continuum, 2008).

Torres, Gerald and Bellinger, Nathan, 'The Public Trust: The Law's DNA' (2014) 4, 2, *Cornell Law Faculty Publications*, 218–317.

Tortell, Philip and Al-Essa, Mai, 'Seeking Sustainability and Cost Efficiency: A UNDP Environment Programme for Kuwait', 2011, www.kw.undp.org

Tucker, Mary Evelyn and Grim, John, 'Series Foreword', in Richard C. Foltz, Frederick Denny and Azizan Baharuddin (eds.), *Islam and Ecology: A Bestowed Trust* (Cambridge, MA: Harvard University Press, 2003).

'The Movement of Religion and Ecology: Emerging Field and Dynamic Force', in Jenkins Willis (ed.), *Routledge Handbook of Religion and Ecology* (New York: Routledge, 2017), 3–12.

Turnipseed, Mary, Sagarin, Raphael, Barnes, Peter, Blumm, Michael C., Parenteau, Patrick and Sand, Peter H., 'Reinvigorating the Public Trust Doctrine: Expert Opinion on the Potential of a Public Trust Mandate in U.S. and International Environmental Law' (2010) 52, 5, *Environment: Science and Policy for Sustainable Development*, 6–14.

Ullah, Aman. 'Public Interest Litigation: A Constitutional Regime to Access to Justice in Pakistan' (2018) 19, 2, *Pakistan Vision*, 167–81.

UNEP, UNEA, 4, Faith for Earth Dialogue, Synthesis Paper, 2019, www.unenvironment.org/resources/synthesis-reports/faith-earth-dialogue-synthesis-report

UNEP, Environmental Rule of Law: First Global Report, www.unenvironment.org/resources/assessment/environmental-rule-law-first-global-report

'Engaging with Faith Based Organizations', 2018, 4–5.

The Statute of Climate Change Litigation: A Global Review, 2017.

United Nations Development Programme (UNDP), 'Climate Change Adaptation in the Arab States, Best Practices and Lessons Learned', 2018, www.undp.org/content/dam/undp/library/Climate%20and%20Disaster%20Resilience/Climate%20Change/Arab-States-CCA.pdf

Verbit, Gilbert Paul, *The Origins of the Trust* (Bloomington, IN: Xlibris Corporation, 2002).

Vernon, Valentine Palmer, 'Mixed Legal Systems', in Maurro Bussani and Ugo Mattei (eds.), *The Cambridge Companion to Comparative Law* (Cambridge: Cambridge University Press, 2012), 368–83.

Vincenti, Donatella, '"Green" Islam and Social Movements for Sustainability' (PhD thesis, Liberta University Internationale Degli Studi Sociali, Luiss Guido Carli, Rome, 2017).

Weeramantry, Christopher G., *Islamic Jurisprudence: An International Perspective* (New York: St. Martin, 1988).

Weiss, Bernard, 'Interpretation in Islamic Law: The Theory of Ijtihad' (1978) 26, 2, *American Journal of Comparative Law*, 199–212.

Wescoat, James L., 'The "Right of Thirst" for Animals in Islamic Law: A Comparative Approach' (1995) 13, *Environment and Planning, Society and Space*, 637–54.

'Islam and Environmental Ethics', in Bron Raymond Taylor and Jeffrey Kaplan (eds.), *The Encyclopedia of Religion and Nature* (New York: Thoemmes Continuum, 2005), 866–68.

West Asia–North Africa Institute (WANA), 'Religious Leaders Promoting Environmental Good Governance', December 2016, Amman, Jordan.

Wilkinson, Charles F., 'The Public Trust Doctrine in Public Land Law' (1980) 14, *University California Davis Law Review*, 269–316.

Wood, Mary Christina, 'Advancing the Sovereign Trust of Government to Safeguard the Environment for Present and Future Generations (Part I): Ecological Realism and the Need for a Paradigm Shift' (2009) 39, 43, *Environmental Law*, 78–84.

*Nature's Trust: Environmental Law for a New Ecological Age* (New York: Cambridge University Press, 2014).

'Atmospheric Trust Litigation: Securing a Constitutional Right to a Stable Climate System' (2018) 29, 2, *Colorado Natural Resources, Energy & Environmental Law Review*, 331–39.

Wood, Mary Christina and Galpern, Dan, 'Atmospheric Recovery Litigation: Making the Fossil Fuel Industry Pay to Restore a Viable Climate System' (2015) 45, *Environmental Law*, 259–335.

Wortley Montagu, Mary, *Letters* (Paris: Théophile Barrois Fils, 1816).

# Index

Abdelzaher, Dina, 4, 9
Adaptive management, 96
  Hima, Agdal, 99
*Adat. See* customary law
*Agdal*, **25–26**, 51–52
  adaptive management, 98
  tragedy of the commons, 100
*Al maslaha*, 43–44
  *Waqf*, 74
*Al waqef*, 72
Algeria, 26
Al-Jayyousi, 3
Alliance of Religions and Conservation (ARC), **5**, 11, 115
*amicus curiae briefs*, 90, 120–21, 123, 127–28
  Atmospheric trust litigation, 120
animal welfare, 10, 38
  environmental *Fatwa*, 106
Arnold *v* Mundy (1821)
  Public Trust Doctrine, 77
Assisi Declarations, **4**
*Atmospheric Khilafa* litigation, 120, 122, 128, 135, 140
  grassroots, 128
Atmospheric Trust litigation, 73, 80, 84, 90, 94, 109, 111, 113, 128, 138, 141, 144–45
  Eco-Islam, 112, 119, 145
  environmental justice, 127
  *Laudato Si*, 120
  Muslim countries, 139
  waqf, 139
Atmospheric Trust Litigation
  Eco-Islam, 126
Atmospheric *Waqf*, 44, 121, 137, 142, 144
  global *Waqf*, 110, 137
Atmospheric *Waqf* Doctrine, 86–87, 145

Atmospheric *Waqf* Paradigm, 86–87, 137, 146
  Atmospheric Waqf Doctrine, 29, 43, 88, 95, 110, 119–20, 138–39
Australia, 79, 130–31
Awkaf Public Foundation (KAPF), 130
*Awqaf*, 48–49, 71, 143
Awqaf Property Investment Fund (APIF)
  Islamic Developement Bank (IDB), 134

Bagader, A., 24–25, 96
Bhala, Raj, 24, 40, 42, 44
biodiversity, 16, 18, 44, 88, 115, 133, 136
birdhouses *Waqf*, 50, 104–5
BirdLife International, 131
Blumm, Michael C., 28, 63, 76–80, 83–84
Bogert, George Gleason, 25
British colonies, 19, 24, 64, 74

Case of the Century, 83
  climate change litigation, France, 83
Cash *Waqf*, 50, 129, 134
  Islamic finance, 49
Chancellor, 27, 65
Chaplin, Jonathan, 5, 37, 145
charitable endowment, **14**, **20**, **24**, **27**, **38**, 56, 70
charitable Trust, 71, 74, 76, 79
  common law, 27
  environment, 142
  nature's rights, 109
Charities Act 2013
  England, 109
civil law, 13, 20, 24, 76, 79, 139
  Public Trust Doctrine, 82
Cizakca, Murat, 24, 55–56
Climate Action Network, 114

colonization, 14, 17, 55
common law, 20, 24, 29–30, 80, 138–39
  animal welfare, 109
  Islamic finance, 135
common law countries
  Public Trust Doctrine, 79
comparative law, 12, 28, 30, 76, 141, 144
Constitution, 33, 55, 81–83
  Islamic Supremacy clause, 120, 126
Constitution, Egypt, animal welfare, 106
*corpus iuris civilis*, 13, 76
  civil law, 78
customary law, 14, 24
  *Agdal, Hima*, 45, 101

democracy, 3, 146
duty of care, 73, 94–96

Earth Charter, 2
Eco-Islam, 6, 8–9, 11, 18, 45, 61, 86, 95, 110, 112, 115,
    119, 122, 139–41
ecological public Trust, Nature's Trust, 80
Ecological Spirituality, 2, 6, 8
ecosystem approach
  Islamic law, Sharia', 102
ecosystem services
  green finance, 136
  *Hima, Waqf*, 74, 143
  perpetuity rule, 88
Egypt, 6, 38, 71, 106, 110, 122, 124–26, 140
*Ekopesantren*, ecological religious schools
  Indonesia, 119
El-Ansary, Waleed, 2, 17, 40, 116, 119
England, 27, 65, 70, 74, 76–77, 84, 109 *See* United
    Kingdom
English law, 19, 27, 65, 70, 84
environmental *Fatwa*, wildlife, 11, 36, 44, 106
environmental *Fatwas*, 11, 41, 112, 117–20, 123, 138,
    144
  animal welfare, 106–7
  *Atmospheric Waqf*, 137
  enforceability, 118–19, 121
  examples, 117
  form, 124
  green finance, 133
  *khilafa*, 93
  scriptures, 36
  Waqf, 120
  wildlife, 117
environmental justice, 126, 129, 141
environmental law, 58
Environmental law, 1, 8, 12, 16, 18–20, 29, 44, 58,
    95–96, 139, 145–46
environmental litigation, 138

environmental *Waqf*, 26, 48, 50, 53, 97, 100, 117,
    119, 129–30, 134–35, 137–39, 143
  decline, 56
  revival, 24
Equity, 27, 39, 42, 87
  Trust, 65

faith-based groups, 6–7, 124, 136
Faith for Earth Dialogue, 8
Faith for Earth Initiative, 119, 136
  Eco-Islam, 111
  UNEP, 6–7, 111, 136
*Fatwa*, environmental *khilafa*, 93
fiduciary duty, 73, 82, 145
  environmental *Fatwas*, 120
  *Khilafa*, 93
  public Trust Doctrine, 80
*Fiqh*, 33, 41, 47, 126
  animal welfare, 102
  climate change, 118
*Fiqh* Council of North America, 122
Foltz, Richard, 2–3, 12, 15, 17, 29, 36, 54, 58, 90, 98,
    100–2, 105, 109
France, 130–31
future generations, 2–3, 81
  Public Trust Doctrine, 77
  Waqf, 87

Gaudiosi, Monica M., 91
global Trust, Our Common future, 88
Gottlieb, Roger S., 2, 12, 111
grassroots, 3, 61
  Atmospheric Trust Litigation, 144
  Eco-Islam, 111
green *Khilafa*, 120
green *Sukuk*, 19, 97, 132–33
Green *Waqf*Program, 131
GreenFaith, 114
Grimm, John, 2
Gulf Arab states, 15, 19

*Hadith*
  animal welfare, 50, 101
  *Sunnah*, 33, 33, 38, 41
Hallaq, Wael B., 33–34, 56, 71
Hansen, James, 81
Haram, 25, 100
  origins, 25
Harasani, Hamid, 27–28, 40, 56, 60, 92, 140
Hennigan, Peter C., 24–25, 45, 70, 140
*Hima*, 14, 39
  adaptive management, 98
  Agdal, 51, 58, 83
  conditions, 52

decline, 55, 57
environmental Waqf, 131
*khilafa*, 91
origins, 25, 45, 51
tragedy of the commons, 100
*Hima, Agdal*, 26
definition, 50
types, 52
*Hima, Waqf*
customary law, 45
*Hubs (Habous). See* Waqf
human rights, 10, 83, 138

Ibn Taymiyya, 101
*Ijma'*, **33**, 39–40
*Ijtihad*, **34**, **40–42**, 40, 43, 50, 56, 124, 143
environmental *Waqf*, 62
Islamic environmental law, Waqf, 119
Waqf, 50
Waqf, Hima, 143
*Ikhwane Al Safa*, 102
*Illinois Central Railroad Co. v. Illinois* (1892)
Public Trust Doctrine, 78
Inalienability, 100
Public Trust Doctrine, 73
Public Trust Doctrine, *Waqf*, 74
*Waqf*, Trust, 73
India, 19, 56, 71, 79, 84, 109, 139
Indonesia, 6, 12, 15, 17, 20, 36, 106, 117–18, 124,
    129–32, 138
interfaith movement, **6**
grassroots, 5
International Islamic Fiqh Academy (IIFA), 114
Iran, 6, 14, 26, 33, 113, 140
Iraq, 14, 71
ISESCO, **8**
Islamic Climate Change Symposium, 114
Islamic Declaration on Global Climate Change, 5,
    36, 40, 114, 122, 140, 145
amicus curiae brief, 128
scriptures, 36
Islamic Declaration on Nature, 36, 40, 92, 113
Islamic Declaration on Sustainable Development,
    4, 36, 113
Islamic Development Bank (IDB), 134
Islamic Ecological Paradigm (IEP), 3–4, 6,
    111, 116
Islamic environmental law, 9–10, 12, 32, 43–45, 58,
    86, 92, 111, 119, 121–22, 124, 127, 138, 140–41,
    143–44
decline, 59
dormancy, 17, 54, 60 *See*Sources
nonenforcement, 58
Islamic finance, **13**, 19, **20**, 129

estimates, 131
green finance, 133
Islamic Foundation For Ecology and
    Environmental Sciences (IFEES), 4,
    114–15
Islamic green finance, 136
Islamic law, 8, 10, 18–19, **58**, 84, **145**
See *Sharia'*, 42, 59, 128
Islamic law, *Sharia'*, tragedy of the commons, 100
Islamic Relief Worldwide, 4, 114, 129
Islamic Scientific, Educational and Cultural
    Organization (ISESCO), 4, 8, 113–14, 139
Islamic supremacy clause, 126
See Constitution, 124, 126
*Istihsan*, **34**, **42**, **43**, **45**
IUCN, **4**, **24**, **26**
Izz-Deen, Mawil, 8, 25

Jenkins, Willis, 2–3, 10
Juliana et al. *v.* United States, 72–73, 81, 90
    *amicus curiae brief*, Islamic Declaration on
        Global Climate Change, 127
    fiduciary duty, 94
Justinian, 13, 76

Kamali, Mohammad Hashim, 91
Kaplan, Jeffrey, 2, 7, 9, 35–36, 40, 113
Kenya, 6, 107
Khalfoune, Tahar, 56, 78
Khalid, Fazlun, 3, 9–10, 12, 35, 111, 122, 140
*Khalifa (Caliph)*, 91–92, 113, 145
    *Khalifa*, 91, 145
        animal welfare, 102
        Eco-Islam, 113
        overarching principle, 92
*Khutbahs*, 61
Kinloch *v* Secretary of State for India, 84
Kuwait, 14, 16, 18–19, 130, 138

*Laudato Si*, **5**, 18, 71, **120–21**
Legrand, Pierre, 13, 70, 82
Litigation, Public Trust Doctrine, **71**, **120**
Llewellyn, Abd-Ar-Rahman Othman, 17, 32, 51, 102

Magna Carta, 78
Majliss Ulama Indonesia (MUI), 11, 36, 93, 118
Malaysia, 6, 11, 16, 65, 106, 117, 119, 124, 130, 132–33
Mangunjaya, Fachrudine Majeri, 6, 11, 117, 140
*Maqasid Sharia'*, **34**, 42–43
*Maslaha*
    adaptive management, 96
    *Istislah*, **34**, **43**
*Mawquf*, 48, 50, 72
Mcleod, Elizabeth, 7, 140

Mekouar, Mohammed Ali, 31
Middle East, 6, 13, 15, 19, 131
Middle East and North Africa (MENA), 6, 15, 132
Misali island, Zanzibar, IFEES, 115
Morocco, 1, 14, 17, 58, 105
*Mufti*, 61
*Mutawalli*, 48, 57, 72, 88, 91, 96

*Nagari, See* Customary law, Indonesia, Hima,
     Agdal, 46
National Audubon Society *v.* Superior Court, 80
National Trust, 27
natural resources, 58, 98
Nature's Trust, 64, 76, 89
Netherlands, 81, 95
New Zealand, 130
Nigeria, 14, 116, 130

*Oposa v. Factoran*, 75, 81
Organization of Islamic Cooperation (OIC), 14, 114
Ottoman Empire, 55–56, 104–5
Our Children's Trust, 71
Özdemir, Ibrahim, 4, 12, 35, 38, 92, 101, 111

Pakistan, 6, 19, 33, 71, 79, 95, 109, 126, 129, 138–39
Palmer, Martin, 5, 7, 11, 13, 140
Paris Climate Agreement, 17, 83, 114
     *Waqf*, 140
Perlis Fatwa Committee, Malaysia, 36
Perpetuity rule, 27, 75, 100
     Waqf, 88
     *Waqf*, finance, 134
Philippines, 75, 81, 109
Pollution, 16, 36, 44, 84
Prophet Muhammad, 9, 25, 39, 47, 51
Public domain, Civil law, 76, 78
     and Public Trust Doctrine, 79
     definition, 78
Public interest, 74, 126–27, 142
     *Waqf*, 74
Public Trust, 77–78
     definition, 77
     England, 84
Public Trust Doctrine, 149
Public Trust Doctrine (PTD)
     "public domain", 76
     adaptive management, 96
     and Civil law, 79
     definition, 77
     evolution, 79, 128
     future generations, 75
     *Juliana et al. v. United States*, 81
     overarching principle, 83
     public interest, 75

religious basis, 71
and Trust, 27, 73, 76
*Zoe and Stella Foster et al. v. Washington State
     et al.*, 94
Public Trust litigation, future generations, 75

Qatar, 14
*Qiyas*, 33, 42–43
     water, 42
*Qur'an*, 34, 36, 41
     animal welfare, 101
     environment, 34–35
     Islamic Supremacy clause, 36
     *khilafa*, 90

Rabat Declaration on the "Role of Cultural and
     Religious Factors in the Protection of the
     Environment and Sustainable
     Development", 114, 128, 140, 145
Raissouni (Raysuni) Ahmad, 3–4
Ramadan, 60
Ramlan, Shazny, 12, 121, 140
Revival
     Islamic environmental law, 1, 4, 18, 24, 26,
          29–30, 33, 41, 45, 76, 86–87, 106, 110–11, 121,
          130–31, 139, 141, 143
     Islamic finance, 19
right of thirst, animal welfare, 100, 103, 106
rights of animals, *Sharia'*, 102
Roman law and Common law, 79

Sachs, Wolfgang, 5
Sacred, 2, 10, 25–26, 31, 77, 113
Sadaqah, Zakat, 25–26
Sand, Peter H., 77
Saudi Arabia, 4, 14, 17, 57, 113, 128, 130
Sax, Joseph, 28–29, 76, 80, 84, 144–45
Schacht, Joseph, 10, 33, 41
Schoenblum, Jeffrey A., 28, 60, 100
Scriptures, 115
Sellers, Mortimer, 13, 82
Seyyed Hossein Nasr, 3, 58, 60–61, 111
*Sharia'*, 10, 14, 20, 48, 91, 130, 139
     definition, 8
     *see* Islamic law, 58
Silecchia, Anne Lucia, 18
Singapore, 11, 17, 119
     *khutbahs*, 61
South Africa, 65, 79
Sponsel, Leslie E., 5, 7, 11
Stibbard, Paul, 28, 56, 72
Stilt, Kristen A., 106, 112, 122, 140
storks, *Waqf*, 105
Sunnah, 33, 36, 38, 41, 51

*Surah*, 35, 101, 106
   Al Imran, 48
Sustainable Development Goals (SDGs), 7
   sharia', 89
sustainable development principle, 87

Tanzania, 79, 115–16
Taylor, Bron R., 2, 7, 9, 35–36, 40, 113
tragedy of the commons, 99
tribe, 52, 74, 91
Trust
   Common law, 95
   definition, 25
   origins, 26–27, 65, 70
   and *Waqf*, 24–25, 65, 72
Trustee, 120
Trusteeship, 35, 91
Tucker, Mary Evelyn, 2, 12
Turkey, 17, 99, 104, 107
Turnipseed, Mary, 77, 79–80, 84, 142

*Ulamas*, 114, 118, 120, 124, 137, 140
UN Framework Climate Change Convention
   (UNFCCC), 81
UNEP, 16, 101, 136, 145
   Report on the environmental rule of law 2019, 16
   United Arab Emirates, 14, 132
   United Kingdom, 109, 129–30 *See also* England
   United Nations Framework Convention on
      Climate Change (UNFCCC), 1, 114
   United Sates, 71
   United States, 19, 27–29, 71, 75–76, 78
   *Urf*, Customary law, 45
Urgenda *v.* The Netherlands, 81, 95
   fiduciary duty, 95
*Usul al-fiqh. See* Fiqh
Verbit, Gilbert Paul, 63, 72, 75, 88, 92
Viceregency
   Islamic Declaration on Global Climate
      Change, 115
   *Khilafa*, 35, 38

*Waqef*, 48
*Waqf*, 14, **20**, **24**, **39**, 98, 129, 131, **134**
   animal welfare, 103–4, 108

animals, 50
Atmospheric Trust litigation, 83
climate change, 98, 135
common law, 19
conditions, 48
decline, 55–56, 59
definition, 24, 47
environment, 46, 96
fexibility, 96
future generations, 75
green *Sukuk*, 133
*Hima*, 72
*Hima*, 39, 47
*Hima, Agdal*, protected areas, 25
importance, 24
Islamic Developement Bank (IDB), 134
Islamic finance, 97
*khilafa*, 91
lawsuit, 128
legal basis, 47
origins, 70
public interest, PTD, 127
religious basis, 65
structure, 48
and Trust, 24, 65, 71–72, 74
types, 48
and Zakat, 48
*Waqf* asset, 48
*Waqf* deed, 50, 105, 107
Water, 10, 15–16, 25, 32, 35, 39–40, 42, 49, 58, 73,
   77–78, 88, 93, 100, 102–3, 107, 130
Weeramantry, Christopher G., 25, 33, 42, 63, 70, 90
Wescoat, James L., 40, 100, 103, 106, 113, 140
Wildlife, 36, 80, 93, 96, 131
   environmental *Fatwa*, 106
Wood, Mary Christina, 28, 63–64, 72, 76–77,
   79–80, 83–84, 90, 94–95, 120, 144
World Widlife Fund (WWF), **4**

Yale's Forum on Religion and Ecology, **5**
Yemen, 106, 124

*Zakat*, 26, 137 *See Sadaqah*
*Zoe and Stella Foster et al. v. Washington State
   et al.*, 94